Frommer's®
Portable
Cayman Islands
5th Edition

by Darwin Porter & Danforth Prince

WILEY

John Wiley & Sons, Inc.

Published by:
JOHN WILEY & SONS, INC.
111 River St.
Hoboken, NJ 07030-5774

ISBN 978-1-118-00429-6 (paper); ISBN 978-1-118-16202-6 (ebk);
ISBN 978-1-118-16201-9 (ebk); ISBN 978-1-118-16200-2 (ebk)

Editor: Andrea Kahn
Production Editor: Lindsay Beineke
Cartographer: Guy Ruggiero
Photo Editor: Richard Fox
Production by Wiley Indianapolis Composition Services

Front cover photo: Woman kayaking in the Cayman Islands. ©James D. Watt / Stephen Frink Collection / Alamy Images

For information on our other products and services or to obtain technical support, please contact our Customer Care Department within the U.S. at 877/762-2974, outside the U.S. at 317/572-3993 or fax 317/572-4002.

Wiley also publishes its books in a variety of electronic formats. Some content that appears in print may not be available in electronic formats.

Manufactured in the United States of America

5 4 3 2 1

CONTENTS

List of Maps vii

1 THE BEST OF THE CAYMAN ISLANDS 1

The Best Cayman Island Experiences 1

The Best Beaches 3

The Best Scuba-Diving Sites 3

The Best Snorkeling Sites 7

The Best Honeymoon & Wedding Accommodations 8

The Best Places to Get Away From It All 8

The Best Luxury Hotels 9

The Best Restaurants 10

2 PLANNING YOUR TRIP TO THE CAYMAN ISLANDS 12

The Islands in Brief 12

When to Go 17

CAYMAN ISLANDS CALENDAR OF EVENTS 18

Entry Requirements 21

Getting There 24

GETTING THROUGH THE AIRPORT 27

Getting Around 31

RENTING A CAR 101 32

Money & Costs 34

What Things Cost in Grand Cayman 36

Health 38

Crime & Safety 41

SAFETY & SECURITY FOR SCUBA DIVERS 41

Specialized Travel Resources 42

Responsible Tourism 44

GENERAL RESOURCES FOR GREEN TRAVEL 45

Packages for the Independent Traveler 46

ASK BEFORE YOU GO 47

Staying Connected 48

Tips on Accommodations 50

ONLINE TRAVELER'S TOOLBOX 50

GETTING MARRIED IN THE CAYMAN ISLANDS 54

3 WHERE TO STAY ON GRAND CAYMAN 58

Hotels & Resorts 59

FAMILY FRIENDLY LODGINGS 65

Condos, Villas & Cottages 69

4 WHERE TO EAT ON GRAND CAYMAN 77

Restaurants by Cuisine 79

Very Expensive 81

Expensive 82

Moderate 92

KILL DEVIL, THE DRINK OF CHOICE 96

Inexpensive 98

5 BEACHES & ACTIVE PURSUITS ON GRAND CAYMAN 104

Hitting the Beaches 105

Scuba Diving & Snorkeling 107

WRECK OF THE TEN SAILS 108

THE ISLAND'S NEWEST SHIPWRECK...AND NEWEST REEF 109

YOUR TEMPORARY CAYMANIAN PET: A STINGRAY 113

More Fun in the Surf 113

Other Outdoor Pursuits 116

THE BOOBY, THE PARROT, THE FRIGATE BIRD, ET AL. 117

Indoor Activities for Inclement Weather 120

6 EXPLORING GRAND CAYMAN 121

The Top Attractions 122

STROLL THROUGH HISOTRIC GEORGE TOWN 125

TRY TO AVOID GOING TO HELL 126

Other Attractions 126

THE NATIONAL FLOWER & THE NATIONAL TREE 127

DRIVING TOUR 1: GEORGE TOWN TO RUM POINT 128

DRIVING TOUR 2: GEORGE TOWN TO WEST BAY 134

Organized Tours 139

THE PIRATES OF THE CARIBBEAN 139

7 SHOPPING ON GRAND CAYMAN 141

The Shopping Scene 141

Shopping: A to Z 142

8 GRAND CAYMAN AFTER DARK 152

Clubs 153

Bar/Restaurant Combos 154

Bars 155

Pubs 156

Pool Hall Bars 158

Other Diversions 159

9 CAYMAN BRAC 160

Essentials 161

FAST FACTS: CAYMAN BRAC 162

Where to Stay 163

Where to Eat 168

Beaches & Active Pursuits 170

Shopping 174

Cayman Brac After Dark 175

10 LITTLE CAYMAN 177

Essentials 178

FAST FACTS: LITTLE CAYMAN 179

Where to Stay 180

Where to Eat 184

Beaches & Active Pursuits 185

Exploring Little Cayman 188

BIKING ON WATER 189

Shopping 190

Little Cayman After Dark 190

11 FAST FACTS 192

Index 197

LIST OF MAPS

The Best of the Cayman
    Islands 4

Cayman Islands Factoids 14

Hotels on Grand Cayman 61

Hotels on Seven Mile Beach 63

Restaurants on Seven Mile
    Beach 83

Restaurants in George Town 85

Restaurants on Grand
    Cayman 87

What to See & Do on Grand
    Cayman 123

Driving Tour 1: George Town to
    Rum Point 129

Driving Tour 2: George Town to
    West Bay 135

Hotels & Restaurants on Cayman
    Brac 165

Hotels & Restaurants on Little
    Cayman 181

ABOUT THE AUTHORS

Veteran travel writers **Darwin Porter** and **Danforth Prince** have written numerous Frommer's guides to the Caribbean, Bermuda, and The Bahamas, including books on the Dominican Republic, Puerto Rico, Jamaica, Barbados, and the Virgin Islands. Porter is also a Hollywood columnist, a radio broadcaster, and the author of numerous biographies of American iconic figures. Prince was formerly employed by the Paris bureau of *The New York Times* and is president of Blood Moon Productions.

HOW TO CONTACT US

In researching this book, we discovered many wonderful places—hotels, restaurants, shops, and more. We're sure you'll find others. Please tell us about them, so we can share the information with your fellow travelers in upcoming editions. If you were disappointed with a recommendation, we'd love to know that, too. Please write to:

Frommer's Portable Cayman Islands, 5th Edition
John Wiley & Sons, Inc. • 111 River St. • Hoboken, NJ 07030-5774

TRAVEL RESOURCES AT FROMMERS.COM

Frommer's travel resources don't end with this guide. Frommer's website, **www.frommers.com**, has travel information on more than 4,000 destinations. We update features regularly, giving you access to the most current trip-planning information and the best airfare, lodging, and car-rental bargains. You can also listen to podcasts, connect with other Frommers.com members through our active-reader forums, share your travel photos, read blogs from guidebook editors and fellow travelers, and much more.

FROMMER'S STAR RATINGS, ICONS & ABBREVIATIONS

Every hotel, restaurant, and attraction listing in this guide has been ranked for quality, value, service, amenities, and special features using a star-rating system. In country, state, and regional guides, we also rate towns and regions to help you narrow down your choices and budget your time accordingly. Hotels and restaurants are rated on a scale of zero (recommended) to three stars (exceptional). Attractions, shopping, nightlife, towns, and regions are rated according to the following scale: zero stars (recommended), one star (highly recommended), two stars (very highly recommended), and three stars (must-see).

In addition to the star-rating system, we also use seven feature icons that point you to the great deals, in-the-know advice, and unique experiences that separate travelers from tourists. Throughout the book, look for:

special finds—those places only insiders know about

fun facts—details that make travelers more informed and their trips more fun

kids—best bets for kids and advice for the whole family

special moments—those experiences that memories are made of

overrated—places or experiences not worth your time or money

insider tips—great ways to save time and money

great values—where to get the best deals

The following abbreviations are used for credit cards:

AE American Express	DISC Discover	V Visa
DC Diners Club	MC MasterCard	

THE BEST OF THE CAYMAN ISLANDS

I n the Cayman Islands, you can hike through untouched woodlands, pay a visit to colorful reefs and fish on a scuba-diving or snorkeling excursion, or plunk yourself down on the islands' white sands with a frosted drink in hand. You can rent an isolated West Indian cottage or stay in a luxurious resort. You can chow down on fresh fried fish at a waterside shack or indulge in a world-class five-course meal in a fine restaurant. Whatever your tastes and budget, this chapter will guide you to the best that the Cayman Islands have to offer.

THE best CAYMAN ISLAND EXPERIENCES

o **"Petting" the Stingrays:** Called the "world's best 4m (13-ft.) dive site," Stingray City lies in Grand Cayman's North Sound. Adventuresome snorkelers and divers can swim among, pet, and feed 30 to 50 graceful, "tame" Atlantic Southern stingrays. Stingray City is a phenomenon unique to the Cayman Islands. See p. 113.

o **Scuba Diving in the Cayman Islands:** Rainbow-hued marine life and an incredible variety of dive sites, including shipwrecks and dramatic "wall dives," combine to make the Cayman Islands perhaps the single most popular spot for scuba diving in the Western Hemisphere. Many sites lie offshore of Grand Cayman, but the archipelago's smaller islands, Little Cayman and Cayman Brac, are also filled with pristine reefs and dramatic drop-offs, including Little Cayman's Bloody Bay Wall, hailed as the most sensational wall dive in the Caribbean. See "Scuba

Diving & Snorkeling" in chapter 5, "Scuba Diving" in chapter 9, and "Scuba Diving & Snorkeling" in chapter 10.

- **Exploring Deep into the Wild Interior:** On Grand Cayman, you can wander back in time on the 3.2km (2-mile) Mastic Trail, which runs through the Caribbean's best example of a dry subtropical forest. A wide variety of plants and animals unique to the Cayman Islands live in this area, where the woodland has evolved undisturbed for 2 million years. See p. 126.

- **Down into the Deep in a Submarine:** Atlantis Adventures and its competitor, Nautilus, will take you under the sea to explore the vivid, colorful life of one of the most incredible marine habitats on the planet, all without getting wet. The companies cover the full spectrum of submarine experiences, from trips to the teeming shallow reefs and shipwrecks of George Town Harbour, to voyages to coral canyons at 30m (98 ft.). You can even take a trip to the Cayman Wall at 300m (984 ft.). See p. 114.

- **Spending the Day on Seven Mile Beach:** This strip of golden sand, running the length of the western side of Grand Cayman, is what makes this island a year-round destination. Soft sands, roped-off swimming sections, and casuarina shade trees make for perfect Caribbean beachfront charm. For jogging, sunning, swimming, windsurfing, kayaking, water-skiing, parasailing, snorkeling, scuba diving, or just plain strolling, this is one of the greatest beachfronts in the Western Hemisphere, complemented by a string of hotels, restaurants, and shops along the entire length of the beach. See p. 105.

- **Visiting the World's Only Green Sea Turtle Farm:** The Cayman Turtle Farm was created to provide a safe habitat for the endangered green sea turtle. Thousands of these magnificent creatures are hatched and raised here. See p. 122.

- **Going Fishin':** Fishing is the "national sport" of the Cayman Islands—a tremendously popular pastime for locals and visitors alike. The catches (which can turn up as close as .4km/¼ mile offshore on all three islands) include such prizes as blue marlin, wahoo, dolphin (mahimahi), tuna, and other species. Bonefishermen will be lured to the flats off Little Cayman. See p. 116 for fishing off Grand Cayman, p. 172 for fishing off Cayman Brac, and p. 187 for fishing off Little Cayman.

- **Snorkeling in an Underwater Paradise:** Great snorkeling, which can be fun for the entire family, is found close to the shore of all three islands. From encounters with the rays of Stingray City to explorations of shipwrecks, underwater thrills galore await you. See "The Best Snorkeling Sites," below, for our favorite sites.

o **Escaping to Little Cayman:** As much as we like to visit Grand Cayman, we also like to escape from it sometimes. If you want a place where the only footprints in the sand will be yours, head for Little Cayman, a tiny, cigar-shaped island only 16km (10 miles) long. Here, you'll enjoy deserted, pearl-white-sand beaches; spectacular bonefishing; barbecue cookouts under the stars; and some of the best scuba diving and snorkeling in the world. See chapter 10.

o **Boating Over to Owen Island for a Picnic:** Our favorite picnic spot in all of the Caribbean is Owen Island, 180m (591 ft.) off the shores of Little Cayman. Easily accessible by rowboat, these 4.4 hectares (11 acres) are pure bliss. You'll find a white sand beach and a blue lagoon. See p. 186.

THE best BEACHES

o **Seven Mile Beach:** Did we already mention that Caribbean beaches don't get much better than Seven Mile Beach on Grand Cayman? The powdery sands here are free of litter and souvenir hawkers, and they're set against a backdrop of resorts, beach bars, restaurants, and shops. This is the Miami Beach of the Caribbean. See p. 105.

o **Southwest Coast of Cayman Brac:** A series of nearly deserted white sand beaches on Cayman Brac is anchored on the southwest coast. These are small and relatively undiscovered beaches that remind many visitors of the Caribbean "the way it used to be." Book into the Brac Reef Beach Resort and you'll be able to walk straight from your room to the sands. See p. 170.

o **Point of Sand:** At the southeastern tip of Little Cayman is the best beach on the island, with a strip of luminescent pink sand. Point of Sand is also ideal for snorkeling. On many weekdays, you'll have much of the beach to yourself. See p. 185.

THE best SCUBA-DIVING SITES

The Cayman Islands are an ideal destination for scuba divers of all experience and skill levels. We've listed our favorite dive sites below, but as the Caymans are surrounded by coral reefs, the options are nearly boundless. Throughout this book, you'll find listings of recommended dive operators who will be able to advise on which sites are right for you.

o **Eden Rock Dive Center:** One of Grand Cayman's most popular dive sites, this area has two alluring reefs, Eden Rock and Devil's

The Best of the Cayman Islands

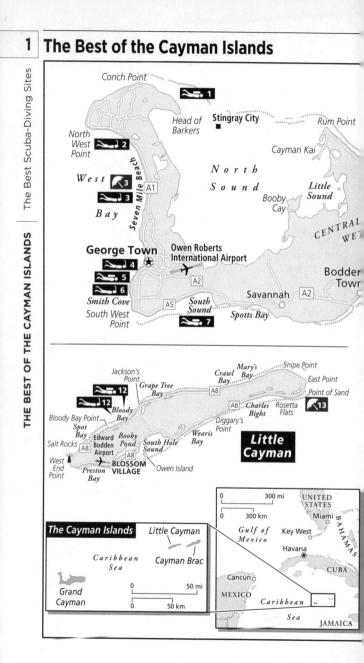

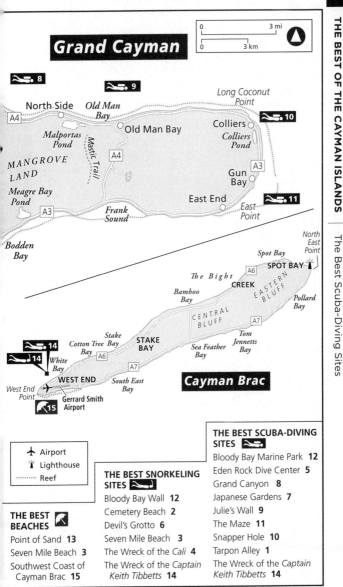

Grand Cayman

0		3 mi
0		3 km

≤. 8

≤. 9

≤. 10

North Side   *Old Man Bay*

A4

Malportas Pond

Mastic Trail

Old Man Bay

Long Coconut Point

Colliers

Colliers Pond

A4

MANGROVE LAND

Meagre Bay Pond

Gun Bay

A3

≤. 11

A3

East End

Frank Sound

East Point

Bodden Bay

North East Point

Spot Bay

SPOT BAY

The Bight

A6

CREEK

Bamboo Bay

EASTERN BLUFF

Pollard Bay

CENTRAL BLUFF

A7

Stake Bay

Cotton Tree Bay

STAKE BAY

A6

Sea Feather Bay

Tom Jennetts Bay

A7

≤ 14

≤ 14

White Bay

WEST END

A7

South East Bay

Cayman Brac

West End Point

Gerrard Smith Airport

15

✈ Airport
☀ Lighthouse
······· Reef

THE BEST SNORKELING SITES ≤

Bloody Bay Wall 12
Cemetery Beach 2
Devil's Grotto 6
Seven Mile Beach 3
The Wreck of the *Cali* 4
The Wreck of the *Captain Keith Tibbetts* 14

THE BEST BEACHES 🏖

Point of Sand 13
Seven Mile Beach 3
Southwest Coast of Cayman Brac 15

THE BEST SCUBA-DIVING SITES ≤

Bloody Bay Marine Park 12
Eden Rock Dive Center 5
Grand Canyon 8
Japanese Gardens 7
Julie's Wall 9
The Maze 11
Snapper Hole 10
Tarpon Alley 1
The Wreck of the *Captain Keith Tibbetts* 14

5

Grotto, that are close to shore at a depth of 14m (46 ft.). You'll find caves, grottos, and a miniwall, plus tunnels that rise up 12m (39 ft.) from the sand. Divers and snorkelers are treated to an array of colorful fish, sea fans, and sponges, along with an "in-residence" family of tarpon.

o **The Maze:** Located in Grand Cayman's South Channel, close to the famous **Wreck of the Ten Sails** (p. 108), this honeycomb of deep, narrow coral ravines evokes an underwater labyrinth. Sponges and soft corals greet you at every turn, along with such creatures as Caribbean reef sharks, green turtles, and spotted eagle rays. Depths range from 17 to 30m (56–98 ft.).

o **Snapper Hole:** One of the top dive sites in the islands and a favorite with beginners, this network of chutes, tunnels, and caverns at a depth of 20m (66 ft.) is located off Grand Cayman, southeast of Morritt's Tortuga Club. Tarpon occupy many of the caverns and tunnels, and schools of snapper swim by, sharing the water with nurse or black-tip sharks, eagle rays, and other denizens of the deep. Visibility is in excess of 24m (79 ft.).

o **Tarpon Alley:** Near Stingray City, this Grand Cayman wall is at a depth of 15 to 24m (49–79 ft.). It's named for the many (at least 100) tarpon who find food and refuge in the reef. Many of these "silver kings" are 1m (3¼ ft.) long, and some can reach a length of 1.2m (4 ft.). Hawksbill turtles also inhabit the site, as do barracuda, stingrays, yellowtail snapper, and other creatures. Because of its drop-offs and canyons, Tarpon Alley is a favorite with underwater photographers.

o **Julie's Wall:** Opposite the town of Old Man Bay on Grand Cayman, this exposed and rather windy, intermediate-level dive site has excellent underwater visibility at depths ranging from 20 to 30m (66–98 ft.). The wall here is home to stunning black coral formations, as well as stingrays and other marine life.

o **Grand Canyon** (also called White Stroke Canyon and 3-Bs Wall): Along the North Wall, off Grand Cayman, lies this undersea canyon. At a depth of 15 to 30m (49–98 ft.), two mammoth coral buttresses form a wide recess, which is filled with a variety of sponges and soft corals. Visibility is usually around 30m (98 ft.). Bermuda chub, purple Creole Wrasse, spotted eagle rays, and green sea turtles inhabit the site.

o **Japanese Gardens:** This site, with depths of 9 to 15m (30–49 ft.), is located inside Grand Cayman's South Wall drop-off. It has a maze of passageways and is known for its schools of Bermuda chub and the tiny, bright blue "juvenile fish" that hide in its dramatic strands of elkhorn coral.

o **The Wreck of the Captain Keith Tibbetts:** A 5- to 20-minute boat ride from most resorts on Cayman Brac, the *Captain Keith*

Tibbetts is one of the most famous wreck dives in the Caribbean. A Russian frigate sent over from Cuba, it was deliberately sunk in 1996 on the north side of Cayman Brac at a depth ranging from 17 to 34m (56–112 ft.). The wreck is home to barracudas, green moray eels, big groupers, scorpionfish, and an array of other tropical species. The coral formations, including beautiful yellow tube sponges, are stunning. See p. 171.

o **Bloody Bay Marine Park:** This dive site, located off Little Cayman, is one of the best in the Caribbean. It roughly covers the area between Jackson Point in the east and Spot Bay to the west, and encompasses 22 of this little island's dive sites. Many of the dives here are deep, as the reef plummets to 1,800m (5,906 ft.). However, the reef starts at 6m (20 ft.), so shallower dives are possible. Grouper, horse-eye jacks, triggerfish, and many small tropical fish call this area home. See p. 186.

THE best SNORKELING SITES

Several beaches and dive sites around the Cayman Islands also happen to be great spots for snorkeling. Below is a list of our favorites, including sites not listed elsewhere in this guide.

o **The Wreck of the Cali:** Wreck sites aren't just for scuba divers. Just a short swim from George Town's shores you will find the wreck of the *Cali,* sitting in shallow water and an easy snorkeling adventure. The wreck rests in 6m (20 ft.) of calm waters about 30m (98 ft.) offshore. Built in 1944, the *Cali* was a 66m (217-ft.) masted schooner that was labeled a shipping hazard in 1957. It was blown up by the British Corps of Army Engineers and has since been a popular snorkeling site. This is an especially intriguing site for snorkelers because it lies close to the shoreline. Its location in relatively shallow water also makes it relatively easy for snorkelers to explore, and it's richly rewarding because of its abundant marine life in rainbow-hued colors.

o **Seven Mile Beach & Cemetery Beach:** Many snorkelers staying on Grand Cayman snorkel off Seven Mile Beach because it's easily accessible from many resorts and rented villas and condos, and colorful reefs lie right offshore. The snorkeling near the Marriott and Westin resorts is excellent. To the north, Cemetery Reef and its public beach are good spots for underwater exploration. At Cemetery Reef we've seen shoals of parrotfish and sergeant majors and even the elusive reef shark. See p. 105.

o **Devil's Grotto:** Just south of Eden Rock, this popular Grand Cayman snorkeling site is a mere 45m (148 ft.) off Parrot's Landing Rock. You can wind your way through a series of long and intricate tunnels here. The fun begins at a depth of 3m (9¾ ft.). Tarpon are often seen at rest during daylight hours.

o **The Wreck of the Captain Keith Tibbetts:** Cayman Brac's celebrated diving site, a Russian frigate wreck, is also loved by snorkelers. See p. 171.

o **Bloody Bay Wall:** Little Cayman's fantastic diving attraction boasts some excellent spots for snorkelers who frequent many of the island's shallower dive sites. The best snorkel site is Jackson Point. Other interesting sites include the amusingly named Nancy's Cup of Tea, lying just west of Jackson Point. For more details, see chapter 10.

THE best HONEYMOON & WEDDING ACCOMMODATIONS

o **Westin Casuarina Resort & Spa, Grand Cayman** (© 800/503-7800 Honeymoon Concierge or 800/937-8461; www.starwood hotels.com): On Seven Mile Beach, with landscaped grounds and romantic suites, it offers one of the best honeymoon packages on Grand Cayman. The deal is for a 4-night minimum stay and includes a bottle of champagne, a 1-day jeep rental, a couples massage, and a sunset cruise on a ferry to Rum Point. This package costs from US$2,132 to US$2,939 per couple year-round. See p. 62.

o **Grand Cayman Marriott Beach Resort, Grand Cayman** (© 888/236-2427; www.marriott.com): With its enviable location on Seven Mile Beach, it doesn't offer honeymoon packages, but it caters to honeymooners nonetheless. The hotel can make all wedding arrangements for you if given sufficient notice. The price depends on your requirements. See p. 64.

o **Grand Cayman Beach Suites, Grand Cayman** (© 345/949-1234; www.grand-cayman-beach-suites.com): The place to go if you're looking to spend your honeymoon in the most posh, luxurious hotel on Grand Cayman (complete with a first-rate golf course). The hotel staff is experienced at making wedding plans. See p. 59.

THE best PLACES TO GET AWAY FROM IT ALL

o **Cobalt Coast Resort and Suites, Grand Cayman** (© 888/946-5656; www.cobaltcoast.com or www.divetech.com): The best resort for divers on Grand Cayman (and great for nondivers as well). Opening onto Boatswains Bay, in the residential community of West Bay, it is a charming, self-contained community that houses its guests in a series of well-furnished accommodations, including oceanfront suites. See p. 64.

o **Retreat at Rum Point, Grand Cayman** (📞 866/947-9135; www.theretreat.com.ky): The retreat opens onto a white sand beach located on an isolated, tranquil point. Although this condo complex is only 35 minutes by car from the bustle of George Town, it seems worlds away. See p. 74.

o **Morritt's Tortuga Club and Grand Resort, Grand Cayman** (📞 800/447-0309; www.morritt.com): Located on 3 hectares (7½ acres) bordering a beach at the eastern end of the island. The area around the condos offers some of Grand Cayman's best diving, but you need not be a diver to enjoy this secluded resort. See p. 73.

o **Reef Resort, Grand Cayman** (📞 888/232-0541; www.thereef. com): A timeshare/condo complex, it's situated on the remote East End, a 32km (20-mile) drive from the airport and a 45-minute trip from George Town. The large, luxurious beachfront units, each boasting a balcony, overlook serene Colliers Bay. See p. 73.

o **Walton's Mango Manor, Cayman Brac** (📞 888/866-5809; www.waltonsmangomanor.com): Set within a lush garden on 1.2 hectares (3 acres) of land on Cayman Brac's remote north shore, it is an excellent B&B. See p. 164.

o **Almond Beach Hideaways, Cayman Brac** (📞 503/472-7628; www.almondbeachhideaways.com): Features two-bedroom villas that open onto a beachfront of white sand and coconut palms, guaranteeing tranquillity and privacy. See p. 166.

o **Little Cayman Cottage, Little Cayman** (📞 800/235-5888; www.caymanvillas.com): A two-bedroom cottage set on a white sandy beach—the perfect hideaway. You'll have an instant home here, with a fully equipped kitchen and room enough for six of your closest friends and family (or whomever you choose). The only sound you'll hear is the pounding surf. See p. 182.

THE best LUXURY HOTELS

o **Ritz-Carlton, Grand Cayman** (📞 800/241-3333; www. ritzcarlton.com): Set on both sides of a boulevard next to Seven Mile Beach, feels like Europe in the Tropics with a golf course. Only problem is, it's very expensive. See p. 60.

o **Grand Cayman Beach Suites, Grand Cayman** (📞 345/949-1234; www.grand-cayman-beach-suites.com): A luxurious and stylish retreat opening onto one of the most beautiful stretches of Seven Mile Beach, 3km (1¾ miles) north of George Town. For golfers, the excellent golf course makes this the obvious lodging choice. See p. 59.

o **Westin Casuarina Resort & Spa, Grand Cayman** (✆ 800/937-8461; www.starwoodhotels.com): Opens onto the sands of Seven Mile Beach and is set on its own luxurious grounds. This resort is so complete that some visitors barely leave the complex until it's time to catch their plane back home. With excellent facilities for watersports, golf, diving, and dining, it is among the top three resorts in the entire Cayman archipelago. See p. 62.

o **Club at Little Cayman, Little Cayman** (✆ 888/756-7400; www.theclubatlittlecayman.com): The club stands on lush grounds and affords the most luxurious living on this sparsely populated island. The private villas here open onto a beach, and the complex has the island's finest pool. See p. 180.

THE best RESTAURANTS

o **Cracked Conch, Grand Cayman** (✆ 345/945-5217; www. crackedconch.com.ky): A longtime favorite and now better than ever with its vastly improved seafood and international cuisine. Of course, conch is the specialty, but you can also order the elusive turtle steak, served here because the endangered turtles are commercially raised on the island and not harvested at sea. See p. 84.

o **Kaibo Beach Bar & Grill, Grand Cayman** (✆ 345/947-9975; www.kaibo.ky): Located at the Kaibo Yacht Club, the grill serves superb international cuisine, often focusing on recipes from Louisiana. The fun, exciting Kaibo Beach Bar has a Polynesian setting that features flaming torches and multilevel terraces. The "Upstairs" restaurant is the gem here and evokes a cross between a pagan temple and a tree house. See p. 88.

o **Grand Old House, Grand Cayman** (✆ 345/949-9333; www. grandoldhouse.com): Set in a converted plantation house south of George Town. The restaurant combines American, Caribbean, and Pacific Rim cuisine. Each dish is prepared exceedingly well, especially the fresh seafood and lobster. See p. 86.

o **Hemingway's, Grand Cayman** (✆ 345/949-1234): Known for serving the finest seafood on the island, along with first-rate international cuisine. It features one of the most imaginative menus on Grand Cayman. Don't miss the catch of the day. See p. 86.

o **Reef Grill at Royal Palms, Grand Cayman** (✆ 345/945-6358; www.reefgrill.com): Nestled in the Royal Palms at the heart of Seven Mile Beach, it has some of our favorite seafood offerings.

From the memorable chowder to the lobster-filled ravioli, the dishes here are prepared with fresh, top-quality ingredients and plenty of skill. See p. 90.

o **Captain's Table, Cayman Brac** (© 345/948-1418): At the Brac Caribbean Beach Resort, it is the most exquisite place to eat on Cayman Brac. It serves the finest-quality American cuisine on the island, prepared with a deft hand. Enjoy your conch fritters and catch of the day outside by the pool. See p. 169.

o **Pirates Point Resort Restaurant, Little Cayman** (© 345/948-1010; www.piratespointresort.com): By far the best restaurant on Little Cayman, serving international cuisine created by the restaurant's owner and manager, Gladys Howard, a graduate of Cordon Bleu in Paris. Try the smoked salmon cheesecake; you won't regret it. See p. 185.

PLANNING YOUR TRIP TO THE CAYMAN ISLANDS

2

This chapter is devoted to the where, when, and how of your trip—the advance planning required to get it together and take it on the road. Because you may not know exactly where in the Cayman Islands you want to go or what to do after you're there, we begin with a quick rundown of the various islands and their attractions. For additional trip-planning information and further on-the-ground resources in the Cayman Islands, see chapter 11, "Fast Facts."

THE ISLANDS IN BRIEF

First things first—just what, and where, are the Cayman Islands? A British Overseas Territory, the Cayman archipelago comprises Grand Cayman (the largest island), Cayman Brac, and Little Cayman (the smallest). Lying 433km (269 miles) south of Havana and about 700km (435 miles) from Mexico's Yucatán Peninsula, it is part of the geographic entity known as the Cayman Ridge, which extends westward from Cuba. The archipelago is actually the top of the underwater Sierra Maestra Range, which runs north into Cuba. The Cayman Trench, the deepest part of the Caribbean Sea with a depth of just over 6.4km (4 miles), separates the Cayman Islands from Jamaica, which lies 290km (180 miles) to the southeast.

Columbus found the Cayman Islands by accident when he was blown off course en route from Panama to Hispaniola in 1503. The Caymans remained, for many decades, a lair for pirates, the home of simple fishermen, and a haven for refugees from the British justice system and, in some cases, runaway slaves. The sandy soil isn't particularly fertile, and as such, the islands never developed the extensive "plantation economy" that became prevalent on neighboring Jamaica and Cuba. The economy was dependent on fishing and trade, and life for the Caymanians was hard, with many residents eking out a living from the sea.

The Cayman Islands were granted independence from Britain in 1962. They remain a staunch member of the British Commonwealth, and pro-Anglo sentiment runs high. In the 1970s, due to their growing role as a financial center and tourist destination, the Cayman Islands began to develop rapidly. Today, Grand Cayman is the condominium capital of the Caribbean and a major center of the offshore financial industry.

It's been said that residents of the Cayman Islands fall into one of three categories: foreign financial services workers (mostly British or Northern Europeans); foreign hotel and restaurant workers (mostly British, Americans, or Slavic Europeans); and local indigenous Caymanians, the descendants of fishermen, pirates, and traders, whose families have been on the islands since the late 1700s, in some cases.

If you're a beach buff, you're in luck here. The sand on the Caymans is sugary white, the surf is typically warm and gentle, and the colors are primarily aqua and turquoise. Grand Cayman is celebrated for its magnificent stretch of white sands, known as Seven Mile Beach, which is lined with hotels and condos. Crowding is rarely a problem on the beach, even with frequent cruise ship arrivals. To satisfy your inner Robinson Crusoe, explore the many hidden coves, beautiful sheltered bays, and expanses of coastline where you can escape the crowds and find your own paradise. The other islands, Cayman Brac and Little Cayman, also have hidden beaches and coves.

When you tire of the beach—if that's possible—you'll find some of the world's best scuba diving and snorkeling here, from the plunge at Bloody Bay Wall off Little Cayman to the calm waters and gentle stingrays at Stingray City off Grand Cayman. The variety of dive sites, the clear waters and abundant marine life, and some of the best scuba-diving and snorkeling outfitters in the world make the Caymans a top diving and snorkeling destination.

In addition to little divers' inns, Grand Cayman has some of the grandest resort hotels in the Caribbean, along with dozens of beachfront condos and timeshares along Seven Mile Beach. The drawback is that there are few modest budget inns; the Caymans,

Cayman Islands Factoids

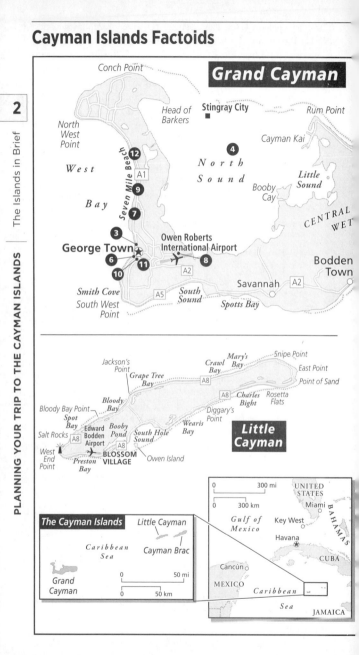

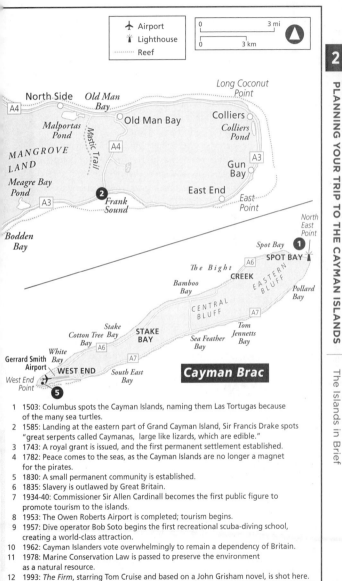

1 1503: Columbus spots the Cayman Islands, naming them Las Tortugas because of the many sea turtles.
2 1585: Landing at the eastern part of Grand Cayman Island, Sir Francis Drake spots "great serpents called Caymanas, large like lizards, which are edible."
3 1743: A royal grant is issued, and the first permanent settlement established.
4 1782: Peace comes to the seas, as the Cayman Islands are no longer a magnet for the pirates.
5 1830: A small permanent community is established.
6 1835: Slavery is outlawed by Great Britain.
7 1934-40: Commissioner Sir Allen Cardinall becomes the first public figure to promote tourism to the islands.
8 1953: The Owen Roberts Airport is completed; tourism begins.
9 1957: Dive operator Bob Soto begins the first recreational scuba-diving school, creating a world-class attraction.
10 1962: Cayman Islanders vote overwhelmingly to remain a dependency of Britain.
11 1978: Marine Conservation Law is passed to preserve the environment as a natural resource.
12 1993: *The Firm*, starring Tom Cruise and based on a John Grisham novel, is shot here.

for the most part, remain an upmarket destination, doing little to attract the frugal traveler, unlike such Caribbean countries as the Dominican Republic.

The Caymans offer excellent dining. The restaurants on the island are diverse and inventive, and they often boast outstanding chefs. In addition to upscale dining spots, plenty of relatively affordable restaurants serving standard Cayman fare can be found.

While the nightlife scene has improved in recent years, don't expect too much. Sipping tropical punch in a bar remains the preferred form of after-dark activity. If you're a casino devotee, you're out of luck: Gambling is not allowed in the Cayman Islands, so hustle yourself off to Puerto Rico or Aruba.

The islands have one of the highest standards of living in the Caribbean. Most of their residents are hospitable and courteous, and panhandling or aggressive souvenir hawking is rare. If safety is a factor in your choice of a destination for your Caribbean vacation, you can rest assured that the low crime rate in the Cayman Islands is the envy of many small nations in the Caribbean.

The downside? Although the Cayman Islands do have splashes of floral and faunal color, along with rows of royal palms and tall pines swaying in the trade winds, far prettier and more geographically dramatic islands exist in the Caribbean. You won't see any spectacular land vistas, although some of Grand Cayman's beaches, found primarily on the western and northern coasts, rank among the most beautiful in the region.

Most people come to the Cayman Islands to get away from it all in a secluded, safe haven. Many visitors come back after their first sampling, including honeymooners who return to celebrate their anniversaries.

GRAND CAYMAN   The largest of the three islands and a scuba-diving mecca, Grand Cayman has become one of the Caribbean's hottest tourist destinations in recent years. With more than 500 banks, its capital, George Town, is the offshore banking center of the Caribbean. (You won't have any trouble finding an ATM here!) Retirees are drawn to the peace and tranquillity of this British crown colony, site of a major condominium development. Almost all of the Cayman Islands' 55,000-strong population lives on Grand Cayman. The civil manners of the locals reflect their British heritage.

CAYMAN BRAC   Short on sandy beaches and the customary Caribbean attractions (beach bars, golf, and a wide selection of restaurants), Cayman Brac may appear to be a poor sibling of Grand Cayman. However, this island has its devotees, mainly adventure seekers and scuba divers who are drawn to its 30 excellent dive sites, snorkeling, bonefishing and deep-sea fishing, and bird-watching. The island lies 143km (89 miles) northeast of Grand Cayman and 7.4km (4⅔ miles) from Little Cayman, and is 19km (12 miles) long, with an average width of 3.5km (2¼ miles). It has a landmass of only 39 sq. km (15 sq. miles), and its highest point, the Bluff, is 42m (138 ft.) above sea level. The island's population is approximately 2,100.

LITTLE CAYMAN   The smallest island of the archipelago, the aptly named Little Cayman, 109km (68 miles) northeast of Grand Cayman, is only 16km (10 miles) long with an average width of 1.6km (1 mile). Relatively flat, it has a total landmass of only 16 sq. km (6¼ sq. miles), with its highest point 12m (39 ft.) above sea level. About 170 people reside on the island full time, sharing living space with some 20,000 red-footed boobies. Most of Little Cayman's residents aren't Caymanian at all, but long-term expats from the United States and elsewhere, including Great Britain and Canada. Who comes here and why? Little Cayman is hailed as one of the three best scuba-diving areas in the world and is a haven for nature lovers, photographers, and those in search of peace and quiet.

WHEN TO GO
The High Season & the Off Season

Hotels charge their highest prices during the peak winter period, from mid-December to mid-April. If you want to travel over Christmas or in the depths of February, especially around U.S. Presidents' Day weekend, you should make your reservations months in advance.

The off season in the Cayman Islands—roughly from mid-April to mid-December, although this varies from hotel to hotel—is one big summer sale, though summer travel to the Cayman Islands has become more popular in recent years. In most cases, hotels, inns, and condos slash 20% to 50% off their winter rates. Dollar for dollar, you'll spend less money renting a summer house or self-sufficient unit in the Cayman Islands than you would on Cape Cod, Fire Island, or Laguna Beach. You just have to be able to tolerate strong sun.

During the off season, beaches are less crowded and you can get good deals, but restaurants are often closed and hotels provide fewer facilities. Some hotels also use the off season to renovate—so be sure to ask if any work is going on and make sure your room is far away from the noise. If you're traveling alone during the off season, ask about the hotel's occupancy rate—especially if you want crowds!

Because there are such drastic differences between high-season and off-season rates at most hotels, we've included both for every lodging we review. Incredible savings can be enjoyed if you're willing to wait a few months for fun in the sun.

Weather

The weather during high season from mid-December to mid-April is perfect for hanging out on the beach: It's usually dry, and the cooling trade winds from the northeast moderate typically high temperatures. Sometimes a few days will be windy and cloudy, but these periods of inclement weather usually come and go quickly.

Weather-wise, the best month to visit the Cayman Islands is April, which boasts perfect warm weather before the heat of summer hits in May. In spite of the heat, many Europeans prefer a summer visit. As one visitor who hails from Yorkshire told us, "After a cold winter in the north of England, I've come just for the heat."

Rainy season is from late May until late November. However, it does not rain every day. Often the showers are short (albeit intense) bursts that are followed by clear skies and plenty of sun.

Even though the Cayman Islands are one of the world's leading scuba-diving destinations, divers often avoid the islands in August and September, when tropical storms can churn the waters. However, because the islands have so many dive sites, you can almost always find places to dive, even in August and September.

Average Temperature & Rainfall in Grand Cayman

	JAN	FEB	MAR	APR	MAY	JUNE	JULY	AUG	SEPT	OCT	NOV	DEC
TEMP. (°F)	77	77	79	81	82	84	84	84	83	82	81	78
TEMP. (°C)	25	25	26	27	28	29	29	29	28	28	27	26
RAINFALL (IN.)	2.3	1.7	1.2	1.9	5.1	7.2	7.0	6.7	8.3	9.3	4.7	2.3

Cayman Islands Calendar of Events

For an exhaustive catalog of events beyond those listed here, check **http://events.frommers.com**, where you'll find a searchable, up-to-the-minute roster of what's happening in cities all over the world.

JANUARY

Art@Government House. This excellent annual event, featuring displays of various art forms by local and resident artists, takes place on the front lawn of Government House. The day is full of entertainment, food, and local arts and crafts. Children can create their own unique works of art in the Kids Corner. Contact the National Gallery at ⓒ **345/945-8111**. Last Saturday in January.

> ## 📎 A Mighty Wind: Hurricanes on the Cayman Islands
>
> The curse of Cayman weather—the hurricane season—lasts officially from June 1 to November 30. But there's no cause for panic: Satellite forecasts give enough warning that safety precautions can be taken if a storm strikes during your visit.

Taste of Cayman. This event, taking place on Grand Cayman, is the "eatfest" of the islands, showcasing a sampling of different cuisines from more than 40 restaurants. Live entertainment, games for kids, and tasty cooking competitions are also part of the fun. Contact the Cayman Islands Tourism Association at ✆ **345/949-8522;** www.tasteofcayman. org. Last Saturday in January.

FEBRUARY

Little Cayman Mardi Gras Festival. Everybody on this small island turns out for this festive event. Parade participants show up from Grand Cayman and Cayman Brac. The parade begins in the morning at Head O'Bay and continues to the airport. Contact Gladys Howard at ✆ **345/948-1010.** Saturday before Ash Wednesday.

Cayman Islands Jazz Fest. Jazz, classical concerts, educational workshops, and art exhibitions spring up across Grand Cayman, Cayman Brac, and Little Cayman in a multitude of venues. Visit **www.cayman artsfestival.com** for dates and details. Mid-February.

MARCH

The Cayman Islands Orchid Show. This annual orchid show takes place at the Queen Elizabeth II Botanic Park from 9am to 5pm. Stop by the park to view the exquisite displays of orchids in bloom. The Orchid Society also hosts a special orchid talk and demonstration. Contact Queen Elizabeth II Botanic Park (✆ **345/947-9462;** www.botanic-park. ky). Early March.

APRIL

Easter Regatta. The Cayman Islands Sailing Club sponsors this annual event off Grand Cayman. The race attracts many boaters, who show up in catamarans ranging from 6 to 24m (20–79 ft.). Highlights include a race to the Banks, a dinghy regatta, and a sail around the island to North Sound. Contact ✆ **345/947-7913** or go to www.sailing.ky for dates and specific information. Staged right before Easter.

Cayfest (The National Festival of the Arts). This 2-week event celebrates and showcases the art and culture of the Cayman Islands. The expo opens at Seven Mile Beach with a reenactment of a traditional boat launch. In George Town, you'll find open-air events with local bands, arts and crafts, native cooking, and other demonstrations of local talent, such as culinary and song competitions. For more information, contact ☎ **345/949-5477.** Mid-April.

Cayman Islands Million Dollar Run. Launched in 2003 on Grand Cayman, this is a show of power and speed on the water, attracting powerboat aficionados and fun seekers from around the world. The hottest, fastest, and most exotic boats gather for this race, with captains competing for US$10,000 in cash and prizes. For more information, contact ☎ **345/949-8423** or visit www.mdr.ky. Third week of April.

MAY

Annual Batabano Carnival. This Mardi Gras–like event in George Town features popular carnival music and live soca (a type of calypso music with elements of soul, often with lyrics on topical or humorous subjects) and calypso bands. The event is enhanced by concession stands with Caymanian and Caribbean cuisine and delicacies. Call ☎ **345/916-1740** or visit www.caymancarnival.com for more information. Early May.

JUNE

Cayman Islands International Aviation Week. This annual air show, off Grand Cayman, includes aerial feats, displays, safety seminars, and a "fly-in" to Cayman Brac. It's sponsored by Cayman Caravan in Hilton Head, South Carolina. Third week of June.

Queen's Birthday. To honor the British heritage of the Cayman Islands, the Queen's birthday is celebrated every year in George Town on Grand Cayman. The streets of the capital are filled with a full military dress parade, complete with a 21-gun salute. You can attend an open house and garden reception at Government House. Dates vary; the event is not always on the Queen's actual birthday. Contact the Cayman Islands Tourism Association at ☎ **345/949-8522** or visit www.cita.ky for dates and details.

NOVEMBER

Cayman Islands Pirates Week. This is a national festival in which cutlass-bearing pirates and sassy wenches storm George Town, capture the governor, throng the streets, and stage a costume parade. The celebration, which is held throughout the Caymans, pays tribute to the nation's past and its cultural heritage. For the exact dates, contact the **Pirates Week Festival Administration** (☎ **345/949-5078;** www.piratesweek festival.com). Early November.

International Scuba Diving Hall of Fame. Some of the leading scuba divers in the world show up for this annual ceremony at the Harquail Theatre on Grand Cayman. Entertainment at the event includes audiovisual presentations of scuba-diving feats, live music by local bands, and a food-and-cocktail reception. Tickets are available at the tourist office. For more information, contact ☎ **345/949-8522** or click on www. scubahalloffame.com. Early November.

Remembrance Day. This is the Cayman Islands' national day of mourning and remembrance for the military heroes lost during World Wars I and II, and for all sailors and mariners lost at sea during the long maritime history of the Cayman Islands. During this national holiday, all schools, banks, and businesses are closed. In a public ceremony, wreaths are laid on two war monuments near the corner of Fort and North Church streets in downtown George Town, on Grand Cayman. Solemn music is broadcast on the radio and churches hold special ceremonies and Masses. Second Monday in November.

ENTRY REQUIREMENTS

All visitors, including those from the U.S. and the British Commonwealth countries, must have a valid return or ongoing plane ticket. All individuals 12 years of age or older are charged a **departure tax** of CI$20. This tax is included in the cost of airfare.

Passports

All **U.S. citizens** traveling to the Cayman Islands must carry a valid passport. **Canadian** and **U.K. citizens** are not required to carry a passport but need to provide proof of citizenship, such as an original birth certificate with a raised seal or a notarized copy of a birth certificate, in addition to a valid government-issued photo ID. Citizens of all other nations need a passport for entry into the Cayman Islands. Travelers carrying passports must ensure their passport is valid for up to 6 months after the scheduled date of return to the home country.

Remember, if you are not a U.S. citizen and you are stopping in or traveling through the U.S., or a U.S. territory (including Puerto Rico and the U.S. Virgin Islands) before arriving in the Cayman Islands, you will need a passport and possibly a U.S. visa. For the most up-to-date information on obtaining transit visas for the U.S., consult www.travel.state.gov.

For information on how to obtain a passport, contact the following agencies.

FOR RESIDENTS OF AUSTRALIA Contact the **Australian Passport Information Service** at ✆ **131-232,** or visit the government website at www.passports.gov.au.

FOR RESIDENTS OF CANADA Contact the central **Passport Office,** Department of Foreign Affairs and International Trade, Ottawa, ON K1A 0G3 (✆ **800/567-6868;** www.ppt.gc.ca).

FOR RESIDENTS OF IRELAND Contact the **Passport Office,** Setanta Centre, Molesworth Street, Dublin 2 (✆ **01/671-1633;** www.foreignaffairs.gov.ie).

FOR RESIDENTS OF NEW ZEALAND   Contact the **Passports Office** (*©* **0800/225-050** in New Zealand or 04/474-8100; www.passports.govt.nz).

FOR RESIDENTS OF THE UNITED KINGDOM   Visit your nearest passport office, major post office, or travel agency; or contact the **United Kingdom Passport Service** (*©* **0870/521-0410;** www.homeoffice.gov.uk/agencies-public-bodies/ips).

FOR RESIDENTS OF THE UNITED STATES   To find your regional passport office, either check the U.S. State Department website or call the **National Passport Information Center** toll-free number (*©* **877/487-2778**) for automated information.

For a country-by-country listing of passport requirements around the world, go to the "International Travel" Web page of the U.S. State Department at **www.travel.state.gov**.

Visas

Visas for the Cayman Islands are not required for U.S., Canadian, U.K., or E.U. citizens, nor for citizens of several countries in South America and the Middle East. Consult **www.caymanislands.ky**, or your nearest Cayman Islands tourist office, for a full list of nationalities that require a visa for entry. To apply for a visa for the Cayman Islands, you must contact your nearest British Consulate or High Commission Office.

Customs

For answers to complicated questions about what you can and cannot bring into the Cayman Islands, contact Cayman Islands Customs (*©* **345/949-4579;** www.customs.gov.ky).

WHAT YOU CAN BRING INTO THE CAYMAN ISLANDS

Like all Caribbean islands, the Caymans restrict what visitors can bring. There's a ban on raw fruit and vegetables. Also on their official list for exclusion are "firearms of any kind, pole spears, Hawaiian slings, and spear guns." So as not to upset the delicate ecology of these islands, live plants or plant cuttings are also forbidden. Visitors age 18 or over are allowed to bring in—duty-free—4 liters of wine or one case of beer; 1 liter of alcohol; and 200 cigarettes, 25 cigars, or 250 grams of tobacco.

WHAT YOU CAN TAKE HOME FROM THE CAYMAN ISLANDS

If you are thinking of bringing home sea turtle products (sunglasses, boxes, jewelry, and other accessories), first consult the website of the Convention on International Trade in Endangered

Species (www.cites.org). The convention strictly prohibits the importation of sea turtle products into the countries that have signed the agreement. The U.S., U.K., Canada, Australia, and New Zealand are among the 171 countries that adhere to this convention. In addition, U.S. Customs prohibits the transshipment of turtle products through the United States, and any products discovered will be confiscated.

U.S. Citizens: Returning U.S. citizens who have been away for at least 48 hours are allowed to bring back, once every 30 days, US$800 worth of merchandise duty-free. You'll be charged a flat rate of 4% duty on the next US$1,000 worth of purchases. Be sure to have your receipts handy. On mailed gifts, the duty-free limit is US$200. With some exceptions, you cannot bring fresh fruit and vegetables into the United States.

For specifics on what you can bring back, download the invaluable free pamphlet *Know Before You Go* online at www.cbp.gov (click on "Travel," and then on "Know Before You Go"), or contact **U.S. Customs and Border Protection (CBP),** 1300 Pennsylvania Ave. NW, Washington, DC 20229 (*℃* **877/287-8667;** www.cbp.gov), and request the pamphlet.

Canadian Citizens: Canada allows its citizens a C$750 exemption, and you're allowed to bring back duty-free one carton of cigarettes, one can of tobacco, 40 imperial ounces of liquor, and 50 cigars if you meet the minimum age requirements set by the province or territory through which you enter Canada. In addition, you're allowed to mail gifts to Canada valued at less than C$60 each day, provided they're unsolicited and don't contain alcohol or tobacco (write on the package "Unsolicited gift, under C$60 value"). All valuables should be declared on the Y-38 form before departure from Canada, including serial numbers of valuables you already own, such as expensive foreign cameras. *Note:* The C$750 exemption can be used only once a year and only after an absence of 7 days. For a clear summary of Canadian rules, write for the booklet *I Declare,* issued by the **Canada Border Services Agency** (*℃* **800/461-9999** in Canada or 204/983-3500; www.cbsa-asfc.gc.ca).

U.K. Citizens: U.K. citizens have a Customs allowance of 200 cigarettes, 50 cigars, or 250 grams of smoking tobacco; 4 liters of still table wine; 1 liter of spirits or strong liqueurs (over 22% volume) or 2 liters of fortified wine, sparkling wine, or other liqueurs; 60 cubic centimeters (mL) of perfume; 250 cubic centimeters (mL) of toilet water; and £145 worth of all other goods, including gifts and souvenirs. Individuals 17 and under cannot have the tobacco or alcohol allowance. For more information, contact **HM**

Customs & Excise (℡ 0845/010-9000 in the U.K. or 020/8929-0152; www.hmrc.gov.uk).

Australian Citizens: The duty-free allowance for Australia is A$900 or, for those under 18, A$450. Citizens over age 18 can bring back 250 cigarettes or 250 grams of loose tobacco, and 2.25 liters of alcohol. If you're returning with valuables you already own, such as foreign-made cameras, you should file form B263. A helpful brochure available from Australian consulates or Customs offices is *Know Before You Go*. For more information, contact the **Australian Customs Service** (℡ 1300/363-263; www.customs.gov.au).

New Zealand Citizens: The duty-free allowance for New Zealand is NZ$700. Citizens over 17 can bring back 200 cigarettes, 50 cigars, or 250 grams of tobacco (or a combination of all three if their combined weight doesn't exceed 250g); plus 4.5 liters of wine and beer, or 1.125 liters of liquor. New Zealand currency does not carry import or export restrictions. Fill out a certificate of export, listing the valuables you are taking out of the country; that way, you can bring them back without paying duty. Most questions are answered in a free pamphlet available at New Zealand consulates and Customs offices: *New Zealand Customs Guide for Travellers, Notice No. 4*. For more information, contact **New Zealand Customs, The Customhouse,** 17–21 Whitmore St., Box 2218, Wellington (℡ 04/473-6099 or 0800/428-786; www.customs.govt.nz).

Medical Requirements

Unless you're arriving from an area known to be suffering from an epidemic (particularly cholera or yellow fever), inoculations or vaccinations are not required for entry into the Cayman Islands.

GETTING THERE
By Plane

The main gateway to the Cayman Islands is through Grand Cayman. Flights to Grand Cayman arrive at **Owen Roberts International Airport (GCM)** (℡ 345/949-5252; www.grand-cayman-gcm.airports-guides.com). The airport lies just east of George Town, the capital, and is only a short taxi ride from most of the hotels along Seven Mile Beach. Customs can be aggressive at times, and you'll need to show a firmly booked hotel reservation and an ongoing or return plane ticket.

The Department of Tourism operates an **information bureau** (℡ 345/949-2635), which is open daily from 11am to 9pm, right at the airport. You'll also find ATMs in the airport, which can dispense money in either Cayman Island or U.S. dollars.

FROM THE UNITED STATES The Cayman Islands are easily accessible from the U.S. Flying time from Miami is 1 hour 20 minutes; from Houston, 2 hours 45 minutes; from Tampa, 1 hour 40 minutes; and from Atlanta, 1 hour 30 minutes. Boston and New York are hubs for flights from the U.S. Northeast. Only a handful of nonstop flights are available from the U.S. Midwest, so most visitors use Miami as their gateway. Residents flying from the West Coast to the Caymans usually have a connecting flight from New York or Miami.

Cayman Airways (℃ 800/422-9626 in the U.S. and Canada, or 345/949-2311; www.caymanairways.com) offers the most frequent service to Grand Cayman, with three flights a day from Miami, five flights a week from Tampa, and three flights a week from New York. Also available is seasonal service from Chicago and Washington, D.C.

Many visitors also fly to Grand Cayman on **American Airlines** (℃ 800/433-7300; www.aa.com), which offers direct nonstop flights from Miami to Grand Cayman daily. **Delta Airlines** (℃ 800/221-1212; www.delta.com) flies to Grand Cayman daily from Atlanta and Detroit. **US Airways** (℃ 800/622-1015; www.usairways.com) offers daily nonstop flights from Charlotte, North Carolina; it also has Saturday flights to George Town from Philadelphia and once-a-week service from Boston during the winter. **Continental Airlines** (℃ 800/231-0856; www.continental.com) offers daily service between its Houston hub and Grand Cayman. It also flies from Newark, New Jersey, on Sunday, Wednesday, and Friday.

FROM CANADA **Air Canada** (℃ 888/247-2262; www.air canada.com) flies nonstop from Toronto to George Town every Sunday. The flight takes 4 hours.

FROM THE U.K. **British Airways** (℃ 800/AIRWAYS [247-9297] in the U.S., or 0870/859-9850 in the U.K.; www.britishairways.com) has direct flights from London's Heathrow to Grand Cayman on Tuesday, Wednesday, Friday, and Saturday, with return flights on the same days. The plane touches down briefly at Nassau in the Bahamas. Total flight time is 10 hours. British Airways also flies twice daily from Heathrow to Miami, where continuing flights into George Town can be booked on Cayman Airways.

FLYING FOR LESS: TIPS FOR GETTING THE BEST AIRFARE

o Passengers who book their ticket either long in advance or at the last minute, or who fly midweek or at less-trafficked hours, may pay a fraction of the full fare. If your schedule is flexible, see if you can secure a cheaper fare by adjusting your flight plans.

Don't Stow It—Ship It

Though shipping luggage can be pricey, it's sometimes worth-while, particularly if you're toting diving equipment, meetings materials, or baby furniture. Specialists in door-to-door luggage delivery include **First Luggage** (*© 800/224-5781; www.first luggage.com) and **Sports Express** (*© 800/357-4174; www.sports express.com).

- Look online for cheap fares. The most popular online travel agencies are **Travelocity** (www.travelocity.com and www.travelocity.co.uk), **Expedia** (www.expedia.com and www.expedia.co.uk or www.expedia.ca), and **Orbitz** (www.orbitz.com). In the U.K., go to **Travelsupermarket** (*© 0845/345-5708;* www.travelsupermarket.com), a search engine that offers flight comparisons for the budget airlines whose seats often end up in bucket-shop sales. Other websites for booking airline tickets include **Cheapflights.com**, **SmarterTravel.com**, **Priceline.com**, and **Opodo** (www.opodo.co.uk). Meta-search sites (which find and then direct you to airline and hotel web-sites for booking) include **Kayak.com**, which includes fares for budget carriers like jetBlue and Spirit as well as major airlines. In addition, most airlines offer online-only fares that even their phone agents know nothing about. British travelers should check **Flights International** (*© 0800/018-7050;* www.flights-international.com) for deals on flights all over the world.
- Keep an eye on local newspapers for promotional specials or fare wars, when airlines lower prices on their popular routes.
- **Consolidators,** also known as bucket shops, are wholesale brokers in the airline ticket game. Consolidators buy deeply discounted tickets ("distressed" inventories of unsold seats) from airlines and sell them to online ticket agencies, travel agents, tour operators, corporations, and, to a lesser degree, the general public. Consolidators advertise in Sunday newspaper travel sections (often in small ads with tiny type), both in the U.S. and the U.K. They can be great sources for cheap interna-tional tickets. On the downside, bucket-shop tickets are often rigged with restrictions, such as stiff cancellation penalties (as high as 50%–75% of the ticket price). And keep in mind that most of what you see advertised is of limited availability. Several reliable consolidators also sell tickets online. **STA Travel** (www.statravel.com) has been the world's leading consolidator for students since purchasing Council Travel, but its fares are

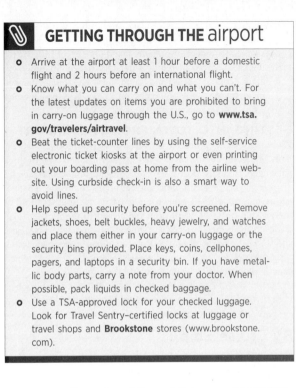

GETTING THROUGH THE airport

- Arrive at the airport at least 1 hour before a domestic flight and 2 hours before an international flight.
- Know what you can carry on and what you can't. For the latest updates on items you are prohibited to bring in carry-on luggage through the U.S., go to **www.tsa. gov/travelers/airtravel**.
- Beat the ticket-counter lines by using the self-service electronic ticket kiosks at the airport or even printing out your boarding pass at home from the airline website. Using curbside check-in is also a smart way to avoid lines.
- Help speed up security before you're screened. Remove jackets, shoes, belt buckles, heavy jewelry, and watches and place them either in your carry-on luggage or the security bins provided. Place keys, coins, cellphones, pagers, and laptops in a security bin. If you have metallic body parts, carry a note from your doctor. When possible, pack liquids in checked baggage.
- Use a TSA-approved lock for your checked luggage. Look for Travel Sentry–certified locks at luggage or travel shops and **Brookstone** stores (www.brookstone. com).

competitive for travelers of all ages. **Flights.com** (© **201/541-3826**; www.flights.com) has excellent fares worldwide, particularly to Europe. It also has "local" websites in 12 countries. **AirTicketsDirect** (© **888/858-8884**; www.airtickets direct.com) is based in Montreal and leverages the Canadian dollar for low fares; it also books trips to places that U.S. travel agents won't touch, such as Cuba.

- Join frequent-flier clubs. Frequent-flier membership doesn't cost a cent, but it does entitle you to free tickets or upgrades when you amass the airline's required number of frequent-flier points. You don't even have to fly to earn points; frequent-flier credit cards can earn you thousands of miles for doing your everyday shopping. But keep in mind that award seats are limited, seats on popular routes are hard to snag, and more and more major airlines are cutting their expiration periods for mileage points—so check your airline's frequent-flier program so you don't lose your miles before you use them. *Tip:* Award seats are offered almost a year in advance, but seats also open up at the last minute, so if your travel plans are flexible, you may strike gold. To play the frequent-flier game to your best advantage, consult the community bulletin boards on **FlyerTalk** (www.flyertalk.com) or go to Randy Petersen's **Inside Flyer** (www.insideflyer.com). Petersen and friends review all the programs in detail and post regular updates on changes in policies and trends.

GETTING INTO TOWN FROM THE AIRPORT

Plenty of taxis are available at Owen Roberts International Airport. The government sets taxi fares, which apply to one to three passengers sharing a ride. Each additional person beyond a group of three pays 25% of the fare. Typical prices (subject to change) are as follows: US$30 from the airport to the southern end of Seven Mile Beach; US$30 from the airport to the northern end of Seven Mile Beach; US$69 from the airport to the East End; and US$72 from the airport to Rum Point on the north shore.

To protect taxi drivers and their livelihood, the government doesn't allow buses between town and the airport.

Many car rental agencies operate kiosks in the airport. It's best to reserve a car before you leave home. For specifics, see "Getting Around," later in this chapter.

By Cruise Ship

Here's a brief rundown of some of the major cruise lines that serve the Caribbean. For more detailed information, pick up a copy of *Frommer's Caribbean Cruises & Ports of Call.*

BOOKING A CRUISE

If you have a favorite travel agency, then by all means, leave the details to the tried-and-true specialists. Many agents will propose a package deal that includes airfare to your port of embarkation. It's possible to purchase your air ticket on your own and book your cruise ticket separately, but in most cases you'll save big bucks by purchasing the fares as a package.

You're also likely to save money—sometimes *lots* of money—by contacting a specialist who focuses on cruise bookings. He or she will be able to match you with a cruise line whose style suits you, and to steer you toward any special sales or promotions.

Here are some travel agencies to consider: **Cruises Inc.** (© 888/282-1249 or 800/854-0500; www.cruiseinc.com); **CruisesOnly** (© 800/278-4737; www.cruisesonly.com); the **Cruise Company** (© 800/289-5505 or 402/339-6800; www.thecruisecompany.com); **Kelly Cruises** (© 800/837-7447 or 630/990-1111, www.kellycruises.com); **Hartford Holidays Travel** (© 800/828-4813 or 516/746-6670; www.hartfordholidays.com); and

Mann Travel and Cruises (ⓒ **800/849-2028;** www.mann travels.com). Cruise lines don't profit if their megaships don't fill up to near peak capacity, so price wars happen frequently. The companies listed above are tuned in to last-minute sales resulting from price wars.

You're likely to sail to the Caymans from Miami, which has become the cruise capital of the world. Other departure ports in Florida include Port Everglades (at Fort Lauderdale), Port Canaveral, and Tampa.

CRUISE LINES

o **Carnival Cruise Lines** (ⓒ **888/CARNIVAL** [2276-4825]; www.carnival.com): Offering affordable vacations on some of the biggest and most vividly decorated ships afloat, Carnival is the brashest and most successful mass-market cruise line in the world. More than 17 of its vessels depart for the Caribbean from Miami, Tampa, New Orleans, Port Canaveral, and San Juan, and some of them specialize in 7-day or longer tours that feature stopovers at selected ports throughout the eastern, western, and southern Caribbean, including Grand Cayman. The cruises are a good value and feature nonstop activities, plus lots of brightly colored drinks. Passengers tend to be young at heart, ready to party, and keyed up for nonstop, round-the-clock fun. While it's one of the best lines to choose if you're single, Carnival's ships certainly aren't overrun by singles—families (who appreciate the well-run children's programs) and couples are definitely in the majority. The average onboard age is a relatively youthful 42. *Note:* Guests are required to be 21 years old (on embarkation day) to travel alone. Those under the age of 21 must be accompanied in the same stateroom by a parent or guardian 25 or older. The exceptions to this rule are a documented married minor couple or pair of legal domestic partners/same-sex union.

o **Celebrity Cruises** (ⓒ **800/647-2251** or 316/554-5961; www. celebritycruises.com): Celebrity maintains stylish, medium-to-large ships with cruises that last between 7 and 15 nights and visit ports such as Key West, San Juan, Grand Cayman, St. Thomas, Ocho Rios (Jamaica), Antigua, and Cozumel (Mexico), to name a few. The ships themselves are works of art—gorgeously designed and featuring clean lines and modern materials—and the onboard atmosphere is classy without being at all stuffy. Accommodations are roomy and well equipped, cuisine is the most refined of any of its competitors, and service is impeccable. The ships also feature beautiful spas. Plus, cruises are competitively priced (though you should watch out for the pricey extras). Clients choose Celebrity because it offers a well-balanced cruise, with lots of activities and a glamorous, exciting atmosphere that's both refined (think champagne and cozy lounges) and fun (think "dress your husband up in women's clothes" contests). Most passengers are couples in their mid-30s and up, with decent numbers of honeymooners and couples celebrating anniversaries, as well as families with children in summer and during the holidays.

o **Costa Cruises** (© **800/462-6782;** www.costacruises.com): Costa sails the 1,358-passenger *Costa Magica* and the 2,112-passenger *Costa Mediterranea* on western and eastern Caribbean cruises on alternate weeks, departing from Fort Lauderdale. Ports of call on the eastern Caribbean itineraries include stopovers in San Juan, St. Thomas, and Nassau. Itineraries through the western Caribbean include stopovers at Grand Cayman, Ocho Rios or Montego Bay (Jamaica), Key West, and Cozumel (Mexico). There's an Italian flavor and lots of Italian design onboard here and an atmosphere of relaxed indulgence. The food is above average. Costa attracts passengers of all ages who want lots of action and who deliberately avoid all-American megaships like those of Carnival. In the Caribbean, Costa appeals both to retirees and to young couples, though there are more passengers over 50 than under. Typically you won't see more than 40 or 50 kids on any one cruise except during holidays such as Christmas and spring break. While about 80% to 90% of passengers are from North America, there's usually a healthy percentage from Europe and South America as well.

o **Holland America Line** (© **877/932-4259;** www.hollandamerica. com): Holland America offers the most Old World–style cruise experience of the mainstream lines, aboard a fleet of respectably hefty and good-looking ships. The cruise line provides solid value, with few jolts or surprises, and attracts a solid, well-grounded clientele of primarily older travelers (so late-night revelers and serious partyers might want to book cruises on other lines, such as Carnival). The 7-day and 10- to 14-day cruises stop at deepwater mainstream ports throughout the Caribbean, including Key West, Grand Cayman, St. Martin, St. Lucia, Curaçao, Barbados, and St. Thomas. Although younger faces are starting to pepper the mix in greater numbers, most HAL passengers still tend to be low-key, fairly sedentary, 55-plus North American couples. Only about 30 or 40 people per cruise will be traveling solo.

GETTING INTO TOWN FROM THE CRUISE SHIP TERMINAL

Cruise ships anchor off George Town and then ferry passengers to the terminals along Harbour Drive, which is in the heart of the shopping and sightseeing district. The waters are often choppy here, so anticipate a rough ride. The Grand Cayman tourist office dispenses information from a little kiosk at the pier when cruise ships arrive. Taxis line up to meet arriving passengers. If you need to call home, there's a phone center accepting credit cards nearby along Shedden Road.

GETTING AROUND

This section includes information on getting around Grand Cayman, the largest island in the Cayman Islands. For information on getting around on Cayman Brac and Little Cayman, see p. 161 and p. 178, respectively.

By Car

Is it necessary to rent a car on Grand Cayman? It depends. If you want to explore the island, you can do so on a far less expensive organized tour. Many visitors prefer to settle into their hotels at Seven Mile Beach for the duration of their visit, perhaps taking one tour or venturing into George Town for a shopping expedition. If you fall into this category, you can easily depend on buses or taxis and save yourself the hassle and expense of a renting a car. However, if you wish to explore the island and don't want to depend on taxis, a rental car is an excellent idea.

The British tradition of **driving on the left** is followed in the Cayman Islands. A driving permit is mandatory if you rent a car. All car rental companies are required by law to issue this permit and collect the fee of US$7.50. Permits, which are valid for 6 months, are also issued at the George Town Police Station on Elgin Avenue (© **345/949-4222**).

Car rental prices depend on the season, with the highest rates charged between mid-December and mid-April. In the off season, prices are often reduced by around 35%. Several car rental companies operate on the island, including **Avis,** which has a kiosk at the Grand Cayman Airport and several at resorts along West Bay Road in George Town (© **800/331-1212** in the U.S., or 345/949-2468; www.avis.com); **Budget,** Grand Cayman Airport (© **800/527-0700** in the U.S., or 345/949-5605; www.budgetcayman.com); **Cayman Auto Rentals,** 135 N. Church St. in George Town (© **345/949-1013;** www.caymanautorentals.com.ky); **Hertz,** Grand Cayman Airport (© **800/654-3001** in the U.S., or 345/949-2280; www.hertz.com); and **Thrifty,** Grand Cayman Airport (© **800-THRIFTY** [847-4389] in the U.S., or 345/949-6640; www.thrifty.com). Avis, Budget, and Cayman Auto Rentals require that reservations be made between 6 and 36 hours before pickup.

RENTING A car 101

All the major car rental companies maintain kiosks within walking distance of the airport terminal on Grand Cayman, although some visitors find it easier to take a taxi to their hotel and arrange for their car to be delivered there.

All major companies suggest that car rentals be reserved at least 6 to 36 hours **in advance** of arrival in the Caymans. In midwinter you should reserve several days in advance because of high demand.

There is definite age "discrimination" in the Cayman Islands. Always check the age requirement with the rental agency before cementing a deal. At Avis you can be 21 years old, but at Hertz, for example, you must be 25. Budget also requires that you be 25 years old and—get this—not above 75 years of age.

The speed limit is 48kmph (30 mph) in built-up areas such as George Town and along Seven Mile Beach, and 64kmph (40 mph) on most other island roads. The highest speed limit on the island is in the East End, where posted speeds go up to 81kmph (50 mph). All gas prices are published at **www.planning.gov.ky**. Stations charge more or less the same prices, ranging from CI$3 to CI$4 per gallon. The busiest stations include **Jose's Service Center** across from the airport (© **345/949-5500**); **Savannah Texaco** across from Countryside Shopping Village (© **345/947-3660**); and **Texas 7-Mile Beach Star Mart** at Seven Mile Beach (© **345/949-0175**).

By Taxi or Limo Bus

Taxicabs, with drivers who are generally informative and friendly, are plentiful at the airport and in front of the cruise ship terminals in George Town. You'll also find them parked in front of the major resorts along Seven Mile Beach. For the most part, drivers are among the most honest you are likely to find in the Caribbean. Shirtless, wet, or damp passengers are frowned upon and may not be taken at all. If you're going out at night, a member of the staff at your resort will often call a taxi for you. Many cabs can be hired for a tour of the island.

The government sets cab prices and regulates the cabbies, so every driver should have the official government rate sheet. Inform the driver where you're heading and agree on the fare before getting into the cab. You may want to ask to see the official rate sheet. If you're paying in U.S. dollars, don't expect the driver to accept denominations larger than US$20. Tipping cabbies between 15% and 20% is the local custom.

The island's major taxi companies include **Burtons Taxi Service** (✆ 345/926-8294; www.burtons.ky) and **A.A. Transportation** (✆ 345/949-7222). If you're going to be out late, you'll have to make advance arrangements with either of these companies for pickup. Contact the companies from Monday to Friday between 7am and 11pm or Saturday between 7am and 6pm to arrange late-night pickup times.

McCurley's Tours, North Side (✆ 345/947-9626) provides transport to and from the airport in air-conditioned limo buses. **Elite Transportation** (✆ 345/949-5963) also arranges airport transfers and personalized sightseeing charters at US$100 per hour. It is the only transport service on the island that provides wheelchair transportation.

By Bus

Buses are mainly used by islanders going to and from work, although visitors who have endless patience and plenty of time to get around also take advantage of them. George Town has had bus service since 1998. A modern terminal adjacent to the Public Library on Edward Street in the center of George Town serves as the dispatch point for buses to all districts. In total, there are 38 minibuses serving eight routes. The most useful line runs from George Town along Seven Mile Beach every 20 minutes during the day. Bus service runs daily from 6am to midnight, with most fares costing CI$1.50 to CI$3.

Buses serve all the main points on the island, including Seven Mile Beach, West Bay, Bodden Town, East End, and North Side. There is no central number to call, since most of the buses are independently operated. For complaints and feedback, call ✆ 345/945-5100, though often you'll get only a recording.

By Bike or Scooter

Grand Cayman is one of the best Caribbean islands for biking, as its main arteries are relatively flat, decently paved, wide, and properly signposted. If you stick to the coastal route, you'll experience few difficulties except for unexpected downpours. Side roads, however, can be difficult, especially if you're attempting to venture a bit into the interior. You should avoid the morning and evening rush hours at George Town and along Seven Mile Beach if possible.

In spite of Grand Cayman's reputation for safety, bicycle theft is a problem. If you're going to leave your bike unguarded, perhaps while going for a swim on a beach, make sure that it's secured, just as you would in any urban area.

A reliable independent outfitter for bike and scooter rentals on Grand Cayman is **Cayman Cycle Rentals,** Coconut Place, West Bay Road (© **345/945-4021**), which is open daily from 9am to 5pm, offering a fleet of scooters, 10-speed bikes, and mountain bikes. They also provide locks and maps. Some bikes have baskets. Bikes cost US$25 per day, and scooters are US$45 a day. A US$100 deposit is required for a bike and a US$200 deposit is required for a scooter. If you don't have a credit card, a cash deposit of US$500 is required for a bike or a scooter. Insurance (which is optional) costs an additional US$26 per day.

Before arranging a bike rental at Cayman Cycle Rentals, check with your hotel to see if they rent bikes—many of them do. Cayman Islands law requires that all cyclists and scooter riders wear helmets.

MONEY & COSTS

The Cayman Islands dollar is the official currency of the Cayman Islands, although U.S. dollars are readily accepted everywhere. Although some international banks abbreviate it as KYD, the country's currency is usually identified within the Cayman Islands as CI$.

The Cayman Islands Dollar & the U.S. Dollar: At the time of this writing, CI$1 = US$1.22. Inversely stated, US$1 is worth approximately CI82¢.

The Cayman Islands Dollar & the British Pound: At the time of this writing, CI$1 = 74p. Inversely stated, £1 is worth approximately CI$1.34.

The Cayman Islands Dollar & the Canadian Dollar: At the time of this writing, CI$1 = C$1.19. Inversely stated, C$1 is worth approximately CI83¢.

The Cayman Islands Dollar & the Euro: At the time of this writing, CI$1 = €0.85. Inversely stated, €1 is worth approximately CI$1.17.

The Cayman Islands Dollar & the Australian Dollar: At the time of this writing, CI$1 = A$1.15. Inversely stated, A$1 is worth approximately CI87¢.

The Cayman Islands Dollar & the New Zealand Dollar: At the time of this writing, CI$1 = NZ$1.50. Inversely stated, NZ$1 is worth approximately CI66¢.

THE VALUE OF THE CAYMAN ISLANDS DOLLAR VS. OTHER CURRENCIES

CI$	US$	UK£	C$	Euro(€)	A$	NZ$
1.00	1.22	0.74	1.19	0.85	1.15	1.50

Frommer's lists exact prices in the local currency; however, hotel rates are quoted in US$ in this guide. The currency conversions quoted above were correct at press time. However, rates fluctuate, so before departing, consult a currency exchange website such as **www.oanda.com** or **www.xe.com** to check up-to-the-minute rates. Although the rate between the CI$ and the US$ is permanently fixed as part of an international banking agreement, the ratios between the CI$ and other currencies fluctuate, based on frequently changing financial and political factors.

Warning: Be alert about which currency is being quoted at any given time. Hotels tend to quote their rates in U.S. dollars, while restaurants, nightclubs, and gift shops tend to quote their prices in Cayman Islands dollars. We do the same when quoting prices in this guide. Misunderstanding the currency quoted for any given transaction can be embarrassing and expensive.

It's always advisable to bring money in a variety of forms when traveling: a mix of cash, credit cards, and traveler's checks. You should also exchange enough cash to cover airport incidentals, tipping, and transportation to your hotel before you leave home, or withdraw money upon arrival at an airport ATM.

In many international destinations, ATMs offer the best exchange rates. Avoid exchanging money at commercial exchange bureaus and hotels, which often have the highest transaction fees.

The Cayman Islands are one of the most upmarket destinations in the Caribbean, although prices aren't as sky-high as on the French island of St. Barts or the British-affiliated island of Anguilla. Nevertheless, a frugal traveler will do better in Puerto Rico or the Dominican Republic. The cost of living is about 20% higher in the Cayman Islands than it is in the United States.

Brace yourself for the high prices that resorts charge. There is almost nothing in the budget category. To give you an idea of the price structure, an "inexpensive" room in Grand Cayman is one charging US$150 a night for a double, a price that might buy you a first-class hotel in many parts of America.

Most of the big hotels along Seven Mile Beach don't offer meal plans such as the MAP (the Modified American Plan, which

WHAT THINGS COST IN GRAND CAYMAN	CI$
Taxi from airport to Seven Mile Beach	12.00
Average bus fare	2.00
Lunch for one at Chicken! Chicken! (inexpensive)	7.00
Dinner for one, without wine, at Grand Old House (expensive)	40.00
Dinner for one, without wine, at Bacchus (moderate)	24.00
Dinner for one, without wine, at Al la Kebab (inexpensive)	8.00
Double room, high season, at Ritz-Carlton (very expensive)	590.00
Studio, high season, at Comfort Suites (moderate)	210.00
Double room, high season, at Eldemire's Guest House (inexpensive)	100.00
Half a liter of beer	5.00
Coca-Cola or Pepsi in a restaurant	2.25
Cup of coffee	2.50
Glass of wine	9.00
Movie ticket	12.50

includes breakfast and either lunch or dinner). You'll often have to pay for your food a la carte. Food prices are high since almost everything is imported, but they're not nearly as exorbitant as hotel prices; US$20 to US$35 will get you a main course at a typical restaurant. "Budget" would refer to any restaurant serving main courses for US$18 and under.

ATMs

The easiest and most economical way to get cash away from home is from an ATM (automated teller machine), sometimes referred to as a "cash machine," or a "cashpoint." The **Cirrus** (© 800/424-7787; www.mastercard.com) and **PLUS** (www.visa.com) networks span the globe. Go to your bank card's website to find ATM locations in the Cayman Islands. Be sure you know your Personal Identification Number (PIN) and your daily withdrawal limit before you depart. It's a good idea to also notify your bank of your travel plans, as international withdrawals may be interpreted as fraud, causing your account to be blocked. *Note:* Many banks

Show Me the Cash (and Small Change)

When you change money, ask for some small bills or loose change. It's always a good idea to carry around some cash and change for small expenses like cab rides, public transportation, tips, or for when a restaurant or small shop doesn't take plastic, which can happen if you're dining at a neighborhood joint or buying from a small vendor. Consider keeping the change separate from your larger bills, so that it's readily accessible and to avoid being a target for pickpockets. Remember that U.S. dollars are accepted almost everywhere on the islands.

impose a fee every time you use a card at another bank's ATM, and that fee can be higher for international transactions (up to US$5 or more) than for domestic ones (where they're rarely more than US$2). In addition, the bank from which you withdraw cash may charge its own fee. For international withdrawal fees, ask your bank.

Note: Banks that are members of the **Global ATM Alliance** charge no transaction fees for cash withdrawals at other Alliance member ATMs; these include Bank of America, Scotiabank (Canada, Caribbean, and Mexico), Barclays (U.K. and parts of Africa), Deutsche Bank (Germany, Poland, Spain, and Italy), and BNP Paribas (France).

Although ATMs are hard to come by on Cayman Brac and Little Cayman, banks with ATMs are easy to find in George Town, the capital of Grand Cayman. You can request U.S. dollars or Cayman dollars at most banks and ATMs.

Credit Cards

Credit cards are another safe way to carry money. They also provide a convenient record of all your expenses, and they generally offer relatively good exchange rates. You can withdraw cash advances from your credit cards at banks or ATMs, but high fees make credit card cash advances a pricey way to get cash. Keep in mind that you'll pay interest from the moment of your withdrawal, even if you pay your monthly bills on time. Also, note that many banks now assess a 1% to 3% "transaction fee" on **all** charges you incur abroad (whether you're using the local currency or your native currency).

Traveler's Checks

You can buy traveler's checks at most banks. They are offered in denominations of US$20, US$50, US$100, US$500, and

Dear Visa: I'm Off to Seven Mile Beach!

Some credit card companies recommend that you notify them of any impending trip abroad so that they don't become suspicious when the card is used numerous times in a foreign destination and block your charges. Even if you don't call your credit card company in advance, you can always call the card's toll-free emergency number if a charge is refused—a good reason to carry the phone number with you. But perhaps the most important lesson here is to carry more than one card with you on your trip; a card might not work for any number of reasons, so having a backup is the smart way to go.

sometimes US$1,000. Generally, you'll pay a service charge ranging from 1% to 4%.

The most popular traveler's checks are offered by **American Express** (© 800/807-6233 or 800/221-7282 for cardholders—this number accepts collect calls, offers service in several foreign languages, and exempts Amex gold and platinum cardholders from the 1% fee); **Visa** (© 800/732-1322—AAA members can obtain Visa checks for free for checks up to US$1,500 at most AAA offices or by calling © 866/339-3378); and **MasterCard** (© 800/223-9920).

Be sure to keep a record of the traveler's checks' serial numbers separate from your checks in case they are stolen or lost. You'll get a refund faster if you know the numbers.

American Express, Thomas Cook, Visa, and **MasterCard** offer **foreign currency traveler's checks,** useful if you're traveling to one country or to the Euro zone; they're accepted at locations where dollar checks may not be.

Another option is prepaid traveler's check cards, reloadable cards that work much like debit cards but aren't linked to your checking account. The **American Express Travelers Cheque Card,** for example, requires a minimum deposit, sets a maximum balance, and has a one-time issuance fee of US$14.95. You can withdraw money from an ATM (for a fee of US$2.50 per transaction, not including bank fees), and the funds can be purchased in dollars, euros, or pounds. If you lose the card, your available funds will be refunded within 24 hours.

HEALTH
Staying Healthy

There are no particular health concerns for travelers to the Cayman Islands. It is one of the safest destinations in the Caribbean.

The best and most comprehensive health care facilities can be found on Grand Cayman.

GENERAL AVAILABILITY OF HEALTH CARE

No shots are required prior to travel to the Cayman Islands (see "Medical Requirements," p. 24). While Grand Cayman has extensive medical facilities, Little Cayman and Cayman Brac have only small clinics. If someone becomes seriously ill or injured on the two smaller islands, he or she will be airlifted to George Town. Grand Cayman also has a decompression chamber. All victims of scuba-diving accidents in the Cayman Islands are taken immediately to this facility.

It's easy to get over-the-counter medicine on Grand Cayman, but more difficult on Cayman Brac or Little Cayman. If you'll be visiting the two smaller islands, stock up on whatever medication you think you'll need. For details on drugstores, hospitals, and medical emergencies on Grand Cayman, see chapter 11, "Fast Facts." For details on hospitals and clinics on Cayman Brac and Little Cayman, see p. 162 and p. 179, respectively.

Pack prescription medications and prescriptions in your carry-on luggage. Many people try to slip drugs such as cocaine into the Cayman Islands (or pick them up there). Drugs are often placed into a container for prescription medication after the legal medications have been removed. Customs officials are well aware of this type of smuggling and often check medications against prescriptions if they suspect a passenger is bringing illegal drugs into or out of a country. Carry written prescriptions in generic, not brand-name, form (as local pharmacists may not recognize foreign brand names), and keep all prescription medications in their original labeled vials.

COMMON AILMENTS

See also "Water" in chapter 11, "Fast Facts."

SUN EXPOSURE   The Cayman sun can be brutal. Wear sunglasses and a hat, and use sunscreen liberally. Limit your time on the beach during the first day. If you do overexpose yourself, stay out of the sun until you recover. If you experience extended periods of fever, chills, headache, nausea, or dizziness following overexposure to the sun, see a doctor.

BUGS & BITES   One of the biggest menaces is the "no-see-ums," which appear mainly in the early evening. You can't see these gnats, but you sure can feel them. Mosquitoes are also a nuisance. Window screens often fail to keep these critters out, so carry bug repellent.

Safe Travels

The following government websites offer up-to-date health-related travel advice.

o **Australia:** www.smartraveller.gov.au

o **Canada:** www.hc-sc.gc.ca/index_e.html

o **U.K.:** www.healthy-travel.co.uk

o **U.S.:** www.fco.gov.uk/en/travel-and-living-abroad

What to Do If You Get Sick Away from Home

Finding a good doctor in the Cayman Islands is not a problem, and all of them speak English. See chapter 11, "Fast Facts," for hospitals on Grand Cayman, and chapters 9 and 10 for hospitals and clinics on the smaller islands.

When you travel abroad, you will often have to pay all medical costs upfront and be reimbursed later. Medicare and Medicaid do not provide coverage for medical costs outside the U.S. Before leaving home, find out what medical services your health insurance covers. To protect yourself, consider buying medical travel insurance (see "Insurance" in chapter 11, "Fast Facts"). Be aware that the Cayman Islands and the U.K. do not have a mutual insurance agreement; though the islands are part of the British Commonwealth, British visitors are not entitled to free treatment under the British health system, and will be charged in the Caymans for any services rendered. For advice for U.K. citizens on healthy travel and medical insurance, see **www.fco.gov.uk/en/travel-and-living-abroad**.

Very few health insurance plans will pay for medical evacuation back to the U.S. (which can cost US$10,000 and up). A number of companies offer medical evacuation services worldwide. If you're ever hospitalized more than 150 miles from home, **MedjetAssist** (© **800/527-7478;** www.medjetassistance.com) will pick you up and fly you to the hospital of your choice virtually anywhere in the world in a medically equipped and staffed aircraft 24 hours day, 7 days a week. Annual memberships are US$225 individual, US$350 family; you can also purchase short-term memberships.

If you suffer from a chronic illness, consult your doctor before your departure. Drugstores and pharmacies are not plentiful, but adequate. They stock most generic drugs; however, if you are on special drugs, it is best to arrive in the Caymans with an adequate supply and not count on local pharmacies. At Cayman hospitals, you will need to be covered by health insurance—or else be prepared to pay in cash or with a credit card.

Contact the **International Association for Medical Assistance to Travellers (IAMAT)** (© **716/754-4883** or 416/652-0137 in Canada; www.iamat.org) for tips on travel and health concerns and for lists of local doctors. The United States **Centers for Disease Control and Prevention** (© **800/CDC-INFO** [232-4636]; www.cdc.gov) provides up-to-date information on health hazards by region or country and offers tips on food safety. **Travel Health Online** (www.tripprep.com), sponsored by a consortium of travel medicine providers, also offers helpful advice on traveling abroad. You can find listings of reliable medical clinics overseas at the **International Society of Travel Medicine** (www.istm.org).

CRIME & SAFETY

Violent crime is rare in the Cayman Islands, but petty thefts, pickpocketing, and purse snatchings occasionally occur. There have been incidents of sexual assault, some reportedly involving the use of so-called "date rape" drugs, such as Rohypnol. To avoid being the victim of a crime, visitors should exercise common sense and take basic precautions, including being aware of their surroundings, not walking alone after dark or in remote areas, and using reasonable caution when offered food or beverages by strangers. Also, gays and lesbians should be aware that discrimination based on sexual orientation remains an issue in the Caymans (see below).

The loss or theft of a passport abroad should be reported immediately to the local police. U.S. citizens may refer to the Depart-

SAFETY & SECURITY FOR
scuba divers

On average, one American citizen per month drowns or suffers cardiac arrest while snorkeling or scuba diving in the Cayman Islands. These deaths are often attributed to tourists overestimating their abilities given their training and physical fitness, or ignoring preexisting medical conditions potentially exacerbated by snorkeling or diving. Know and respect your limits. Inexperienced or first-time divers should obtain proper training, and may wish to undergo a physical examination before diving. **Divers Alert Network** (© **800/446-2671** or 919/684-4326; www.diversalertnetwork.org) insures scuba divers.

ment of State's pamphlet, *A Safe Trip Abroad,* for tips on dealing with this and similar situations. The pamphlet is available by mail from the Superintendent of Documents, U.S. Government Printing Office, Washington, DC 20402; via the Internet at **www.gpo.gov/fdsys**; or via the Bureau of Consular Affairs home page at **www.travel.state.gov**.

SPECIALIZED TRAVEL RESOURCES

In addition to the destination-specific resources listed below, visit **www.frommers.com** for further specialized travel resources.

LGBT Travelers

Most of the gay and lesbian community regards the Cayman Islands as gay-hostile as opposed to gay-friendly. None of the islands in the Caribbean are completely gay-friendly, even more liberal destinations like Puerto Rico and St. Croix. But the government of the Cayman Islands has been particularly vocal and unapologetic in expressing its anti-gay attitudes.

In 1998 the Cayman Islands government notoriously turned away Norwegian Cruise Lines *Leeward,* which was carrying 900 gay passengers. The tourism directors at George Town stated at the time: "We cannot count on this group to uphold the standards of appropriate behavior expected of visitors to the Cayman Islands." The decision drew massive protest in America, with many groups, even travel agents, discouraging travel to the Cayman Islands or calling for a complete boycott of the Cayman Islands.

Although the government officially sanctioned the ban of the *Leeward,* such intolerance is often not endorsed by individual hotel owners, who have told us privately that they welcome gay and lesbian patronage. Nonetheless, the official attitude doesn't make for a happy vacation, and displays of same-sex affection are severely frowned upon in Cayman Islands society. There are no gay bars or clubs and the local gay and lesbian community congregates privately, within individual homes. As a gay or lesbian traveler, you have to make a personal choice whether you want to spend your vacation dollars in the Cayman Islands, or whether you would prefer to vacation in a friendlier and more tolerant climate.

The **International Gay and Lesbian Travel Association (IGLTA)** (© **800/448-8550** or 954/630-1637; www.iglta.org) is the trade association for the gay and lesbian travel industry and offers an online directory of gay- and lesbian-friendly travel businesses; go to their website and click on "Members."

Many agencies offer tours and travel itineraries specifically for gay and lesbian travelers. Among them are **Now, Voyager** (📞 800/255-6951; www.nowvoyager.com) and **Olivia Cruises & Resorts** (📞 800/631-6277; www.olivia.com).

The Canadian website **GayTraveler** (www.travelgaycanada.com) offers ideas and advice for gay travel all over the world.

The following travel guides are available at many bookstores, or you can order them from any online bookseller: *Spartacus International Gay Guide, 36th Edition* (Bruno Gmünder Verlag; www.spartacusworld.com/gayguide) and the *Damron* guides (www.damron.com), with separate, annual books for gay men and lesbians.

Travelers with Disabilities

Like most islands in the Caribbean, the Cayman Islands should do more to welcome vacationers with disabilities. If you have a disability, we'd recommend that you confine your visit to Grand Cayman and not venture to the remote islands of Cayman Brac or Little Cayman. Your best bet is to check into one of the major resorts along Seven Mile Beach, which are far more accessible than the smaller lodgings on the island. It is always advisable to call a hotel and discuss your individual needs before booking a stay there.

Organizations that offer a vast range of resources and assistance to travelers with disabilities include **MossRehab** (📞 800/CALL-MOSS [2255-6677]; www.mossresourcenet.org), the **American Foundation for the Blind (AFB)** (📞 800/232-5463 or 212/502-7600; www.afb.org), and **Society for Accessible Travel & Hospitality (SATH)** (📞 212/447-7284; www.sath.org). **Air Ambulance Card** (📞 877/424-7633 or 205/297-0060; www.airambulancecard.com) is now partnered with SATH and allows you to preselect top-notch hospitals in case of an emergency.

Access-Able Travel Source (📞 303/232-2979; www.access-able.com) offers a comprehensive database of travel agents from around the world with experience in accessible travel; destination-specific access information; and links to such resources as service animals, equipment rentals, and access guides.

Many travel agencies offer customized tours and itineraries for travelers with disabilities. Among them are **Flying Wheels Travel** (📞 507/451-5005; www.flyingwheelstravel.com) and **Accessible Journeys** (📞 800/846-4537 or 610/521-0339; www.disabilitytravel.com).

Flying with Disability (www.flying-with-disability.org) is a comprehensive information source on airplane travel. **Avis Rent a Car** (📞 800/331-1212 in the U.S.; www.avis.com) has an "Avis Access" program that offers services for customers with special travel needs. These include specially outfitted vehicles with swivel seats, spinner knobs, and hand controls; mobility scooter rentals; and accessible bus service. Be sure to reserve well in advance.

Also check out the quarterly magazine **Emerging Horizons** (www.emerginghorizons.com), available by subscription online (US$16.95 a year in the U.S.; US$21.95 outside the U.S.).

The "Accessible Travel" link at **Mobility-Advisor.com** offers a variety of travel resources to individuals with disabilities.

British travelers should contact **Tourism For All** (✆ 0845/124-9971 in the U.K. only; www.tourismforall.org.uk) for a wide range of travel information and resources for the elderly and individuals with disabilities.

Family Travel

The Cayman Islands welcome families with kids. For accommodations, restaurants, and attractions that are particularly kid-friendly, look for the "Kids" icon throughout this guide.

Recommended family travel websites include **Family Travel Forum** (www.myfamilytravels.com), a comprehensive site that offers customized trip planning; **Family Travel Network** (www.familytravelnetwork.com), an online magazine providing travel tips; and **TravelWithYourKids.com,** a comprehensive site written by parents and for parents, which provides sound advice for long-distance and international travel with children.

Senior Travel

Mention that you're a senior when you make your travel reservations in the Cayman Islands. Members of **AARP,** 601 E St. NW, Washington, DC 20049 (✆ 888/687-2277; www.aarp.org), get discounts on hotels, airfares, and car rentals. AARP offers members a wide range of benefits, including *AARP The Magazine* and a monthly newsletter. Anyone over 50 can join.

Recommended publications with travel resources and discounts for seniors include the quarterly magazine *Travel 50 & Beyond* (www.travel50andbeyond.com) and *Unbelievably Good Deals and Great Adventures That You Absolutely Can't Get Unless You're Over 50, 2009–2010, 18th Edition* (McGraw-Hill), by Joan Rattner Heilman.

RESPONSIBLE TOURISM

The spectacular coral reefs that fringe the Cayman Islands are the islands' greatest natural resource. Strict laws prevent cruise ships from dropping anchor in the reefs near George Town and punish any entity caught tampering with underwater wildlife.

GENERAL RESOURCES FOR green TRAVEL

In addition to the resources for the Cayman Islands listed above, the following websites provide valuable wide-ranging information on sustainable travel.

- **Responsible Travel** (www.responsibletravel.com) is a great source of sustainable travel ideas; the site is run by a travel industry spokesperson for ethical tourism.

- **Sustainable Travel International** (www.sustainabletravel international.org) promotes ethical tourism practices and manages an extensive directory of sustainable properties and tour operators around the world.

- **Carbonfund.org, TerraPass** (www.terrapass.org), and the **CoolClimate Network** (http://coolclimate.berkeley.edu) provide info on "carbon offsetting," or offsetting the greenhouse gas emitted during flights.

- **"Green" Hotels Association** (www.greenhotels.com) recommends green-rated member hotels around the world that fulfill the company's stringent environmental requirements. **Environmentally Friendly Hotels** (www. environmentallyfriendlyhotels.com) offers more green accommodations ratings.

- For information on animal-friendly issues throughout the world, visit **Tread Lightly** (www.treadlightly.org).

- **Volunteer International** (www.volunteerinternational.org) has a list of questions to help you determine the nature and intentions of a volunteer program. For general info on volunteer travel, visit **www.goabroad.com/volunteer-abroad** and **www.idealist.org**.

Grand Cayman has developed rapidly over the past 30 years, although new laws aim to curb large-scale development. Increasing emphasis is being put on low-rise construction of beachfront condos. The Ritz-Carlton, built in a series of multistory towers, required a special zoning permission and post-Ritz, these will be increasingly difficult to obtain. If you'd like to check into the "greenest" hotel on Grand Cayman, head for **Lighthouse Point** (p. 70).

The best eco-tours on Grand Cayman are offered by Geddes Hislop of **Earthfoot's Ecotours** (www.earthfoot.org). Geddes is a wildlife biologist, and he has a variety of mostly half-day walks and tours, including visits to the Queen Elizabeth II Botanic Park. His most popular jaunt is a nature walk tour, lasting nearly 5 hours and costing from US$50 to US$55 per person or US$40 to US$45 for ages 12 and under. A guided tour of the botanic park costs US$55 or US$45 per child age 12 and under. Customized tours can also be arranged.

All three of the Caymans are ideal for bike riding, and depending on your plans, you may not need to rent a car at all. Cayman Brac and Little Cayman are easily traversed by bike, and many hotels provide them free to their guests.

Each time you take a flight or drive a car, carbon dioxide is released into the atmosphere. You can help neutralize this danger to our planet through "carbon offsetting"—paying someone to reduce carbon dioxide emissions by the same amount you've augmented them. Carbon offsets can be purchased in the U.S. from companies such as **Carbonfund.org** and **TerraPass** (www.terra pass.org), and from **Climate Care** (www.jpmorganclimatecare. com) in the U.K.

Although one could argue that any vacation that includes an airplane flight can't be truly "green," you can travel internationally and still contribute positively to the environment. Patronize forward-looking hotels, restaurants, and businesses that embrace responsible development practices, helping preserve destinations for the future. An increasing number of sustainable tourism initiatives can help you plan a family trip and leave as small a "footprint" as possible on the places you visit; see "General Resources for Green Travel" below for ideas.

PACKAGES FOR THE INDEPENDENT TRAVELER

Before you start your search for the lowest airfare, you may want to consider booking your flight as part of a travel package. Package tours are not the same thing as escorted tours. Package tours are simply a way to buy the airfare, accommodations, and other elements of your trip (such as car rentals, airport transfers, and sometimes even activities) at the same time and often at discounted prices. In most cases, a package to the Cayman Islands will include airfare, hotel, and transportation to and from the airport—and it'll often cost you less than the hotel alone if you booked it yourself. Packages are sold in bulk to tour operators, who resell them to the public at a cost that usually undercuts standard rates. A package deal might not be for you if you want to stay in a more intimate inn or guesthouse, but if you like resorts, read on.

Many land-and-sea packages include meals, and you might find yourself locked into eating in your hotel dining room every night if your meals are prepaid. If you're seeking a more varied dining

ASK before **YOU GO**

Before you invest in a package deal or an escorted tour:

o Always ask about the **cancellation policy.** Can you get your money back? Is a deposit required?

o Ask about the **accommodations choices and prices** for each. Then look up the hotels' reviews and check their rates online for your specific dates of travel. Also find out what types of rooms are offered.

o For escorted tours, request a complete **schedule.**

o For escorted tours, ask about the **size** and **demographics** of the group.

o For escorted tours, discuss what is included in the **price** (transportation, meals, tips, airport transfers, and so forth).

o Finally, look for **hidden expenses.** Ask whether airport departure fees and taxes, for example, are included in the total cost—they rarely are.

experience, avoid the **AP** (American Plan), which means full board, and opt for the **MAP** (Modified American Plan), which means breakfast and either lunch or dinner at your hotel.

One good source of package deals is the airlines themselves. Most major airlines offer air/land packages, including **American Airlines Vacations** (✆ **800/321-2121;** www.aavacations.com), **Delta Vacations** (✆ **800/654-6559;** www.deltavacations.com), and **Continental Airlines Vacations** (✆ **800/301-3800;** www.covacations.com). Several big **online travel agencies—Expedia, Travelocity,** and **Orbitz**—also do a brisk business in packages. If you're unsure about the pedigree of a smaller packager, check with the Better Business Bureau in the city where the company is based, or go to **www.bbb.org.** If a packager won't tell you where it's based, don't fly with them.

Travel packages are also listed in the travel section of your local Sunday newspaper. Or check ads in national travel magazines such as *Arthur Frommer's Budget Travel Magazine, Travel + Leisure, National Geographic Traveler,* and *Condé Nast Traveller.*

The biggest hotel chains and resorts also have package deals. If you already know where you want to stay, call the resort itself and ask if it offers land/air packages.

To save time comparing the prices and value of every package tour, contact **TourScan Inc.** (✆ **800/962-2080** or 203/655-8091; www.tourscan.com). Every season, the company computerizes the contents of travel brochures that contain about 10,000 different vacations at 1,600 hotels in the Caribbean, and selects the best value vacation at each hotel and condo.

Escorted General Interest Tours

For organized tours around Grand Cayman, see p. 139 in chapter 6. Visitors can enjoy private taxi tours or choose from different half- or full-day sightseeing tours around the island.

STAYING CONNECTED

To call the Cayman Islands from the United States or Canada, dial **1,** and then the **345** country code followed by the local number.

To call the Cayman Islands from the U.K., dial **00,** and then the **345** country code followed by the number. To call from Australia, dial **0011-1,** and then **345** followed by the number. From New Zealand, dial **00-1,** and then **345** followed by the number.

From the Cayman Islands, call the U.S. direct by dialing **1,** and then the area code and number. Call Canada by dialing **011,** and then **1,** the area code, and the number. If you're calling the U.K., dial **011,** and then **44** and the number. To call Australia, dial **011,** and then **61** and the number. To call New Zealand, dial **011,** and then **64** and the number.

Call **411** for directory assistance in the Cayman Islands. Dial **0** for internal and external operator assistance. Phone cards and credit cards can be used to make international calls. Nearly everyone has a cellphone, so don't expect to encounter many old-fashioned phone booths.

Note: Numbers beginning with 800 within the Caymans are toll-free, but calling an 800 number in the States from the Caymans is not. In fact, it costs the same as an overseas call.

Major hotels throughout the Cayman Islands are fully capable of routing your phone calls to any destination in the world. Select hotels will directly transfer your call through a switchboard; others allow dialing with a locally purchased calling card, or you can direct-dial from your hotel room. Note that surcharges usually apply for calls dialed directly from within your hotel.

Cellphones

Much of the world's wireless capabilities are defined by **GSM** (Global System for Mobile Communications) and **TDMA** (Time Division Multiple Access), the big digital networks that make for easy cross-border cellphone use throughout dozens of countries worldwide. They function with a removable plastic SIM card, encoded with your phone number and account information. If your cellphone is on a GSM or TDMA system, and you have a world-capable multiband phone, you can make and receive calls across populated areas around much of the globe. Just call your wireless operator and ask for "international roaming" to be activated on your account. A prepaid Cayman Islands SIM card with an international cellphone is a convenient and economical calling solution during your visit to the Caymans.

To an increasing degree, residents of the Cayman Islands—especially the islands' corps of taxi and minivan drivers—rely on cellphones for all telephone communications. Cellphone reception, thanks to relay stations scattered throughout Grand Cayman, is generally very good, though somewhat less reliable on Little Cayman and Cayman Brac. Temporary visitors to the Cayman Islands can buy or rent a cellphone from providers including **Cable & Wireless,** Anderson Square Building on Shedden Road, and Galleria Shopping Mall at Seven Mile Beach, George Town (✆ **345/949-7800;** www.time4lime.com); **Digicel,** Cayman Financial Center, 36A Dr. Roy's Dr., Third Floor, George Town (✆ **345/623-3444;** www.digicelcayman.com/en/plans); and **Lime,** Anderson Square Building on Shedden Road, and Galleria Plaza on West Bay Road, George Town (✆ **345/949-8450;** www.time4lime.com). Rentals are about CI$5 per day, plus the cost of a calling card; international per-minute rates are around CI35¢ to CI60¢.

An alternative plan is to rent a cellphone before you leave home. In North America, rent one from **InTouch USA** (✆ **800/872-7626;** www.intouchglobal.com) or **Roadpost** (✆ **888/290-1616** or 905/272-5665; www.roadpost.com). InTouch will also, for free, advise you on whether your existing phone will work overseas; simply call ✆ **703/222-7161** between 9am and 4pm EST, or go to www.intouchglobal.com/travel.htm.

If you have Web access while traveling, you might consider a broadband-based telephone service (in technical terms, **Voice over Internet protocol,** or **VoIP**) such as **Skype** (www.skype.com) or **Vonage** (www.vonage.com), which allows you to make free international calls if you use their services from your laptop or in a cybercafe. Check their websites for details on restrictions and availability.

Internet & E-Mail

Internet cafes are located in the shopping centers along Seven Mile Beach. They include **Café del Sol/Team Café,** located in the Marquee Shopping Centre and the Aqua World Duty Free Mall (✆ **345/946-2233**), and the **Thirsty Surfer,** located at the Reef Resort in East End (✆ **345/947-2337**). Rates at both cafes range from CI$8 for 24-hour unlimited access to CI$50 for 30-day

ONLINE TRAVELER'S toolbox

Following is a selection of handy online travel tools to book-mark and use.

o **Cayman Islands Department of Tourism** (www.cayman islands.ky)

o **Nature Cayman** (www.naturecayman.com)

o **Professional Association of Diving Instructors** (www. padi.com)

o **Maps** (www.mapquest.com and www.maps.google.com)

o **Travel Warnings** (www.travel.state.gov, www.fco.gov.uk/ travel, www.voyage.gc.ca, or www.smartraveller.gov.au)

o **Universal Currency Converter** (www.xe.com/ucc)

o **Visa ATM Locator** (www.visa.com), **MasterCard ATM Locator** (www.mastercard.com)

o **Weather** (www.weather.com)

unlimited access. On Cayman Brac, Internet access is available at the West End Post Office and at Brac Reef Beach Resort (p. 164). On Little Cayman, Wi-Fi is available only at select hotels (p. 180). For more information, check **www.cybercaptive.com** and **www. cybercafe.com**.

More and more hotels, resorts, airports, cafes, and retailers are becoming "hotspots" that offer free high-speed Wi-Fi access or charge a small fee for usage. Most laptops sold today have built-in wireless capability. Public Wi-Fi hotspots in the Cayman Islands are at the **Hard Rock Cafe** (43 S. Church St., George Town; ✆ 345/945-2020) and **Owen Roberts International Airport.** For more information, go to **www.jiwire.com**; its Hotspot Finder holds the world's largest directory of public wireless hotspots.

For dial-up access, most business-class hotels offer dataports for laptop modems.

Wherever you go, bring a **connection kit** of the right power and phone adapters, a spare phone cord, and a spare Ethernet network cable—or find out whether your hotel supplies them to guests.

TIPS ON ACCOMMODATIONS

The government of the Cayman Islands imposes a 10% surcharge on all hotel room rentals, which is included in the price.

Hotels also charge a room tax. The room tax depends on the quality of the hotel—it might be relatively low for a guesthouse but steeper for a first-class resort. When booking a room, make sure you understand whether the price you've been quoted includes the room tax (which is different from the 10% hotel room surcharge), so that you avoid an unpleasant surprise when it comes time to pay the bill.

Furthermore, most hotels routinely add 10% to 12% for "service," even if you didn't see much evidence of it. That means that with tax and service, some bills are 17% or even 25% higher than the price that was originally quoted! Naturally, it's best to determine before you book just how much the hotel, guesthouse, or inn plans to add to your bill at the end of your stay.

That's not all. Some hotels slip in little hidden extras that mount quickly. For example, it's common for many places to quote rates that include a continental breakfast. Should you prefer ham and eggs, however, you will pay an extra charge. If you request special privileges, like extra towels for the beach, beach chairs, or laundry done in a hurry, surcharges may mount. It pays to watch those extras and to ask questions before you commit.

HOTELS & RESORTS Many budget travelers assume they can't afford the big hotels and resorts. But with so many packages out there and frequent sales, you might be pleasantly surprised, even in the winter.

The rates given in this book are "rack rates"—that is, the officially posted rate that you'd be given if you just walked in off the street. Almost everyone ends up paying less than the rack rate through packages, bargaining, and discounts. Think of the rates in this book as guidelines to help you comparison-shop.

Some hotels are quite flexible about their rates, and many offer discounts and upgrades whenever they have a big block of rooms to fill and few reservations. The smaller hotels and inns are not as likely to be generous with discounts, much less upgrades. A good travel agent may know which hotels have reduced their rates and can help you save serious money.

CONDOS, VILLAS & COTTAGES Particularly if you're traveling with your family or a group of friends, a "housekeeping holiday" can be one of the least expensive ways to vacation in the Caymans. And if you like privacy and independence, it's a good way to go. Accommodations with kitchens are available on all the islands. Some are individual cottages, others are condo complexes with swimming pools, and some are private homes that owners rent out while they're away.

In the simpler rentals, you do your own cooking and laundry and, in a few cases, your own housekeeping. This may not be your idea of a good time in the sun, but it saves money—a lot of money. The savings, especially for a group of three to six people, can range from 50% to 60% of what a hotel would cost. Groceries are often priced 35% to 60% higher than on the U.S. mainland, as nearly all foodstuffs have to be imported, but even so, preparing your own food will be a lot cheaper than eating all your meals at restaurants.

Most villas, condos, and cottages have a staff, or at least a maid who comes in a few days a week, and they also provide the essentials, including linens and housewares. Many places (though not all) include maid service and fresh linens in the price. Condos usually come with a reception desk and are often comparable to a suite in a big resort hotel. Nearly all condo and villa complexes have pools (some more than one). Like condos, villas range widely in price; a "modest" villa may begin at US$750 per week, while a luxurious one can go for over US$50,000 a week.

You can also rent a lavish private home. You'll spend a lot of money, but you'll be staying in the lap of luxury in a prime beachfront setting, usually with maid service (though you may need to arrange this in advance).

Approach all these rental properties with a certain sense of independence. There may or may not be a front desk with someone to answer your questions, and you will most likely have to plan your own watersports activities and excursions. Always ask when you book.

Make your reservations well in advance. Below, we've listed a few agencies that rent condos, villas, and private homes throughout the Caymans. You can also ask each island's tourist office for suggestions.

o **Cayman Villas** (177 Owen Roberts Dr., Grand Cayman (℗ **800/ 235-5888** in the U.S., or 345/945-4144; www.caymanvillas. com), is a booking agency that rents more than 100 private beachfront homes and condos on all three islands. The properties range from cozy studio cottages to large villas that have as many as seven bedrooms. Some properties have the added luxury of a private pool or a maid, and sometimes even a cook. Most of the rentals have kitchenettes, Internet access, a washer and dryer, and kitchenware. Rentals range from budget to deluxe, so most pocketbooks can be accommodated. Prices range from US$150 to US$2,000 per night.

o **Villas of Distinction** (℗ **800/289-0900** in the U.S.; www. villasofdistinction.com) offers upscale private villas, all with a pool, and one to six bedrooms throughout the Caymans. From town houses to beachfront villas, all their lodgings are beautifully furnished.

Tips on Accommodations

PLANNING YOUR TRIP TO THE CAYMAN ISLANDS

o **Hideaways Aficionado** (*©* **888/843-4433** in the U.S., or 603/430-4433; fax 603/430-4444; www.hideaways.com) is a worldwide rental agency that also publishes *Hideaways Collection,* a pictorial directory of home rentals throughout the world, including the Cayman Islands. Rentals range from cottages to staffed villas. Hideaways Aficionado can also help you charter yachts and arrange cruises, flights, car rentals, and hotel reservations. Annual membership is US$195.

Saving on Your Hotel Room

The **rack rate** is the maximum rate that a hotel charges for a room. Hardly anybody pays this price, however, except in high season or on holidays. To lower the cost of your room:

o **Ask about special rates or other discounts.** You may qualify for corporate, student, military, senior, frequent-flier, trade union, or other discounts.

o **Dial direct.** When booking a room in a chain hotel, you'll often get a better deal by calling the individual hotel's reservation desk rather than the chain's main number.

o **Book online.** Many hotels offer Internet-only discounts, or supply rooms to Priceline, Hotwire, or Expedia at rates much lower than the ones you can get through the hotel itself.

o **Remember the law of supply and demand.** You can save big on hotel rooms by traveling during a destination's off season or shoulder seasons, when rates typically drop, even at luxury properties.

o **Look into group or long-stay discounts.** If you come as part of a large group, you should be able to negotiate a bargain rate. Likewise, if you're planning a long stay (at least 5 days), you might qualify for a discount. As a general rule, expect 1 night free after a 7-night stay.

o **Sidestep excess surcharges and hidden costs.** Many hotels have adopted the unpleasant practice of nickel-and-diming their guests with opaque surcharges. When you book a room, ask what is included in the room rate, and what is extra. Avoid dialing direct from hotel phones, which can charge exorbitant rates. And don't be tempted by the room's minibar offerings: Most hotels charge through the nose for water, soda, and snacks.

o **Consider the pros and cons of all-inclusive resorts and hotels.** The term "all-inclusive" means different things at different hotels. Many all-inclusive hotels include three meals daily,

GETTING married IN THE CAYMAN ISLANDS

Those who want to take the plunge and get married on these sun-dappled islands should know that there's some red tape. Visitors have to call ahead and arrange for an authorized person to marry them. The name of the "marriage officer," as the person is called, has to appear on the application for a marriage license. The application for a special marriage license costs US$180 and can be obtained from the **Chief Secretary's Office,** Fourth Floor, Government Administration Building, George Town (© **345/949-7900**). There is no waiting period. Present a birth certificate, the embarkation/disembarkation cards issued by the island's immigration authorities, and, if applicable, divorce decrees or proof of a prior spouse's death.

The Cayman Islands are one of the few Caribbean destinations that allow U.S. citizens to marry the same day they arrive, instead of requiring a minimum stay before the wedding. A relevant brochure, *Getting Married in the Cayman Islands,* is available from **Government Information Services,** Broadcasting House, Grand Cayman (© **345/949-8092;** fax 345/949-5936).

The Cayman Islands are a wedding-friendly destination. (See "The Best Honeymoon & Wedding Accommodations," p. 8, for specific resorts with wedding and honeymoon packages.) The host hotel or a wedding service can handle all ground arrangements. Wedding service companies can perform all the necessary functions

sports equipment, spa entry, and other amenities; others may include most alcoholic drinks. In general, you'll save money going the "all-inclusive" way—as long as you use the facilities provided. The downside is that your choices are limited and you're stuck eating and playing in one place for the duration of your vacation.

o **Carefully consider your hotel's meal plan.** If you enjoy eating out and sampling the local cuisine, it makes sense to choose a **Continental Plan (CP),** which includes breakfast only, or a **European Plan (EP),** which doesn't include any meals and allows you maximum flexibility. If you're more interested in saving money, opt for a **Modified American Plan (MAP),** which includes breakfast and one meal, or the **American Plan (AP),** which includes three meals. If you choose a MAP, make sure you can get a free lunch at your hotel if you decide to do dinner out.

related to the ceremony, providing musicians, catering, flowers, and photography, as well as the marriage application with the civil registrar or marriage officer.

Celebrations, PO Box 10599 APO (© **345/949-2044;** fax 345/949-6947; www.celebrationsltd.com), is an excellent wedding planner, offering packages ranging from US$800 to US$3,000-plus. Bridal packages include everything from prerecorded wedding music to a personal wedding coordinator on the day of the grand event.

Competitor **Cayman Weddings,** PO Box 678 GT (© **345/949-8677;** fax 345/949-8237; www.caymanweddings.com.ky), is another good choice, with packages starting at US$625 and going up into the stratosphere for deluxe weddings. You get such thoughtful extras as 36 candid photographs, two crystal memento glasses, and a two-tier wedding cake.

After arrival, rest, and perhaps a rehearsal dinner, guests usually convene the following day for a sumptuous island-style wedding. Choose from many romantic, tropical locations: a hotel, chapel, or church; the Caymanian-style Bride House; a beach at sunset; an oceanfront gazebo; a waterside restaurant; or perhaps the depths of the ocean (underwater weddings are extremely popular with divers).

o **Book an efficiency.** A room with a kitchenette allows you to shop for groceries and cook your own meals. This is a big money saver, especially for families on long stays.

o **Consider enrolling in hotel chains' "frequent-stay" programs,** which have been stepping it up recently to win the loyalty of repeat customers. Frequent guests can now accumulate points or credits towards free hotel nights, airline miles, in-room amenities, merchandise, tickets to concerts and events, and discounts on sporting facilities. Perks are awarded not only by many chain hotels and motels (Hilton HHonors, Marriott Rewards, Wyndham ByRequest, to name a few), but also by individual inns and B&Bs. Many chain hotels partner with other hotel chains, car rental firms, airlines, and credit card companies to give consumers additional incentive to do repeat business.

Landing the Best Room

Somebody has to get the best room in the house. It might as well be you. You can start by joining the hotel's frequent-guest program, which may make you eligible for upgrades. A hotel-branded credit card usually gives its owner "silver" or "gold" status in frequent-guest programs for free. Always ask about corner rooms. They're often larger and quieter, with more windows and light, and they often cost the same as standard rooms. When you make your reservation, ask if the hotel is renovating; if it is, request a room away from the construction. Ask about nonsmoking rooms and rooms with views. Be sure to request your choice of twin, queen-, or king-size beds. If you're a light sleeper, ask for a quiet room away from vending or ice machines, elevators, restaurants, bars, and discos. Ask for a room that has been recently renovated or refurbished.

If you aren't happy with your room when you arrive, ask for another one. Most lodgings will be happy to accommodate you if other rooms are available.

You might ask the following questions before booking a room:

o **What's the view like?** Cost-conscious travelers may be willing to pay less for a back room facing the parking lot, especially if they don't plan to spend much time in their room.

o **Does the room have air-conditioning or ceiling fans? Do the windows open?** If they do, and the nighttime entertainment takes place alfresco, you may want to find out when showtime is over.

o **What's included in the price?** Your room may be moderately priced, but if you're charged for beach chairs, towels, sports equipment, and other amenities, you could end up spending more than you bargained for.

o **How far is the room from the beach and other amenities?** If it's far, is there transportation to and from the beach, and is it free?

Online Bookings

In addition to the online travel booking sites **Travelocity, Expedia, Orbitz, Priceline,** and **Hotwire,** you can book hotels through **Hotels.com, Quikbook** (www.quikbook.com), and **Travelaxe** (www.travelaxe.com).

HotelChatter (www.hotelchatter.com) is a daily webzine offering smart coverage and critiques of hotels worldwide. Go to **Trip**

Advisor.com or **HotelShark.com** for helpful independent consumer reviews of hotels and resort properties.

It's a good idea to **get a confirmation number** and **make a printout** of any online booking transaction.

You can often find some very good scuba-diving packages online, especially from late April to mid-December.

WHERE TO STAY ON GRAND CAYMAN

3

The good news: The Cayman Islands have some of the finest and most elegant resorts in the Caribbean, opening onto one of the grandest strips of sand in the entire Caribbean Basin.

Now for the bad news: The cost of living here is about 20% higher than in the United States. Winter vacations in the Caymans can be pricey affairs. Because so much food has to be imported from the U.S. mainland, restaurant tabs are second only to those on the high-priced French islands such as St. Barts and Martinique.

But you can make a trip here affordable. The key is to plan in advance and to visit the islands between mid-April and mid-December, when room rates are 20% to 40% lower than in the winter. In addition, you might consider staying in one of several low-cost or moderately priced lodgings that have opened in recent years. Many of these accommodations include facilities for cooking simple meals. Be forewarned, however, that so-called moderate or inexpensive hotels in the Cayman Islands might be judged "super-expensive" in other parts of the world, including the United States.

Nearly all the hotels on Grand Cayman are lined up along Seven Mile Beach. Hotels farther out on the island will be more isolated, but may not front a hospitable sand beach. Unlike many Caymanian restaurants, hotels quote prices in U.S. dollars. **All prices in this chapter are listed in U.S. dollars.** When choosing a hotel, keep in mind that the quoted rates include neither the 10% government tax nor the 10% hotel service tax.

Consider booking a package tour to make your stay at an expensive resort more affordable. See "Packages for the Independent Traveler," p. 46, before you book. See "Tips on Accommodations," p. 50, for descriptions of various lodgings and tips on saving money.

HOTELS & RESORTS
Very Expensive

Cotton Tree ★   Book in here and spend your stay in a modern, West Indian–style cottage at the northernmost point on the island's West Bay. Staying at this secluded retreat is like having your own vacation home on the Caribbean Sea. Cottages are designed for comfort and convenience, with fully equipped kitchens, spa-like bathrooms, spacious living areas, and a library of books, music, and DVDs. The units are decorated with art and artifacts from around the globe. The staff can arrange on-site art and cooking classes, island tours, and horseback riding, as well as provide a laptop on request. A free shuttle carries you to nearby restaurants, beaches, and attractions.

West Bay, Grand Cayman, B.W.I. ℂ **345/943-0700.** Fax 345/943-0707. www. caymancottontree.com. 4 units. Winter US$950 cottage; off season US$650 cottage. Minimum 3-night stay. DISC, MC, V. **Amenities:** Babysitting; bike rentals; concierge; exercise room; outdoor pool. *In room:* A/C, TV, DVD player, Wi-Fi (free).

Grand Cayman Beach Suites ★ ☺   This stylish all-suite resort is set directly on the sands of Seven Mile Beach. The property originated as part of a 36-hectare (89-acre) resort development. The beach suites—originally conceived in 2004 as an afterthought to the larger resort—are now some of the most sought-after accommodations on Grand Cayman. And although the land on which the truncated resort sits is relatively compact, the owners have placed lots of diversions on-site. There are two restaurants, including the acclaimed **Hemingway's** (p. 86). The resort also has direct access to the beach. Rooms are well appointed and have private verandas with views of the sea. Each suite is compact, yet artfully designed. There are a number of additional restaurants nearby, and also some convenient markets if you want to cook in your suite.

Seven Mile Beach (PO Box 32348), George Town, Grand Cayman, B.W.I. ℂ **345/949-1234.** Fax 345/949-8528. www.grand-cayman-beach-suites.com. 53 units. Winter US$390–US$450 1-bedroom suite, US$870–US$1,170 2-bedroom suite; off season US$270–US$330 1-bedroom suite, US$540–US$660 2-bedroom

What the Abbreviations Mean

Travelers to the Cayman Islands may at first be confused by classi-
fications on rate sheets.
MAP (Modified American Plan) includes room, breakfast, and dinner, unless the room rate has been quoted separately, in which
case the rate covers only breakfast and dinner.
CP (Continental Plan) includes room and a light breakfast.
EP (European Plan) includes room only.

3

Hotels & Resorts

WHERE TO STAY ON GRAND CAYMAN

suite. AE, DISC, MC, V. **Amenities:** 2 restaurants; 4 bars; babysitting; children's
programs; golf course (9 holes); health club & spa; 2 outdoor pools. *In room:* A/C,
TV, fridge, Wi-Fi (US$13 per day).

The Ritz-Carlton ★★★ ☺ With amenities and a service level
that's rivaled only by the Westin Casuarina (p. 62), the Ritz-Carlton
is the largest, plushest, most prestigious, most spectacular, and
most awe-inspiring resort in the Cayman Islands. In a league and
a class of its own, this property defies comparison to anything else
on Grand Cayman. And unless you make a concentrated effort to
explore other parts of the island, it's very easy, once you've checked
in, never to venture beyond its boundaries. The whole resort is set
atop 58 hectares (143 acres) that cover the entire width of the
island, from Seven Mile Beach to North Sands.

Straddling the boulevard that parallels Seven Mile Beach, the
resort is divided into two regal and very large, but distinctly separate, buildings—each painted the color of sand. Binding the com-
ponents together is a climate-controlled catwalk that stretches
above the congested rush-hour traffic of West Bay Street. Thanks
to a changing array of artwork, elaborate soundproofing, and the
fact that the windows of the catwalk are inset with frosted glass,
you'll have absolutely no sense of the workaday world below. Everything in both buildings is climate-controlled, meticulously mani-
cured, and covered with marble, stone, expensive hardwoods, and
ultraplush wall-to-wall carpeting. No other hotel in the Cayman
Islands so effectively evokes Europe in the Tropics. This is a richly
decorated, sedate, and luxurious architectural fantasy that's run by
a bright, hardworking, and polite staff. Unfortunately, it is bone-
chillingly expensive, with hidden fees everywhere, as many visitors
are apt to discover upon checkout.

You expect—and get—accommodations with elegant and tasteful furnishings that remind you of a hotel in an expensive neighborhood of London. All of the rooms are lovely, but the Residential

Hotels on Grand Cayman

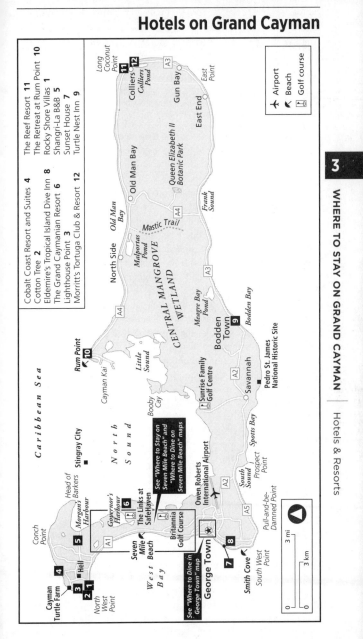

Cobalt Coast Resort and Suites **4**
Cotton Tree **2**
Eldemire's Tropical Island Dive Inn **8**
The Grand Caymanian Resort **6**
Lighthouse Point **3**
Morritt's Tortuga Club & Resort **12**

The Reef Resort **11**
The Retreat at Rum Point **10**
Rocky Shore Villas **5**
Shangri-La B&B **5**
Sunset House **7**
Turtle Nest Inn **9**

Suites are an especially extravagant collection of two dozen ocean-front condos with large living and dining areas and wide terraces.

West Bay Rd., Grand Cayman, B.W.I. ✆ **800/241-3333** or 345/943-9000. Fax 345/943-9001. www.ritzcarlton.com. 365 units. Winter US$459–US$959 double, US$1,100–US$3,400 suite; off season US$449–US$779 double, US$900–US$1,500 suite. AE, DC, MC, V. **Amenities:** 5 restaurants; 2 bars; babysitting; children's programs; concierge; golf course; health club & spa; 2 outdoor pools; room service; extensive watersports equipment/rentals. *In room:* A/C, TV/DVD, movie library, CD player, minibar, Wi-Fi (free).

The Westin Casuarina Resort & Spa ★★ ☺ After the Ritz, this is the best-accessorized, most elegant, and plushest resort in the Cayman Islands. Elaborate but tasteful, this five-story block-buster is, by anyone's standards, a very fine and well-managed property. Set on the sands of Seven Mile Beach, the Westin is filled with artfully landscaped gardens; plenty of facilities, includ-ing a dive shop; and a beautiful oval-shaped swimming pool that was once the largest on Grand Cayman, until it was surpassed in size by one of the pools at the Ritz. Most of the bedrooms have French doors that open onto private balconies, and conservative but attractive furnishings. Units are a bit small for a luxury hotel, but are well equipped and very comfortable; bathrooms are a bit less upscale, considering the overall elegance of the hotel, but all have marble trim and oversize tubs. Thanks to the building's lay-out in the form of a giant U, about two-thirds of the units have sea views, a higher percentage than at the Ritz-Carlton, although the others simply look out on the parking lot and West Bay Road. Ask questions when you reserve to avoid getting stuck with a view of your rental car.

West Bay Rd. (PO Box 30620), Seven Mile Beach, Grand Cayman, B.W.I. ✆ **800/937-8461** in the U.S., or 345/945-3800. Fax 345/949-5825. www.starwoodhotels.com. 343 units. Winter US$409–US$578 double, from US$1,050 suite; off season US$324–US$555 double, from US$650 suite. AE, MC, V. **Ameni-ties:** 3 restaurants; 3 bars; children's programs; concierge; exercise room; out-door pool; room service; spa. *In room:* A/C, TV, Internet (US$15 per day), minibar.

Expensive

Beach Club Colony Hotel & Dive Resort We like to think of this resort as a beach club for nondivers. Directly on the sands of Seven Mile Beach, the Beach Club Colony has fewer organized activities than its dive-focused competitors, although certified div-ers can still enjoy generous dive packages and free shore diving. For those interested, the on-site dive shop can schedule night dives and trips to Stingray City, along with diving courses. All 41 units are efficiently decorated, comfortable but not particularly plush, although each does have a terrace or patio. The on-site restaurant

Hotels on Seven Mile Beach

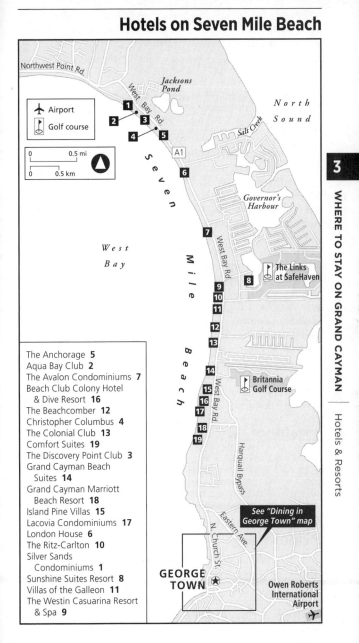

The Anchorage **5**
Aqua Bay Club **2**
The Avalon Condominiums **7**
Beach Club Colony Hotel
  & Dive Resort **16**
The Beachcomber **12**
Christopher Columbus **4**
The Colonial Club **13**
Comfort Suites **19**
The Discovery Point Club **3**
Grand Cayman Beach
  Suites **14**
Grand Cayman Marriott
  Beach Resort **18**
Island Pine Villas **15**
Lacovia Condominiums **17**
London House **6**
The Ritz-Carlton **10**
Silver Sands
  Condominiums **1**
Sunshine Suites Resort **8**
Villas of the Galleon **11**
The Westin Casuarina Resort
  & Spa **9**

is one of the friendliest hangouts on Seven Mile Beach, and makes for a great lunchtime retreat from the sun. Rates are all-inclusive and even include nonmotorized watersports activities.

West Bay Rd. (PO Box 903GT), Grand Cayman, B.W.I. © **800/48-2DIVE** (23483) in the U.S., or 345/949-8100. Fax 345/949-5167. www.beachclubcolony.ky/index. htm. 41 units. Winter US$150–US$250 per person double; off season US$125– US$175 per person double. Children ages 7–12 US$75, ages 13–17 US$80 each per night, in parent's room. Rates are all-inclusive. Diving packages available. AE, MC, V. **Amenities:** Restaurant; bar; babysitting; outdoor pool; watersports equipment/rentals. *In room:* A/C, TV, Internet (US$3 for 15 min.).

Grand Cayman Marriott Beach Resort ★ ☺ It may be way down in the pecking order from the Ritz-Carlton and the Westin, but this five-story resort on Seven Mile Beach is still among the island's top-ranked hotels. A favorite with large package-tour groups and conventions, it's a 5-minute drive north of George Town. Its ochre-colored, vaguely Hispanic-designed buildings contain roofed loggias that open onto views of either the sea, a verdantly landscaped interior courtyard, or the side of the hotel. Ask which way your room faces when booking. Regrettably, the complex sits astride a relatively narrow portion of Seven Mile Beach, resulting in a particularly densely populated strip of sand immediately in front of the hotel, and just a bit too much congestion around the swimming pool. But there's plenty to do at this family-friendly resort, with lots of emphasis on organized activities. The resort has its own watersports facilities, including a dive shop, with good snorkeling a mere 15m (49 ft.) offshore. Each of the spacious units has been remodeled and has modern art, dark-grained wood furniture, pastel walls, tropical-patterned fabrics, large closets, and a private balcony.

389 West Bay Rd. (PO Box 30371), Seven Mile Beach, Grand Cayman, B.W.I. © **888/236-2427** in the U.S., or 345/949-0088. Fax 345/949-0288. www. marriott.com. 295 units. Winter US$340–US$475 double, US$740 junior suite, US$1,150 1-bedroom suite, US$1,400 2-bedroom suite; off season US$199–US$299 double, US$570 junior suite, US$950 1-bedroom suite, US$800–US$1,250 2-bedroom suite. 10% surcharge applies over Christmas. AE, DISC, MC, V. **Amenities:** 3 restaurants; 2 bars; babysitting; children's programs; concierge; small health club w/Jacuzzi; outdoor pool; room service. *In room:* A/C, TV, fridge, Wi-Fi (US$9.95 per day).

Moderate

Cobalt Coast Resort and Suites ★★ 🎁 Fans of this resort liken it to a contemporary B&B where most clients are deeply involved with diving. It's one of the best resorts for divers on Grand Cayman, thanks to the on-site, full-service dive operation (**Divetech,** p. 109) and a deep drop-off (the North Wall), a short distance offshore, that's loaded with marine life. You have to drive

FAMILY-FRIENDLY lodgings

The Discovery Point Club (p. 71) This series of condos allows families to create a home away from home on Grand Cayman. Children under 12 stay free in the parent's room and cribs and rollaway beds are provided when needed. In the main lobby, the hotel has games, and kids can watch videos.

The Grand Caymanian Resort (p. 66) Families can create an "instant home" in these spacious, well-furnished apartments that feature well-equipped kitchens for home-cooked meals. The staff organizes many activities for kids.

Silver Sands Condominiums (p. 74) Right on the beach, this complex of apartments allows large families to lodge all in one place (their accommodations house up to eight people) and to prepare meals in their own fully equipped kitchen. Children up to age 12 also stay free with parents.

Villas of the Galleon (p. 75) This is a family favorite on Seven Mile Beach. Such extras as cribs are readily provided. Families meet other families at the popular outdoor grill.

through Hell (p. 126) to get there, though. Don't expect a sand beach: The coastline on this part of the island is infamously composed of jagged rocks, and swimmers use a series of ladders and metal steps to lower themselves into the surf. Even the diving boats have to moor at the end of an extensive pier to avoid damage. Rooms include oceanfront suites and standard rooms, which are all spacious, modern, cozy, and soothing, with Marimekko fabrics from Finland and European plumbing fixtures. On-site is a well-managed, well-run restaurant, **Duppies,** which serves well-prepared light fare, including platters of local food and sandwiches.

18 Seafan Dr., West Bay, Grand Cayman, B.W.I. ⓒ **888/946-5656** or 345/946-5656. Fax 345/946-5657. www.cobaltcoast.com or www.divetech.com. 18 units. Winter US$290 double, US$330 1-bedroom suite for 2, US$525 2-bedroom suite or villa for 4; off season US$170 double, US$195 1-bedroom suite for 2, US$355 2-bedroom suite or villa for 4. Dive packages available. AE, DC, MC, V. **Amenities:** Restaurant; bar; free airport transfers; Jacuzzi; watersports equipment/rentals. *In room:* A/C, TV, Wi-Fi (free).

Comfort Suites Streamlined, efficient, and relatively cost-effective, this hotel is often cited as one of the less expensive accommodations along Seven Mile Beach. Rising five sand-colored stories above the southern end of the fabled beach, it follows a time-tested, generic, and familiar layout that has proven successful in hundreds of other locations within North America. Each of the comfortable bedrooms has a large writing table, a boon to business travelers, and is comfortably if predictably outfitted in tones of blue and white. Unfortunately, none of the rooms has a balcony or veranda to let the light in, and only some have worthwhile views. All units have refrigerators, coffeemakers, and microwaves. One- and two-bedroom suites also contain stoves and dishwashers. There's a small pool, direct access to the beach along a sandy footpath, and a simple restaurant and bar set beneath the palm fronds of an open-sided *bohio* (hut) beside the pool. The more extensive bar and restaurant choices of the also-recommended **Marriott** (p. 64) lie immediately next door.

West Bay Rd., Grand Cayman, B.W.I. ✆ **345/945-7300.** Fax 345/945-7400. www.comfortsuites.com. 108 units. Winter US$210–US$299 studio, US$240–US$360 1-bedroom suite, US$350–US$400 2-bedroom suite; off season US$146–US$239 studio, US$230–US$290 1-bedroom suite, US$300–US$340 2-bedroom suite. Rates include breakfast. AE, DC, MC, V. **Amenities:** Restaurant; bar; babysitting; bikes; exercise room; Jacuzzi; watersports equipment/rentals. *In room:* A/C, TV, kitchenette (in studios), kitchen (in suites), Wi-Fi (free).

The Grand Caymanian Resort ★★ ☺ This is the most upscale apartment-hotel resort on the North Sound. This government-rated five-star facility was originally built on scrubland that had been shunned by many other developers.

Within a short drive of the island's biggest golf course, facing the rocky beachfront of North Sound, you'll find an opulent cluster of beige-yellow apartments, each designed in a modernized version of the British colonial style. Accommodations occupy a series of two- and three-story wings, and furnishings in each unit are more elegant than the major resort competitors. The granite-trimmed private kitchens are genuinely plush. Sound-insulated doors can be locked and unlocked to allow configurations of units ranging from studios to full-blown two-bedroom suites. Each bedroom contains a veranda or balcony. The social center is a well-designed and pleasant restaurant and bar, which is more casual and relaxed than you might expect for such an upscale venue.

278 Crighton Dr. (PO Box 31495 SMB), Crystal Harbour, Grand Cayman, B.W.I. ✆ **345/949-3100.** Fax 345/949-3161. www.grandcaymanian.ky. Winter US$159 studio, US$189 1-bedroom suite, US$230–US$459 2-bedroom suite; off season US$139 studio, US$169 1-bedroom suite, US$209–US$339 2-bedroom suite. AE, DC, MC, V. **Amenities:** Restaurant; bar; babysitting; children's center; concierge; 2 outdoor pools; 2 tennis courts (lit); watersports equipment/rentals; Wi-Fi (free). *In room:* A/C, TV, kitchen.

Shangri-La B&B ★★ 🎁 This is the most elegant bed-and-breakfast on the island, the creation of George Davidson, an entertainer who plays the piano at various venues on the island, including the Westin Hotel. He and his wife, Eileen, welcome you to their charming lakeside home, an epitome of good taste and comfort. The decor is stylish and tasteful, from the carved hardwood furnishings to the embroidered pillows. There is a screened patio that provides views of the bird life on the lagoon. Special features include a hot tub and a waterfall pool. Bedrooms are equally elegant, often with plantation-style four-posters or else canopied beds. Patrons are also granted kitchen privileges and space to store food in the communal refrigerator.

Sticky Toffee Lane, West Bay, Grand Cayman, B.W.I. ℭ **941/876-6868** or 345/526-1170. Fax 345/946-6491. www.shangrilabandb.com. 6 units. Winter US$139–US$189 double, US$249 1-bedroom apt, US$349 2-bedroom apt; off season US$119–US$169 double, US$199 1-bedroom apt, US$299 2-bedroom apt. AE, MC, V. **Amenities:** Outdoor pool. *In room:* TV/DVD, fridge, Wi-Fi (free).

Sunset House   Set on a coastal road about 1.2km (¾ mile) south of George Town, this middle-bracket hotel has rooms divided among a quartet of two-story pink-sided outbuildings. These well-recommended, no-nonsense lodgings are relatively comfortable. The location is favored by divers and snorkelers, who appreciate the jagged, mostly rocky shoreline for its excellent snorkeling opportunities, the extensive on-site diving programs, and the dive shop. Guests interested in sand, sun, and swimming shouldn't expect to take a dip off the shore here: You must lower yourself via ladders directly into the sea, thanks to the rocky shoreline.

Guests are given a number of options for accommodations, ranging from the cheapest—a unit opening onto the courtyard—to the most expensive—a roomy suite that contains extras such as private balconies, two double beds, a full kitchen, and a living room. The latter is ideal for families or groups of four or more who like to do their own cooking. The midrange standard bedrooms open onto views of the sea and contain more space than the courtyard units.

390 S. Church St. (PO Box 479), George Town, Grand Cayman, B.W.I. ℭ **800/854-4767** or 345/949-7111. Fax 345/949-7101. www.sunsethouse.com. 59 units. Winter US$220–US$310 double, US$320 suite, US$365 apt; off season US$200–US$250 double, US$260 suite, US$280 apt. AE, DISC, MC, V. **Amenities:** Seaharvest Restaurant (p. 102); bar; Jacuzzi; 2 outdoor pools; Wi-Fi (free in pool and at bar). *In room:* A/C, TV, fridge (in suites), kitchen (in apts).

Sunshine Suites Resort   Built on a flat-as-a-pancake stretch of scrubland and separated from Seven Mile Beach by a 5-minute trek across the busy traffic of West Bay Street, this is a well-designed resort compound. Along with the also-recommended Comfort Suites, it is acknowledged as one of the least expensive lodgings in the Seven Mile Beach area. The resort resembles a decent but somewhat anonymous and uncluttered apartment complex on the outskirts of, say, Washington, D.C., that just so happens to be next to the beach. Both inside and out, the design reflects British colonial architecture. Each of the units has its own kitchen, so many guests prepare their meals on-site, avoiding the high cost of nearby restaurants and contributing to a hands-off laissez-faire dynamic that suits many of the guests here just fine. Each of the units is equipped with a midsize private bathroom with tub and shower.

1465 Esterley Tibbetts Hwy. (PO Box 30095), Grand Cayman, B.W.I. ☏ **877/786-1110** or 345/949-3000. Fax 345/949-1200. www.sunshinesuites.com. 132 units. Winter US$200–US$220 double, US$230 1-bedroom suite; off season US$125–US$135 double, US$145 1-bedroom suite. Rates include continental breakfast. AE, DISC, MC, V. **Amenities:** Restaurant; bar; access to nearby health club; outdoor pool; watersports equipment/rentals. *In room:* A/C, TV, kitchen, Wi-Fi (free).

Turtle Nest Inn 🔑   This cluster of fully furnished apartments opening onto a beach is an attractive and affordable alternative to the pricey condos and chain hotels such as the Marriott. The beach out front is a bit narrow but always has good snorkeling (equipment available at the inn), and guests usually find it uncrowded. Otherwise, guests relax on the terrace. The architecture is vaguely Spanish, with arches and a red-tiled roof, along with whitewashed walls and cooling terra-cotta tiles in the private, well-furnished units. The inn is located in the somewhat remote village of Bodden Town, the original capital of the island, which is a 10-minute drive from George Town and the airport.

166 Bodden Town Rd. (PO Box 187), Bodden Town, Grand Cayman, B.W.I. ☏ **345/947-8665.** Fax 345/947-6379. www.turtlenestinn.com. 8 units. Winter US$149; off season US$99–US$119. AE, DC, MC, V. **Amenities:** Bikes/mopeds; outdoor pool. *In room:* A/C, TV, fridge, kitchen (in some), Wi-Fi (free).

Inexpensive

Eldemire's Tropical Island Dive Inn   Set within a quiet and completely unpretentious residential neighborhood on the landward side of South Church Road, 1.5km (1 mile) south of downtown George Town, this is one of only two B&Bs on Grand Cayman. Basic and completely free of glitter, it's run with a relaxed sense of humor by Carol "Tootie" Eldemire-Huddleston, the congenial but outspoken and no-nonsense Jamaica-born entrepreneur who lives across the street. Accommodations lie in either the main house or a handful of outbuildings. Each of the rooms is a simple, sparsely furnished affair, with well-worn furniture and few frills. Residents of the standard rooms have access to the house's communal kitchen, and each of the suites contains a simple kitchenette. Dive courses are available. Smith Cove Beach lies within a 5-minute walk.

18 Pebbles Way, George Town, Grand Cayman, B.W.I. ☏ **704/469-2635** in the U.S. and Canada, or 345/916-8369. Fax 345/949-4595. www.eldemire.com. 13

units. Winter US$119 double, US$144 studio suite, US$159 1-bedroom suite, US$240 2-bedroom suite; off season US$85 double, US$105 studio suite, US$115 1-bedroom suite, US$175 2-bedroom suite. Dive packages available. MC, V. **Amenities:** Bikes; outdoor pool. *In room:* A/C, TV, kitchenette (in suites), Wi-Fi (free).

Rocky Shore Villas 🎁   This little guesthouse is a real find. Blissfully far removed from the action along overcrowded Seven Mile Beach, it lies to the north in the West Bay area, near the **Cayman Turtle Farm** (p. 122). It is only steps away from a tranquil beach and has easy access to good snorkeling and scuba diving. Massage therapy and traditional arts-and-crafts classes are offered on-site. This hotel can connect you to local life more than any other lodging on the island, as the on-site owners are involved in a number of the island's social and cultural events and can recommend excursions and activities you might not otherwise hear about.

30 Grass Piece Lane, West Bay, Grand Cayman, B.W.I. ✆ **866/845-6943** or 345/926-0119. Fax 345/946-0118. 7 units, 2 with private bathroom. Winter US$120–US$385 double; off season US$99–US$265 double. MC, V. **Amenities:** Babysitting. *In room:* A/C, TV/DVD, fridge, no phone, Wi-Fi (free).

CONDOS, VILLAS & COTTAGES
Very Expensive

The Avalon Condominiums ★★   One of Grand Cayman's best condo complexes is the Avalon, which occupies prime real estate on a stretch of Seven Mile Beach. Painted a distinctive shade of blue-violet (the staff refers to it as "orchid"), it consists of 27 oceanfront three-bedroom/three-bathroom units, 19 of which are available for rent. Only a short distance from restaurants, and about a 10-minute drive from George Town, the Avalon is well maintained, pleasant, and stylish. The three-story design ensures a lower density of people on the beachfront than you're likely to find in front of newer properties with six or seven stories. Children under 12 are allowed on-site, but overall, they're rather carefully "policed" for misbehavior and loud noises, a policy that contributes to a sense of calm and sedate well-being that residents and investors work hard to maintain. The well-appointed, spacious units have an English colonial motif; durable, flowered or pastel-colored upholsteries; and king-size or twin beds. Each condo has a fully equipped, open-sided kitchen with amenities (including granite or Corian countertops) upgraded in 2006 and a screened lanai overlooking a stretch of beach.

West Bay Rd. (PO Box 31236), Grand Cayman, B.W.I. ✆ **305/395-4503** or 345/945-4171. Fax 345/945-4189. www.avaloncayman.com. 27 units. Winter US$975 apt for 4, US$1,175 apt for 6; off season US$595 apt for 4, US$695 apt for

Condos, Villas & Cottages

6. Surcharges of up to 10% apply during Christmas, Thanksgiving, and Easter. AE, MC, V. **Amenities:** Exercise room; Jacuzzi; sauna; tennis court (lit). *In room:* A/C, TV, kitchen, Wi-Fi (free).

The Beachcomber ★   In the center of Seven Mile Beach, this is one of the older condo complexes, but it's still well maintained and inviting. The fabled sands of Seven Mile Beach lie right outside your rental. You're made to feel welcome from the very beginning of your stay: Upon your arrival, you're given a piece of rum cake and discount coupons for shops and attractions. The condos are spacious, but rather simply furnished. Each is a two-bedroom apartment that sleeps four people comfortably and six people in a somewhat cramped fashion. Tile floors and rattan furnishings make up the decor, and each unit opens onto a view of the sea from a screened-in private patio. For those who want to make use of their kitchenettes, at least for preparing simple meals, there's a grocery store across the street. Even if you don't have a car, you'll find a deli, three dive shops, liquor stores, and scooter rentals nearby. The restaurants and bars of the **Westin Casuarina** (p. 62) and the **Grand Cayman Beach Suites** (p. 59) are also within walking distance. You'll find good snorkeling on the reef right offshore.

PO Box 1799, Seven Mile Beach, Grand Cayman, B.W.I. ☎ **345/943-6500.** Fax 345/943-6550. www.beachcomber1.com. 24 units. Winter US$800–US$1,325 double; off season US$450–US$800 double. AE, MC, V. **Amenities:** Babysitting; access to nearby health club; outdoor pool. *In room:* A/C, TV, CD player, kitchen, Wi-Fi (free).

The Colonial Club ★★   Built in 1985, this pastel-pink complex is set on a highly desirable stretch of the famous Seven Mile Beach. It's a three-story and rather standard condominium development about 6km (3¾ miles) north of George Town and some 10 minutes from the airport. First-class maintenance, service, and accommodations are provided in the apartments, all of which have a kitchen, maid service, and laundry facilities. Usually only 8 of the 24 apartments are available for rent (the rest are privately owned and occupied, but are sometimes rented out). You can choose units with two bedrooms and three bathrooms or units with three bedrooms and three bathrooms.

West Bay Rd. (PO Box 320WB), Grand Cayman, B.W.I. ☎ **345/945-4660.** Fax 345/945-4839. www.thecolonialclub.com. 24 units. Winter US$725 apt for 4, US$795 apt for 6; off season US$425 apt for 4, US$495 apt for 6. Minimum 5-night stay Dec 16–Apr 15. AE, MC, V. **Amenities:** Outdoor pool; tennis court (lit). *In room:* A/C, TV, Internet (free), kitchen.

Lighthouse Point ★   If you want to travel "green" in Grand Cayman, this condo resort is the most eco-friendly on the island. Located on the northwest point of the island, the resort has rooms with unobstructed views of the Caribbean from private balconies, and it's surrounded by flora and fauna indigenous to the islands. The exterior blends into the landscape, with a number of nautical features such as anchors, cannons, and yes, even a lighthouse. Green amenities include solar power, wind power, and on-demand hot water heating, as well as a water reclamation system. The condos are made of solid wood interiors (from sustainable forests), and there is also a dive shop run by Divetech, one of Cayman's premier operators. Divers can explore a 19th-century shipwreck and, as of January 2011, the USS *Kittiwake,* a World War II American rescue vessel donated and sunk to create a 76m-long (250-ft.) reef teeming with fish. The one- and two-bedroom suites and villas are attractively and comfortably furnished in a Caribbean motif.

Seven Mile Beach, Grand Cayman, B.W.I. ⓒ **345/946-5658.** www.lighthouse-point-cayman.com. 9 units. US$3,150–US$4,200 weekly; off season US$2,625–US$2,800 weekly. MC, V. *In room:* A/C, TV, kitchen, Wi-Fi (free).

Expensive

Aqua Bay Club ★   These privately owned oceanfront condos occupy well-kept grounds with coconut palms, on the western end of Seven Mile Beach, about a 20-minute run from the airport. Short-term rentals are arranged here while the owners are away. Each of the units has the same layout, and most come with two bedrooms and two full bathrooms. In most cases, the master bedroom opens onto a terrace with a view of the water. Each unit comes with a well-equipped kitchen, including a dishwasher. Special features include machines for laundry as well as grills for barbecuing near the beach. As an added bonus, a cellphone is provided for each rental. The location is a bit remote, so you'll probably have to rely on taxi service unless you rent a car.

Seven Mile Beach, Grand Cayman, B.W.I. ⓒ **800/825-8703** or 345/945-4728. Fax 345/945-5681. www.aquabayclub.com. 21 units. Winter US$325–US$495 1-bedroom suite, US$395–US$625 2-bedroom suite; off season US$275 1-bedroom suite, US$325–US$375 2-bedroom suite. AE, MC, V. **Amenities:** Jacuzzi; outdoor pool. *In room:* A/C, TV, Internet (free), kitchen.

The Discovery Point Club ★ ☺   Located at the far end of the northern stretch of Seven Mile Beach in West Bay (10km/6¼ miles from George Town), this tranquil and relatively isolated group of condos is entirely composed of privately owned oceanside suites. The venue here is local, West Indian, and rural—if you're looking for a city atmosphere, forget it and move back south along West Bay Road. When you tire of snorkeling just offshore, retreat to the club's pool or Jacuzzi. Accommodations are comfortable, individually furnished and styled, well maintained, and, in some cases, better than those offered by nearby competitors. Condos have tasteful furnishings and a screened patio, and each has daily maid service. Each renovated unit comes with a fully equipped kitchen. Children under 12 stay free, and cribs and rollaway beds are available. Typically, management will agree to subdivide any two-bedroom suite into studios and one-bedroom suites by locking doors within each individual unit.

West Bay Rd. (PO Box 439), West Bay, Grand Cayman, B.W.I. © **866/384-9980** or 345/945-4724. Fax 345/945-5051. www.discoverypointclub.com. 45 units. Winter US$235 studio, US$495 double, US$675 quad; off season US$210 studio, US$300 double, US$345 quad. AE, DISC, MC, V. **Amenities:** Jacuzzi; outdoor pool; 2 tennis courts (lit). *In room:* A/C, TV, Internet (free), kitchen.

Lacovia Condominiums ★ 🎁

This lovely condo resort opens onto 122m (400 ft.) of white sand on Seven Mile Beach, and is surrounded by tropical gardens and towering shade trees. It features handsomely furnished and comfortable two- and three-bedroom condos, complete with kitchens. Although it's not quite home away from home, it's almost there. The accommodations are well maintained by an efficient housekeeping staff, and the decor is a modern Caribbean motif. If you're cooking in, you can walk to a grocery store; otherwise, opt for one of the excellent restaurants nearby. In spite of a lot of traffic on the beach road, life in the courtyard is secluded and tranquil. Of course, you must pay the piper for all this luxury.

Seven Mile Beach, Grand Cayman, B.W.I. © **345/949-7599.** Fax 345/949-0172. www.lacovia.com. 35 units. Winter US$415–US$545 1-bedroom condo, US$570–US$685 2-bedroom condo, US$720–US$875 3-bedroom condo; off season US$290–US$345 1-bedroom condo, US$335–US$435 2-bedroom condo, US$435–US$530 3-bedroom condo. AE, DISC, MC, V. **Amenities:** Exercise room; Jacuzzi; outdoor pool; tennis court (lit). *In room:* A/C, TV, Internet (free), kitchen.

London House ★

At the tranquil northern end of Seven Mile Beach, London House is a good choice if you'd like your own upscale apartment. Thanks to Hurricane Ivan in 2004, the hotel has undergone a massive renovation in recent years and been rebuilt essentially in its original style. Each unit has a fully equipped kitchen, spacious living and dining areas, and a private patio or balcony overlooking the water. Floral prints, rattan, tile floors, and Caribbean pastels set a tropical tone in most units.

The complex has a seaside swimming pool (but try to get a room away from the pool area if you're bothered by noise, as parties are sometimes staged on the patio), plus a volleyball court. You'll find a stone barbecue for private poolside cookouts and many restaurants nearby.

Seven Mile Beach, Grand Cayman, B.W.I. © **345/945-4060.** Fax 345/945-4087. www.londonhouse.ky. 21 units. Winter US$390 US$450 1 bedroom apt, US$375–US$575 2-bedroom apt, US$800 3-bedroom apt; off season US$320–US$350

1-bedroom apt, US$315–US$450 2-bedroom apt, US$400–US$550 3-bedroom apt. Extra person US$30 per day. AE, MC, V. **Amenities:** Babysitting; outdoor pool. *In room:* A/C, TV/DVD, kitchen, Wi-Fi (free).

Morritt's Tortuga Club & Resort ★

On 3 beachfront hectares (7½ acres) in the East End, this resort offers some of the island's best windsurfing and diving within waters that drop off quickly into Grand Cayman's "West Wall." **Tortuga Divers** (p. 111) runs a branch on the premises and focuses on the diving and windsurfing trade that has developed offshore from this isolated but surprisingly busy hotel.

About a 40km (25-mile) drive from the airport, the resort and club are composed of clusters of three-story beachfront condos opening onto the water. Each was built in the Antillean plantation style from the wreckage of a former hotel. There's a bit more space within the Grand Resort units, with kitchens that are somewhat of an upgrade from those in the Tortuga Club. Grand Resort rooms rent at a premium between 10% and 15% more than the rates noted below. Many are rented as timeshare units, often to visiting British and Canadian residents who appreciate the calm of this resort's isolated position on Grand Cayman's distant East End. Each of the comfortably furnished apartments has a fully equipped kitchen, although many guests opt for meals in the complex's simple restaurant.

PO Box 496GT, East End, Grand Cayman, B.W.I. © **800/447-0309** in the U.S., or 345/947-7449. Fax 345/947-7669. www.morritts.com. 160 units. Winter US$320 studio, US$440 1-bedroom apt, US$470 2-bedroom apt; off season US$250 studio, US$300 1-bedroom apt, US$350 2-bedroom apt. AE, DISC, MC, V. **Amenities:** Restaurant; 4 bars; babysitting; exercise room; Internet (free); 3 outdoor pools. *In room:* A/C, TV, kitchenette.

The Reef Resort ★ 🎁

A bit of a discovery, this well-maintained and exceedingly comfortable timeshare/condo complex is located in the less trampled East End, a 32km (20-mile) drive from the airport. Guests who stay here will need a car, as the property lies about a 45-minute ride from George Town. Spacious beachfront units range from luxury studios to suites. The studio units, favorites among honeymooners, are the smallest and feature their own balcony, a full bathroom, an oversize Jacuzzi, and a kitchenette. The one-bedroom suites are a good option for a family, and are mainly the same as the studios except that they are larger and feature two pullout Murphy beds in the living room. These units are suitable for four guests. The largest, best, and most expensive of the accommodations are the two-bedroom villas, which are a combination of the one-bedroom suite and the studio. The spaciousness of these particular lodgings makes them a favorite with larger families. The many activities here range from stargazing to diving instruction.

Queen's Hwy. (PO Box 3865), Colliers Bay, East End, Grand Cayman, B.W.I. *©* **888/232-0541** in the U.S., or 345/947-3100. Fax 345/947-9920. www.thereef. com. 30 units. Year-round US$250–US$290 studio, US$340 1-bedroom suite, US$465 2-bedroom villa. AE, MC, V. **Amenities:** Restaurant; bar; babysitting; health club & spa; 3 outdoor pools; room service; tennis court (lit); watersports equipment/rentals. *In room:* A/C, TV/DVD, CD player (in some), kitchenette, Wi-Fi (US$8 per day).

The Retreat at Rum Point ★ This secluded, remote group of privately owned condominiums, located on Rum Point peninsula, opens onto 390m (1,280 ft.) of white sand beach. The beach, shaded by casuarina trees, is a bit narrow and can hardly compare to the wide sands of Seven Mile Beach, but the place draws tranquillity-seekers for its relative isolation. The retreat is a 35-minute drive from George Town or the airport. The condos are owner-occupied for part of the year and are rented the rest of the time. Each condo has been individually decorated by its particular owner, and most feature typical Caribbean decor, with wicker and rattan. All units contain private balconies. Each condo has a fully equipped kitchen, as well as a washer and dryer. Small groups ranging from two to six people can be accommodated here in one- to three-bedroom beachfront condos. All units receive maid service. The **Lighthouse Restaurant at Breakers** (p. 88) is within walking distance. Right next door to the Retreat is an office of **Red Sail Sports** (p. 107), an excellent watersports outfitter.

PO Box 46, North Side, Grand Cayman, B.W.I. *©* **866/947-9135.** Fax 345/947-9135. www.theretreat.com.ky. 23 units. Winter US$330–US$450 double, US$550 triple; off season US$230–US$325 double, US$400 triple. AE, DISC, MC, V. **Amenities:** Exercise room; outdoor pool; tennis court (lit); nearby watersports equipment/rentals; Wi-Fi (free by pool). *In room:* A/C, TV, kitchen.

Silver Sands Condominiums ★ ☺ A good choice for families, this modern complex is arranged around a rectangular pool on a relatively low-density stretch of sandy beachfront, 11km (6¾ miles) north of George Town. The eight three-story apartment blocks, each painted pale blue, were solidly built to high standards in the late 1970s, and in some ways are more substantial than recently constructed projects nearby. Each is configured as either a two-bedroom/two-bathroom or three-bedroom/three-bathroom unit. Each apartment comes with a balcony and a fully equipped kitchen. In all, this is a smoothly run operation, which, in spite of its high costs, satisfies most guests.

West Bay Rd. (PO Box 752WB), Seven Mile Beach, Grand Cayman, B.W.I. *©* **345/949-3343.** Fax 345/949-1223. www.silversandscondos.com. 42 units. Winter US$410–US$550 1-bedroom apt, US$520–US$570 2-bedroom apt,

US$610–US$710 3-bedroom apt; off season US$300–US$395 1-bedroom apt, US$340–US$570 2-bedroom apt, US$410–US$480 3-bedroom apt. Additional person US$25 extra. Children 12 and under stay free in parent's room. Minimum 7-night stay in winter; minimum 3-night stay off season. AE, MC, V. **Amenities:** Outdoor pool; 2 tennis courts (lit). *In room:* A/C, TV, kitchen, Wi-Fi (free).

Villas of the Galleon ★ ☺ This condo complex is on the widest strip of sand along Seven Mile Beach, across the road from the Links at SafeHaven golf course. Inside the stucco cottages, you'll find impressive, well-maintained rooms with rattan furnishings and pastels, along with creamy tiles, all evoking the easy, breezy Caribbean lifestyle. Each of the rentals contains one, two, or three bedrooms along with a fully equipped kitchen and a private balcony or patio overlooking Seven Mile Beach and the ocean. The closets are especially large. The villas lie just 2 blocks from grocery and liquor stores and several top restaurants. Families like to check in here because each unit comes with baby cribs and rollaway beds. You'll find beach towels, patio furniture, beach loungers, and outdoor barbecue grills. There is even daily maid service.

PO Box 1797, Seven Mile Beach, Grand Cayman, B.W.I. ✆ **866/665-4696** or 345/945-4433. Fax 345/945-4705. www.villasofthegalleon.com. 59 units. Winter US$420–US$510 1-bedroom, US$525–US$650 2-bedroom, US$650–US$850 3-bedroom; off season US$295–US$360 1-bedroom, US$300–US$425 2-bedroom, US$400–US$600 3-bedroom. Extra person US$50. AE, DISC, MC, V. *In room:* A/C, TV/DVD, CD player, Internet (free).

Moderate

The Anchorage On a tranquil stretch of Seven Mile Beach, this villa complex includes a series of well-furnished, privately owned, and individually decorated units. Each has two bedrooms and two bathrooms and can accommodate up to four (great for two couples traveling together or a family with kids). Units opening onto the garden are the least expensive; you'll pay more for oceanfront accommodations. Each villa has a screened porch or balcony. Good snorkeling can be found right offshore.

PO Box 30986, Seven Mile Beach, Grand Cayman, B.W.I. ✆ **813/333-6532** in the U.S., or 345/945-4088. Fax 345/945-5001. www.theanchoragecayman.com. 15 units. Winter US$295–US$505 2-bedroom apt; off season US$160–US$330 2-bedroom apt. MC, V. **Amenities:** Outdoor pool; tennis court (lit). *In room:* A/C, TV, kitchen, Wi-Fi (free).

Christopher Columbus ★ ☺ This is an intimate condo complex and hideaway tucked away at the northern end of Seven Mile Beach, with some of the best snorkeling right off its beach. The choice is ideal for families because the lodgings consist of either two- or three-bedroom units. Thatched cabanas line the beach in front of the hotel. Spacious, well-equipped kitchens and large living rooms are found in each of the condos, which are decorated with pastel colors, handsomely furnished, and well maintained. There's a private swimming pool if you tire of the beach. There are also laundry facilities on-site. However, you'll need transportation to reach most restaurants and attractions.

2013 West Bay Rd., Seven Mile Beach, Grand Cayman, B.W.I. © **866/311-5231** or 345/945-4354. Fax 345/945-5062. www.christophercolumbuscondos.com. 30 units. Winter US$340 2-bedroom unit, US$490 3-bedroom unit, US$540 penthouse; off season US$250 2-bedroom unit, US$325 3-bedroom unit, US$350 penthouse. AE, DISC, MC, V. **Amenities:** Outdoor pool; 2 tennis courts (lit). *In room:* A/C, TV, kitchen, Wi-Fi (free).

Island Pine Villas   Located right on Seven Mile Beach, this unpretentious villa complex is comfortable and casual, though it's far less elegant than the Colonial Club. A family-friendly complex of one- and two-bedroom condos close to George Town, it's a practical and affordable choice. Inside and outside, it looks like a Days Inn motel along the Florida Turnpike. The units are well furnished, with fully equipped kitchens and daily maid service. There's a choice of queen- or king-size beds, and the best accommodations overlook the beach.

PO Box 30197-SMB, Seven Mile Beach, Grand Cayman, B.W.I. © **866/878-7477** or 345/949-6586. Fax 345/949-0428. www.caribbeancoast.com/nHotels/IslandPineVillas. 40 units. Winter US$200 double; off season US$150 double. AE, MC, V. **Amenities:** Watersports equipment/rentals. *In room:* A/C, TV, kitchen.

WHERE TO EAT ON GRAND CAYMAN

On his trip to the West Indies in 1859, Anthony Trollope, the British novelist, was not impressed with the food his plantation-owning hosts served him. Ignoring the rich bounty of their islands, including local fruit and vegetables, they fed him canned potatoes, tinned meats, and cheeses imported from England. At the time, British expats felt that if a food item didn't come from their homeland, it wasn't worth putting on the table.

Regrettably, Trollope did not visit the Cayman Islands as part of his sojourn. Had he paid a call, he would have found that the enterprising Caymanians were eating what they raised. Or, more accurately, what they caught. There was little reliance on imported goods in the 19th-century Cayman Islands. Today, Caymanian cuisine continues to take advantage of the islands' natural provisions, and locally caught fish dominates menus throughout the islands.

Today, many Caymanian chefs showcase international recipes on their menus, and some Caymanians claim that you have to be invited to a local home to sample real island cuisine. This is simply not true. Numerous restaurants still feature West Indian cooks who prepare food as their grandmothers did, and we've recommended several of them. Unless a restaurant is devoted to a particular foreign cuisine, it is likely to offer a handful of authentic Caymanian dishes.

Although Grand Cayman hotels quote their rates in U.S. dollars, nearly all restaurants list prices in both Cayman and U.S. dollars. (This is based on the assumption that islanders patronize their local restaurants, but have little need for hotel rooms.) Most restaurants add a 10% to 15% charge in lieu of a tip, so check your bill carefully.

Following are a few traditional menu items you can expect to see at Caymanian restaurants:

SEA TURTLE   Turtle meat that appears on menus in the Cayman Islands is from the local **Cayman Turtle Farm** (p. 122), which raises turtles specifically for commercial purposes.

QUEEN CONCH   The national food of the Cayman Islands is conch. The firm white meat of this mollusk—called the "snail of the sea"—tastes somewhat bland until local chefs work their magic. Conch has a chewy consistency, which means that it has to be tenderized. It's often served at happy hour in taverns and bars, as a main dish, in salads, and as an hors d'oeuvre.

Every cook has a different recipe for conch chowder, but a popular version includes tomatoes, potatoes, sweet peppers, onions, carrots, salt or pork bacon, bay leaves, thyme, and (of course) salt and pepper. Conch fritters are served with hot sauce and are made with finely minced peppers, onions, and tomato paste, among other ingredients. They are deep-fried in oil.

Cracked conch (or "fried conch," as the old-timers used to call it) is prepared like a breaded veal cutlet. The conch is tenderized and dipped in batter, and then sautéed. Conch is also served steamed, in Creole sauce, curried, "scorched," creamed on toast, and stewed. You'll even see "conch burgers" listed on menus.

Marinated conch is frequently enjoyed right on the water, courtesy of the numerous Caymanian sea captains who operate North Sound excursions that include lunch. They will scoop a conch right out of the sea, remove it from its shell (an art unto itself), slice it up, and serve it with lime juice and onions—as fresh as it can possibly be.

The High Price of Imported Ingredients

Because many ingredients must be imported into the Cayman Islands, restaurants here are among the most expensive in the Caribbean. Even so-called moderate restaurants can become expensive if you order steak or lobster. For the best value, opt for West Indian fare at local restaurants.

THE MAIN EVENT Red snapper, mahimahi (which is also called dorado or dolphin), swordfish, yellowfin tuna, and grouper are the most commonly available fish.

The most elegant item you'll see on nearly any menu is the local spiny lobster. This tropical cousin of the Maine lobster is also called crayfish or rock lobster. Only the tail is eaten. You get fresh lobster when it is in season, from the beginning of April until the end of August. Otherwise it's frozen.

Chicken and pork, the meats that are most often prepared island-style, are frequently roasted, grilled, curried, or "jerked"— that is, rubbed with spices and slow-smoked for hours over a low fire, preferably made with pimento wood. Each cook has his or her own spice blend, but jerk spices usually include allspice, hot Scotch bonnet pepper, thyme, nutmeg, salt, garlic, onion, and green onion. Other popular meat dishes that are easily found at restaurants serving island cuisine include braised beef liver, curried goat, oxtail, and salt beef and beans.

THE SIDES The most frequent companion for main dishes is "rice and peas," a dish that's also popular in Jamaica, which is actually composed of rice and red beans cooked in coconut milk. Along with rice and peas, ripe plantains (larger, less sweet relatives of the banana) are fried or baked with brown sugar and served alongside main dishes.

RESTAURANTS BY CUISINE

AMERICAN
Chicken! Chicken! (Seven Mile Beach, $, p. 98)
Corita's Copper Kettle ★ (George Town, $, p. 99)
Eats Café (Seven Mile Beach, $, p. 99)
Grand Old House ★★ (South of George Town, $$$, p. 86)
Hard Rock Cafe Cayman Islands (George Town, $, p. 100)
Rackham's Pub & Restaurant (George Town, $$, p. 96)

ASIAN
Casa Havana ★★ (Seven Mile Beach, $$$, p. 84)

CAFE/COFFEEHOUSE
Full of Beans (George Town, $$, p. 95)

CARIBBEAN
Aqua Beach Restaurant & Bar (Seven Mile Beach, $$, p. 92)
Bacchus Restaurant and Wine Bar ★ (George Town, $$, p. 92)
The Brasserie ★★ (George Town, $$$, p. 82)

KEY TO ABBREVIATIONS:
$$$$** = Very Expensive   **$$$** = Expensive   **$$** = Moderate   **$ = Inexpensive

Breezes by the Bay (George Town, $$, p. 93)
Corita's Copper Kettle ★ (George Town, $, p. 99)
Grand Old House ★★ (South of George Town, $$$, p. 86)
Harry's Caribbean Bar & Grill (George Town, $, p. 100)
The Lighthouse Restaurant at Breakers ★ (Breakers, $$$, p. 88)
Over the Edge (Old Man Bay, $$, p. 96)
Portofino Wreckview Restaurant ★ (Colliers, $$$, p. 90)
Rackham's Pub & Restaurant (George Town, $$, p. 96)
The Wharf ★ (Seven Mile Beach, $$$, p. 91)

CONTINENTAL

The Brasserie ★★ (George Town, $$$, p. 82)
Deckers Grille & Lounge (Seven Mile Beach, $$, p. 94)
The Wharf ★ (Seven Mile Beach, $$$, p. 91)

CUBAN

Casa Havana ★★ (Seven Mile Beach, $$$, p. 84)

ENGLISH PUB FARE

Triple Crown (Seven Mile Beach, $, p. 102)

INDIAN

Gateway of India (Seven Mile Beach, $$, p. 95)

INTERNATIONAL

Breezes by the Bay (George Town, $$, p. 93)
The Brick House (Red Bay, $$, p. 93)
Calypso Grill ★★ (Morgan's Harbour, $$$, p. 82)
Cimboco Caribbean Cafe (Seven Mile Beach, $, p. 98)
Eats Café (Seven Mile Beach, $, p. 99)
Hemingway's ★★ (Seven Mile Beach, $$$, p. 86)
Icoa Cafe ★ (Seven Mile Beach, $, p. 101)
Kaibo Beach Bar & Grill ★ (North Side, $$$, p. 88)
Lobster Pot ★ (George Town, $$$, p. 89)
Mezza (Seven Mile Beach, $, p. 101)
Portofino Wreckview Restaurant ★ (Colliers, $$$, p. 90)
Seaharvest Restaurant ★ (South of George Town, $, p. 102)

ITALIAN

Casanova's ★ (George Town, $$$, p. 84)
Edoardo's (Seven Mile Beach, $$, p. 94)
The Lighthouse Restaurant at Breakers ★ (Breakers, $$$, p. 88)
Neptune's ★ (Seven Mile Beach, $$$, p. 89)
Portofino Wreckview Restaurant ★ (Colliers, $$$, p. 90)
Ristorante Pappagallo ★ (Conch Point, $$$, p. 91)
Ristorante Ragazzi (Seven Mile Beach, $$, p. 97)

WHERE TO EAT ON GRAND CAYMAN | Restaurants by Cuisine

JAMAICAN
Seymour's Jerk Centre (George Town, $, p. 102)

LIGHT FARE
Full of Beans (George Town, $$, p. 95)

MIDDLE EASTERN
Al la Kebab (Seven Mile Beach, $, p. 98)

PACIFIC RIM
Grand Old House ★★ (South of George Town, $$$, p. 86)

SEAFOOD
Blue by Eric Ripert ★★★ (Seven Mile Beach, $$$$, p. 81)

Calypso Grill ★★ (Morgan's Harbour, $$$, p. 82)

Casanova's ★ (George Town, $$$, p. 84)

The Cracked Conch/Macabuca Oceanside Tiki Bar & Grill ★★ (West Bay, $$$, p. 84)

Hemingway's ★★ (Seven Mile Beach, $$$, p. 86)

The Lighthouse Restaurant at Breakers ★ (Breakers, $$$, p. 88)

Lobster Pot ★ (George Town, $$$, p. 89)

The Reef Grill at Royal Palms ★★★ (Seven Mile Beach, $$$, p. 90)

Ristorante Pappagallo ★ (Conch Point, $$$, p. 91)

THAI
Thai Orchid (Seven Mile Beach, $$, p. 97)

WEST INDIAN
Vivine's Kitchen ★ (Gun Bay, $, p. 103)

VERY EXPENSIVE

Blue by Eric Ripert ★★★ SEAFOOD   This is Grand Cayman's premier restaurant, a showcase for the deluxe culinary wares of master chef Eric Ripert. The mother restaurant is Le Bernardin, one of the most celebrated in Manhattan. You're presented with a choice of three-course fixed-price menus or else a fabulous tasting menu that food critics have labeled "hedonistic." The chef has perfected a wonderfully rich, inventive cuisine full of diverse flavors and textures, all presented harmoniously and artistically on your plate. Both visitors and Caymanians are beguiled by the epicurean skill of the seafood menus inspired by the bounty of island fisherman. The appetizers dazzle, including a trio of conch ceviche or a velvety combo of yellowfin tuna and foie gras. The main courses are sensual delights, especially the sautéed cobia with an avocado and coconut cream or bread-crusted striped bass with grilled mango and a roasted chili emulsion. One of the most celebrated wine cellars in the Caribbean features more than 650 selections.

At the Ritz-Carlton, Grand Cayman, West Bay Rd. ⓒ **345/943-9000.** www.ritzcarlton.com/en/Properties/GrandCayman/Dining/Blue-byEricRipert. Reservations required. 3-course fixed-price menus CI$66–CI$88; tasting menus CI$96–CI$135. AE, DC, MC, V. Tues–Sat 6–10pm.

EXPENSIVE

The Brasserie ★★ CARIBBEAN/CONTINENTAL   Elegant and stylish, and favored by members of Grand Cayman's investment community, this restaurant seems very far removed from the hubbub of Seven Mile Beach and other tourist-geared areas. Expect a Caribbean colonial decor with high ceilings, artfully carved teakwood and mahogany furniture, spinning ceiling fans, and a cool, breezy layout that might evoke an upscale private club in a long-gone British colonial empire. Lunches focus on exquisite and elaborate salads such as a fresh yellowfin tuna tataki with pine nuts, feta cheese, and sweet basil vinaigrette; pasta dishes; and the fresh catch of the day. Dinners are more elaborate, featuring such appetizers as a slab of Hudson Valley foie gras with chocolate foam, or warm white asparagus with prosciutto and a lemon velouté. Main courses are a Lucullan treat, especially the pan-seared scallops with a celeriac mousseline, and the braised lamb shank with roasted garlic mashed potatoes and red wine cabbage.

171 Elgin Ave., Cricket Sq., George Town. ⓒ **345/945-1815.** www.brasserie cayman.com. Reservations recommended, especially at lunch. Lunch salads and platters CI$6.50–CI$12; dinner main courses CI$15–CI$25. AE, DC, MC, V. Mon–Fri 11:30am–2:30pm; tapas menu daily 4:30–7pm; dinner daily 6–10pm.

Calypso Grill ★★ 🍴 SEAFOOD/INTERNATIONAL   At first glance, you might think this is little more than a waterfront shack. But when you enter, you'll find a charming, funky, and slightly psychedelic bar and restaurant that absolutely drips with Creole colors, a sense of whimsy, and even a bold and creative elegance. If the wind isn't too brisk, you can sit on a wooden deck directly above the water, watching workaday fishing craft depositing their loads at West Bay's busiest fishing port. The place feels very authentic, with a clientele from many walks of Caymanian life, ranging from the moneyed to the bohemian—resulting in an atmosphere that's a far cry from the congestion and glitter of Seven Mile Beach. Perch at the rectangular bar here for a cocktail or any of a dozen kinds of wine by the glass, or, if a table isn't likely to become

Restaurants on Seven Mile Beach

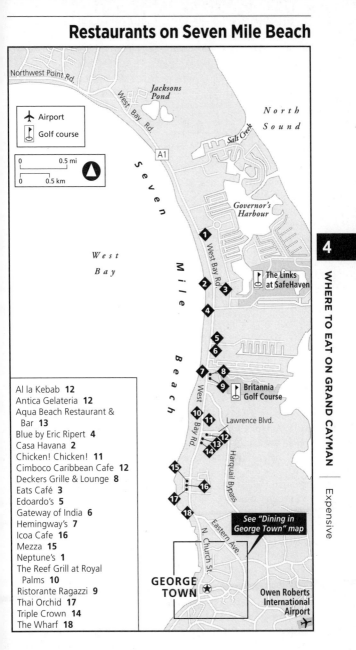

Al la Kebab **12**
Antica Gelateria **12**
Aqua Beach Restaurant & Bar **13**
Blue by Eric Ripert **4**
Casa Havana **2**
Chicken! Chicken! **11**
Cimboco Caribbean Cafe **12**
Deckers Grille & Lounge **8**
Eats Café **3**
Edoardo's **5**
Gateway of India **6**
Hemingway's **7**
Icoa Cafe **16**
Mezza **15**
Neptune's **1**
The Reef Grill at Royal Palms **10**
Ristorante Ragazzi **9**
Thai Orchid **17**
Triple Crown **14**
The Wharf **18**

available, opt for a full meal. The best menu items include marinated conch; a creamy version of lobster bisque; Cuban-style shrimp with sherry-flavored cream sauce; fresh fish (ask the waiter what's available) that can be blackened, grilled, or sautéed; veal chops with chanterelles; and a garlic-laced version of shrimp linguine. Favorite desserts include mango crepes and sticky toffee pudding.

Morgan's Harbour, West Bay. © **345/949-3948.** www.calypsogrillcayman.com. Reservations required for dinner. Main courses CI$20–CI$32. AE, DC, MC, V. Tues–Sat 11:30am–2:30pm; Sun 12:30–2:30pm; Tues–Sun 6–10pm.

Casa Havana ★★ CUBAN/ASIAN   As you enter, you expect to see a reincarnated Ernest Hemingway sitting at the bar with his cronies telling tall fish tales. Located in the Westin Casuarina, this upmarket eatery recaptures some of the flavor of pre-Castro Old Havana, with mahogany furnishings and crystal chandeliers. In this elegant oceanfront setting, you experience a Nuevo Latino Caribbean cuisine. Some food critics have called chef Jason Koppinger's fare "Floribbean." With rich yet subtle flavors, the food is inspired enough to appeal even to terminally jaded palates. Here, you might be treated to a seared foie gras with caramelized apple salad that is earthy yet refined, followed by the chef's black cod specialty. The latter dish is crusted with ground macadamia nuts and served with a white truffle essence. The Key lime cheesecake is the dessert supreme, enhanced by a Melba sauce.

In the Westin Casuarina, West Bay Rd. © **345/945-3800.** www.westincasuarina. net. Reservations required. Main courses CI$27–CI$42. AE, MC, V. Daily 6–10pm.

Casanova's ★ ITALIAN/SEAFOOD   This local favorite, right in the heart of George Town, is owned and run by the Crescente family, and the cooks here have mastered the art of Italian cooking. A large number of dishes revolve around the catch of the day. The lunch menu is particularly enticing, with its salads, homemade soup of the day, and conch fritters with jerk mayonnaise. Dinner grows more elaborate, with a choice of both hot and cold appetizers, ranging from tuna sashimi style to sautéed mussels. Main dishes include a penne with fresh lobster, and fresh center-cut yellowfin tuna in a light oregano sauce on a bed of orange seaweed salad.

65 N. Church St., George Town. © **345/949-7633.** www.casanova.ky. Reservations recommended. Main courses CI$11–CI$28. MC, V. Mon–Sat 11:30am–2:30pm; daily 6–10pm.

The Cracked Conch/Macabuca Oceanside Tiki Bar & Grill ★★ SEAFOOD   Nestled among the jagged rocks of West Bay on the seacoast near the northern terminus of Seven Mile

Restaurants in George Town

Bacchus Restaurant
  and Wine Bar **4**
The Brasserie **9**
Breezes by the Bay **6**
Casanova's **3**
Corita's Copper Kettle **5**
Full of Beans **8**
Hard Rock Café
  Cayman Islands **7**
Harry's Caribbean Bar
  & Grill **8**
Lobster Pot **1**
Rackham's Pub
  & Restaurant **2**
Seymour's Jerk
  Centre **10**

(i) Information
✉ Post office

↑ To Seven
Mile Beach

North Church St.
Bodden Rd.
Eastern Ave.
Edward Ave.
School Rd.
Mary St.
Harbour Dr.
Fort St.
Cardinal Ave.
Edward St.
Shedden Rd.
Crewe Rd.
Eastern Ave.
To Airport
George Town Harbour
South Church St.
Cayman Islands National Museum
Elgin Ave.

0   0.2 mi
0   0.2 km

Beach, across the road from the Turtle Farm, this eatery serves some of the island's freshest seafood. It's also a dining and drinking destination in its own right, a magnet for young, attractive residents of Grand Cayman, who frequent the place when they're not otherwise hard at work on other parts of the island.

Kick off an evening here with drinks and perhaps some time spent relaxing by the big-screen TVs at the Macabuca Tiki Bar, and then move to a table on the open-sided veranda at the Cracked Conch. Here you'll enjoy views of flickering torches and the sound of surf crashing against the jagged rocks nearby, hallucinatory rum punches and martinis, and very good food.

Management works hard to define the Macabuca Bar (whose name translates as "No Problem" in Taíno) as informal, relaxed, and irreverent, and the Cracked Conch as a venue for fine dining. Informal menu items available throughout the day and evening at Macabuca and at lunch at the Cracked Conch include salads; fried calamari; breaded and fried conch steaks; and beef, chicken, or conch burgers. More formal and elaborate dishes, available for dinner at the Cracked Conch, feature some of the most creative and elaborate combinations of conch and turtle steak we've ever

Which Dollar? Yours or Mine?

Make sure you know in which currency menu prices are quoted. If the currency is not written on the menu, ask the waiter if the prices are in U.S. or Cayman Islands dollars.

seen. Examples include a steamed-conch-and-snapper-coconut casserole; a skillfully prepared roulade of conch; and turtle steak braised with Parma ham, fresh tomatoes, and basil. Also available is a platter with fresh local tuna prepared three different ways: as marinated sashimi, as fried tuna rice rolls with pickled papaya, and as a tartare with fresh cilantro. Sunday brunches are festive, with buffet stations set up in the gleaming stainless-steel kitchen.

North West Point Rd., West Bay, near Cayman Turtle Farm. ℂ **345/945-5217.** www.crackedconch.com.ky. Reservations required for the Cracked Conch. At Macabuca CI$6.50–CI$19; at Cracked Conch dinner CI$15–CI$39, all-you-can-eat Sun brunch buffet CI$26. AE, MC, V. Cracked Conch daily 11am–3pm and 5:30–10pm. Macabuca Tiki Bar daily 10am–midnight or later.

Grand Old House ★★ AMERICAN/CARIBBEAN/PACIFIC RIM The Grand Old House is the island's premier caterer and hosts everything from lavish weddings and political functions to casual family dinners. This former plantation house lies amid venerable trees 2km (1¼ miles) south of George Town, past Jackson Point. Built on bedrock near the edge of the sea, it stands on 129 ironwood posts that support the main house and a bevy of gazebos.

For appetizers, we recommend the roasted lobster Napoleon or the marinated conch Cayman Islands–style with tomato, cilantro, and Key lime flavorings. Also worth trying is the tequila-infused snow crab and lobster on a mango gazpacho with spicy cucumber noodles. A signature main course is a platter of baked shrimp and scallops gratin in white wine, or the Cayman Islands–style turtle steak in a tomato-and-white-wine sauce. Of the fish dishes, we like the fire-roasted Chilean sea bass in balsamic syrup on a sweet-potato mash with a candied lemon-and-mango beurre blanc.

Petra Plantation, 648 S. Church St. ℂ **345/949-9333.** www.grandoldhouse.com. Reservations required. Main courses CI$21–CI$40. AE, DISC, MC, V. Mon–Sat 11:30am–2pm; daily 6–10pm.

Hemingway's ★★ SEAFOOD/INTERNATIONAL Some of the best seafood on the island can be found at the premier restaurant of the Grand Cayman Beach Suites, 3km (1¾ miles) north of George Town. It occupies a rambling, single-story annex of the hotel, in a spot shoehorned between the beach and two swimming

Restaurants on Grand Cayman

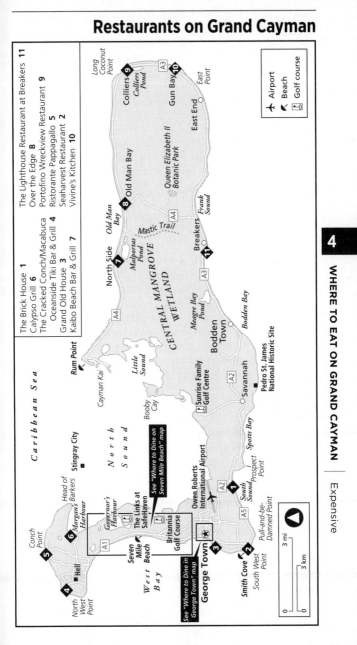

The Brick House **1**
Calypso Grill **6**
The Cracked Conch/Macabuca
Oceanside Tiki Bar & Grill **4**
Grand Old House **3**
Kaibo Beach Bar & Grill **7**

The Lighthouse Restaurant at Breakers **11**
Over the Edge **8**
Portofino Wreckview Restaurant **9**
Ristorante Pappagallo **5**
Seaharvest Restaurant **2**
Vivine's Kitchen **10**

pools. There's a rather plush bar inside, a classic after-work hang-out that's favored by managers of competing, nonaffiliated restaurants nearby; a big-windowed, air-conditioned dining room; and tables set outside, on a shaded colonnade near trails of bougainvillea, with spinning overhead fans. The menu is among the most imaginative on the island and has won acclaim from *Gourmet* magazine. Appetizers include a tasty coconut shrimp with a mango marmalade accent, Cuban-style barbecued turtle steak, well-spiced crab cakes, paella, and an absolutely fantastic deep-fried version of a whole red snapper that's deboned and artfully presented like a piece of sculpture with pickled onions, bell peppers, and garlic-laced mashed potatoes. There's also the catch of the day prepared any way you want it, and citrus-and-cumin-marinated tenderloin of pork.

In the Grand Cayman Beach Suites, West Bay Rd. ✆ **345/949-1234.** Reservations required. Main courses lunch CI$12–CI$19, dinner CI$21–CI$43. AE, DC, DISC, MC, V. Daily 11:30am–2:30pm and 6–10pm.

Kaibo Beach Bar & Grill ★ INTERNATIONAL   Isolated on Grand Cayman's northern coast, adjacent to a busy marina, this place serves good food in an irreverent and gregarious atmosphere. Flaming torches, multilevel terraces, and cabanas with palm-thatched roofs evoke a beach compound in Polynesia. Menu items include juicy burgers, fresh salads, seafood prepared any way you want, steaks, and pasta, all accompanied by sunset-colored drinks that tend to get the party roaring.

585 Water Cay Rd. (in the Kaibo Yacht Club), Cayman Kai, North Side. ✆ **345/947-9975.** www.kaibo.ky. Lunchtime platters, salads, and sandwiches CI$8.10–CI$12; dinner main courses CI$19–CI$39. AE, MC, V. Grill daily 11am–11pm. Bar daily 11am–1am.

The Lighthouse Restaurant at Breakers ★ CARIBBEAN/ITALIAN/SEAFOOD   This cozy, elegant, and nautically decorated landmark lies about a 30-minute drive east of George Town, on the south shore of the island. Its creative menu features fresh local seafood. An experienced chef, backed by a skilled staff, serves well-prepared meals, attracting both locals and visitors. Put yourself in the hands of the mostly European staff and sit back to enjoy such tempting appetizers as penne pasta with shrimp, asparagus, tomatoes, and pesto; or tuna sushi rolled in sesame seeds. For your main course, opt for the mixed grill of Caribbean seafood, lobster with gnocchi and shrimp, filet mignon with brandy-flavored cream sauce, or a veal chop topped with Gorgonzola and pancetta ham. The restaurant has one of the best wine cellars on the island. Immediately adjacent to the restaurant is a towering life-size replica of a lighthouse, its trademark and signature, that's visible for many miles out to sea.

Shamrock Rd. (Rte. A3), Breakers. ℰ **345/947-2047.** www.lighthouse.ky. Reservations recommended. Main courses lunch CI$7.30–CI$13, dinner CI$15–CI$41. AE, DISC, MC, V. Daily 11:30am–3:30pm and 5:30–10pm.

Lobster Pot ★ SEAFOOD/INTERNATIONAL Folksy and charming but not quite as delicious or as polished as Hemingway's, Lobster Pot remains nevertheless an island favorite. It overlooks the water from its second-floor perch at the northern perimeter of George Town, directly beside the road that funnels traffic into the capital from Seven Mile Beach. As its name suggests, it serves lobster prepared in many different ways: Cayman style (broiled in its shell), as lobster bisque, and as a mouth-watering salad. Braised jerk chicken, turtle steak, and stuffed Chilean salmon are also on the menu. Most dishes are right on the mark. A house specialty is the "Cayman Trio," with portions of broiled lobster tail, garlic-sautéed shrimp, and grilled fresh local fish piled onto the same platter. For lunch, you might opt for English-style fish and chips or perhaps lobster quesadillas or lobster-studded pasta.

245 N. Church St., George Town. ℰ **345/949-2736.** www.lobsterpot.ky. Reservations recommended in winter. Main courses lunch CI$11–CI$28, dinner CI$18–CI$40. AE, DISC, MC, V. Mon–Fri 11:30am–2:30pm; daily 5–10pm.

Neptune's ★ ITALIAN Set in a simple concrete building near the northern end of West Bay Road, this is one of a few genuinely appealing and relatively affordable Italian restaurants on Grand Cayman. There's no view of the sea, but you'll get the feeling that you're at the seashore, thanks to a decor featuring pristine ceramic tiles, a blue-and-white color scheme, and a mural of cavorting mermaids. Tables on the large outdoor terrace are centered on a human-size statue of Neptune, Roman god of the sea and the restaurant's namesake. Menu items include a wide array of the usual pastas, plus some nonstandard choices such as "Spaghetti alla Courtney," made with eggplant, fresh tomatoes, garlic, and mozzarella cheese, and "Spaghetti Bella Pesaro," made with grilled zucchini and fresh clams. The seafood options are especially tempting, including shrimp with garlic butter, balsamic vinegar, and fresh herbs; mixed seafood curry; and grilled red snapper served with lobster, shrimp, and tomato-flavored cream sauce.

Trafalgar Place (across from Seven Mile Beach), West Bay Rd. ℰ **345/946-8709.** Reservations recommended Fri–Sat at dinner. Lunch CI$6.50–CI$11; dinner CI$11–CI$24. AE, DC, MC, V. Mon–Sat 11:30am–2:30pm; daily 5:30–10:30pm.

Expensive

Portofino Wreckview Restaurant ★ ITALIAN/INTERNA-TIONAL/CARIBBEAN   In 1962, an American cargo ship, the *Liberty*, sank during a storm on a reef close to Grand Cayman's eastern shore. Today, split into three thoroughly rusted separate sections that rest in shallow water, it provides a focal point for the panoramas that open before you from the terrace of this restaurant. The most popular independent restaurant on Grand Cayman's East End, it draws clients from the hotel and resort complexes nearby. For dinner, you might begin with a satay of beef or chicken, served with a cucumber-and-peanut sauce; then follow with a savory version of *zuppa di pesce* (fish soup), conch steak served in traditional East End style (breaded), turtle steak, any of several kinds of pasta, or the house specialty, baked seafood Portofino, which delectably combines lobster, tiger shrimp, scallops, and mousseline potatoes au gratin. Lunches are simpler, focusing on salads, sandwiches, pastas, and grilled fish.

In Colliers, East End. ✆ **345/947-2700.** Reservations recommended. Lunch platters CI$4.90–CI$13; dinner main courses CI$11–CI$23. AE, DISC, MC, V. Daily 11:30am–10pm.

The Reef Grill at Royal Palms ★★★ SEAFOOD   This is one of the island's finest restaurants, and one of our favorites, a site that manages to be chic, savvy, elegant, hip, and fun all at the same time. It's positioned on a strategic plot of land in the heart of the Seven Mile Beach "golden strip." The savvy entrepreneurs who rent the space maintain a compound of one- and two-story buildings that include a beachfront bar and grill, a nightclub, and a classy citadel of gourmet cuisine. We recommend a brisk walk-through upon your arrival as a means of determining which corner of the place you'd most like to occupy. The inland, "landlocked" bar and dining area is elegant, red, and evocative of an upscale corner of Europe, and the seafront bar offers dance-floor views of some of Grand Cayman's most attractive denizens.

Favorites here include Maytag blue cheese salad with chopped Granny Smith apples and spiced pecans; conch fritters with jerk-flavored mayonnaise; a melt-in-your-mouth honey- and soy-glazed sea bass with Thai-style curried vinaigrette; and lobster risotto with coconut reduction. At lunch, you can order well-stuffed sandwiches, freshly made salads, and fresh oven-baked pizzas. If you opt to dine under the stars on a Friday or Saturday night, you'll hear some of the most talented local musicians playing soca and calypso in the bar pavilion about 100 paces away.

In the Royal Palms Beach Club, Seven Mile Beach. ✆ **345/945-6358.** www. reefgrill.com. Reservations recommended. Main courses lunch CI$7.30–CI$13, dinner CI$18–CI$26. AE, MC, V. Daily 11am–3pm and 5:30–10pm. Closed Sun night May–Dec.

If you're staying at one of the many condos and villas that pepper Grand Cayman, you can call a private caterer and order an island dinner to be delivered. One of the best is **Burton Ebanks** (✆ **345/ 926-8294**).

Ristorante Pappagallo ★ ITALIAN/SEAFOOD   One of the island's most memorable restaurants lies on a 6-hectare (15-acre) bird sanctuary overlooking a natural lagoon, 15 minutes north of George Town. Its designers incorporated Caymanian and Aztec weaving techniques in its thatched roof. Glass doors, black marble, and polished brass mix a kind of Edwardian opulence with a Tahitian decor. Inside, you'll see some of the most beautiful (caged) parrots on the island, separated from the dining and drinking area (for sanitary reasons) by plate-glass windows. For an appetizer, try the lobster-and-scallop bisque in coconut cream or the carpaccio of raw beef with arugula. Pasta dishes are full of flavor, especially the fettuccine with lemon-grilled chicken and sun-dried tomatoes and the penne with homemade sausage. For a main course, choose between well-prepared fish and shellfish options; the peppered West Indian pork tenderloin in an apple-bourbon sauce; or a combination of lobster and shrimp, prepared in the style of the chef, with pepper, garlic, diced tomatoes, mushrooms, and a flaming brandy and tarragon-flavored cream sauce.

Close to the Villas Pappagallo, Conch Point Rd., Barkers, in West Bay (near the northern terminus of West Bay Rd., 13km/8 miles north of George Town). ✆ **345/949-1119.** www.pappagallo.ky. Reservations recommended. Main courses CI$8.10–CI$33. AE, MC, V. Daily 6–10:30pm.

The Wharf ★ CARIBBEAN/CONTINENTAL   On the northern fringe of George Town, at the southernmost edge of Seven Mile Beach, this dining, drinking, and nightlife emporium is fun, tropical, artfully illuminated, and occasionally hip. More than half of the place is built on wharves and piers that jut seaward, allowing fish to swim under your table as you eat and even to make appearances in an open area that's the target of a plethora of spotlights illuminating their every silvery movement. (The feeding of the tarpon, something approaching an underwater frenzy, occurs every night at 9pm.) The restaurant is decorated in tones of turquoise and blue, with dining in an air-conditioned interior, or outside on either an elevated veranda or a waterside terrace. The sound of the surf mingles with chatter from the Ports of Call Bar and music from the strolling Paraguayan harpist, Eugenio Leon.

Many diners begin with the blue-crab-and-shrimp salad with cucumber and mango, or the golden-fried Caribbean lobster cake with a roasted-corn relish. Main dishes are a delight, especially the basil-and-pistachio-crusted sea bass in a creamy champagne sauce or the grilled turtle-and-lobster pie with rice and vegetables. A local favorite is the pork tenderloin Tortuga, marinated with cumin, coriander, and molasses and served with a dark-rum sauce. Fresh fish can be prepared any way you want: blackened, amandine, grilled, or "island-style." The kitchen makes a laudable effort to break away from typical, dull menu items, and they are largely successful.

43 West Bay Rd., Seven Mile Beach. ☏ **345/949-2231.** www.wharf.ky. Reservations recommended. Main courses CI$19–CI$36. AE, MC, V. Daily 6–10pm.

MODERATE

Aqua Beach Restaurant & Bar CARIBBEAN   This restaurant screams fun. Christmas lights hang around the edges of the thatched roof, and neon signs make the bar visible from any part of the restaurant. If you're hoping for a quiet, relaxed dinner, this is not the place. Golf, football, rugby, hockey, basketball, cricket, and baseball can all be seen on one of the many big-screen televisions, and mixologists can create just about any cocktail your heart desires. Depending on what part of the restaurant you're occupying, the walls around you will either be deep red, or neon green and decorated with monkeys. The staff is young and hip, as is much of the clientele. The menu is nothing extraordinary, but the food is made well. Try the Island spicy linguine or the West Indian spice-encrusted tuna. You'll find a kids' menu, but we wouldn't recommend taking children here past 8pm.

426 West Bay Rd., Seven Mile Beach. ☏ **345/946-6398.** Sandwiches and wraps CI$7.30–CI$8.90; main courses CI$8.90–CI$23. MC, V. Mon–Fri 11am–1am; Sat–Sun 11am–midnight.

Bacchus Restaurant and Wine Bar ★ CARIBBEAN   Located in the center of George Town and surrounded by office buildings and shops, this restaurant does most of its business at lunch and late in the afternoon, after nearby businesses have closed. Dozens of regulars enjoy cocktails after work, making late afternoon here an especially good opportunity to gain insight into the inner life of Grand Cayman. The restaurant and bar are decorated like a warm, welcoming tavern, with exposed brick and dark mahogany paneling. Lunches are simple, focusing on salads, sandwiches, light platters, and soups. Dinners are more elaborate and can be accompanied by glasses of any of the house wines, ranging from CI$6.95

to CI$8.95 a glass. Other cocktails, such as a melon-flavored piña colada, go for CI$6.50 to CI$10. If you just want to hang out at the bar and nibble on snacks and tapas, consider ordering the jerk-chicken quesadilla, the flash-fried calamari with jerk-seasoned tartar sauce, or an antipasto platter. Main courses at dinner may include partially seared tuna tataki, baked portobello mushrooms with Gorgonzola cheese, roasted and olive-crusted rack of lamb, and braised salmon with a seafood salad. The wide-ranging vegetarian options are very tasty as well.

Fort St., George Town. ✆ **345/949-5747.** www.bacchus.ky. Main courses CI$13–CI$24. AE, DC, MC, V. Mon–Thurs 10am–1am; Fri 10am–2am; Sat 11am–midnight.

Breezes by the Bay CARIBBEAN/INTERNATIONAL   The "rhum deck" of this tropical grill draws a lot of cruise ship passengers, as it lies right on the harbor—it's also an ideal spot for a sundowner. Happy hours on Friday and Saturday evenings are some of the most popular in the capital. Food is served in a more formal atmosphere upstairs.

The chefs pride themselves on baking what are generally agreed to be the best conch fritters on the island. Conch also appears in a chowder (similar to New England clam chowder, but the meat is more rubbery). The marinated conch is quite good, as are the West Indian crab cakes. Fishermen bring in the day's catch, which might be your best bet. You can also order standard fare such as smoked ribs, Jamaican jerk chicken, and fish and chips. Ever had shrimp cooked with sugar cane? Now's your chance to try it. Bread and even the luscious ice creams are made from scratch.

Harbor Dr., George Town. ✆ **345/943-8439.** www.breezesbythebay.com. Main courses CI$10–CI$27. AE, MC, V. Mon–Sat 7am–10pm; Sun 10am–2pm.

The Brick House INTERNATIONAL   This restaurant offers panoramic views out of floor-to-ceiling windows. Sunshine floods the space during the day, giving it an open-air feel. The friendly staff can recommend items from the extensive menu. Your best bets are the seafood Monterey; grilled ginger tuna with a ginger-soy sauce; the Cayman conch chowder; or the Cayman fettuccine with jerk chicken, shrimp, and red bell peppers. You can also choose from a wide selection of savory pizzas. Parts of the menu have a cheesy wannabe-*Sopranos* feel—for example, "Stallone Calzone," "Mama's Linguini," and "Meatball Ba Da Bing"—but the taste of the food makes up for it.

The Shoppes at Grand Harbour, Red Bay. ✆ **345/947-3456.** www.ourhouse cayman.com. Reservations not required. Pizza CI$6.50–CI$11; main courses CI$11–CI$23. AE, DC, MC, V. Daily 11:30am–10pm.

Deckers Grille & Lounge CONTINENTAL One of the most appealing restaurants in the Caymans, Deckers allows diners to choose between three distinct seating areas. If you want casual dining, choose the terrace, where live music can be heard on weekends. In the air-conditioned dining room, enjoy the original Caribbean paintings and couches for lounging. The backyard is the most tranquil of the areas, as diners listen to the calming sounds of water running in a triple-tier fountain. Our favorite part of the restaurant, however, is the bar. It's housed in an original English double-decker bus and serves everything from fine wines to tropical drinks to Metropolitan Martinis. The wine list has more than 70 labels. The extensive and well-prepared cuisine at this restaurant keeps people coming back. Excellent choices include the homemade portobello mushroom ravioli, macadamia-nut-crusted black grouper, apple-cured and grilled Chilean salmon, and Moroccan spiced rack of lamb. A children's menu is available.

Next to the Grand Cayman Beach Suites, West Bay Rd. ☎ **345/945-6600.** www. deckers.ky. Main courses CI$11–CI$53. AE, DC, MC, V. Daily 5:30–10:30pm.

Edoardo's ITALIAN This Sicilian-owned trattoria-cum-tavern draws a loyal patronage of full-time Grand Cayman residents who make Friday and Saturday dinner their culinary respite from home-cooked meals. The restaurant is located in a less-than-glamorous shopping center on the landlocked side of West Bay Road, completely lacking a view. Ironically, it is also recommended by the concierges of nearby upscale hotels. Food is served in generous portions in a no-nonsense, dark-paneled setting that might have been imported directly from a bar and grill in the suburbs of Detroit or Pittsburgh. However, considering that many of the clients aren't particularly interested in a restaurant theme of "Caribbean romance" (they're probably sick of that restaurant theme anyway), no one seems to care.

Begin your meal with zesty grilled shrimp and calamari in a garlic-and-lemon-flavored sauce, or barbecued Cajun prawns. The cioppino (shellfish stew) is fabulous. Pastas come in dozens of different varieties; a favorite is tossed in a basil sauce with red potatoes. Mussels are piled high with your choice of four sauces—white wine with garlic, spicy marinara, saffron-flavored cream, or red-wine sauce—and served as either a starter or main course. The best fish and meats are a savory snapper *livornese,* made with capers and black olives; veal Edoardo (scaloppine topped with Parma ham and fontina cheese); and tenderloin of beef wrapped in bacon and served with Cambozola cheese and red-wine demi-glace.

WHERE TO EAT ON GRAND CAYMAN | Moderate

If you're in the mood for pizza, choose from nine types, or build your own from 15 toppings, including blackened chicken and shrimp.

Coconut Place, West Bay Rd. (✆) **345/945-4408.** www.edoardos.ky. Reservations recommended on weekends. Main courses lunch CI$5.60–CI$15, dinner CI$19–CI$24; pasta CI$15–CI$22. AE, MC, V. Mon–Fri 11:30am–2pm; daily 5:30–10:30pm.

Full of Beans CAFE/COFFEEHOUSE/LIGHT FARE   Don't you love the name? Even though it's a mere strip-mall cafe, the joint is warmly decorated with old wooden tables and floors, modern Italian chairs, mirror mosaics, and even a fake brick wall to add a more old-fashioned ambience. At this local favorite, you can begin with Belgian waffles in the morning and homemade soups or the lobster medallions later in the day.

Each day a special is posted for lunch, perhaps baked chicken with basmati rice and fresh vegetables. Among the most tempting platters are a cranberry brie salad with toasted nuts, and a sesame-encrusted tuna with a shiitake mushroom salad. You might also go for the chicken tandoori wrap. Desserts are rich and luscious, especially the carrot cake with a cream cheese glaze or the cheesecake with strawberries served with freshly whipped cream.

Pasadora Place, George Town. (✆) **345/943-2326.** Main courses CI$6–CI$12. MC, V. Mon–Fri 7am–5pm; Sat 7am–4pm.

Gateway of India 🔖 INDIAN   Although some island restaurants might feature an Indian dish on their menus from time to time, this is the only truly Indian restaurant in the Cayman Islands, and as such, it's often sought out as a change of pace from Caribbean cuisine. The decor is warm, folkloric, and charming, with the interior illuminated with lanterns of embroidered fabric. Dishes are, as a matter of policy, prepared with a "medium" degree of spiciness, which you can doctor by instructing the staff (most of whom come from either Goa or Mumbai) according to your wishes. There's a wide array of meat, fish, and vegetarian dishes to choose from, but ongoing favorites include chicken *korma* in a mild curry sauce; chicken *tikka masala,* cooked in a medium-spicy, tomato-flavored butter sauce; and lamb vindaloo, served in a tomato-based, spicy curry sauce. All main courses come with saffron-flavored rice, pickles, yogurt, salad, and Indian breads. The lunch buffet is an excellent value on Grand Cayman.

Adjacent to the Strand Shopping Center, West Bay Rd. (✆) **345/946-2815.** Reservations recommended. Lunch CI$7.30–CI$12; lunch buffet CI$11; dinner CI$8.10–CI$21. AE, MC, V. Mon–Fri 11:30am–2:30pm; daily 5:30–10pm.

💬 kill-devil, **THE DRINK OF CHOICE**

Since the late 16th century, rum has been associated with slavery. Slaves were imported to such places as Jamaica to do the backbreaking work of harvesting the sugar cane that would be distilled into rum at various on-island distilleries.

From Jamaica, rum was imported into the Cayman Islands, where it became the drink of choice among islanders. Yankee traders, pirates, and bootleggers ruled the waters between Jamaica and the Caymans, which lie to Jamaica's immediate northwest.

Although the Caymans today have all the imported beer and liquors you could wish for, rum-laced tropical punches are still the most popular drinks. The average bar on all three islands offers a bewildering array of rum punches.

A word of caution: Be aware of your limits, especially if you're driving. The pastel-colored drinks can make visitors very drunk on extremely short notice because of their elevated sugar content, as well as the hot climate.

Over the Edge CARIBBEAN   The ambience at this eatery is just the opposite of what you'll find at the glossy venues of West Bay Road and downtown George Town. This remote and raffish restaurant is something of a mecca for residents of the sparsely populated North Side. A raucous bar crowd greets you at the restaurant's entrance. Inside, the dining room walls block out the sometimes-ferocious winds that batter this place during storms. Outside, you'll find a wharf-style terrace with pilings that extend straight down into the seabed. The views from the terrace have been described as mystical, especially on calm, moonlit nights. Lunches are relatively simple, focusing on Cayman-style steamed fish, pan-fried conch steak, turtle steak with port sauce, sandwiches stuffed with either tuna or mahimahi, and chef's salads. Dinners are more elaborate, featuring charbroiled rock-lobster tail, lobster Thermidor, savory jumbo shrimp in Pernod sauce, grilled wahoo, and grilled breast of chicken with Dijonnaise sauce.

Old Man Bay, North Side. 📞 **345/947-9568.** www.over-theedge.com. Lunch and dinner CI$4.40–CI$29. AE, MC, V. Daily 7am–10pm (bar till 1am).

Rackham's Pub & Restaurant AMERICAN/CARIBBEAN   If you're looking for an extensive menu and open-air dining with a beautiful view, you should try this place. In the morning, you can watch boats coming to port, and in the evening you can see their lights as they head back out to sea. Your best bets here are the Caribbean shrimp, fish and chips, grilled mahimahi marinated in jerk sauce, Caesar salad, pan-fried grouper with rice and beans, and a wide array of curries and pastas.

93 N. Church St., George Town. ✆ **345/945-3860.** Reservations recommended for parties of 6 or more. Main courses CI$9–CI$31. AE, MC, V. Kitchen daily 10:30am–11pm. Bar Mon–Fri 9am–1am; Sat 10am–midnight; Sun 10:30am–midnight.

Ristorante Ragazzi ITALIAN   This is one of our favorite Italian restaurants on Seven Mile Beach. It's located between two banks, in a shopping center adjacent to the entrance of the Grand Cayman Beach Suites. You can dine on a narrow terrace in front, but you'll be struck by the restaurant's real glamour inside, where you'll find a large, northern Italian–style blue-and-gold room with granite trim. This place is hip, fun, stylish, and breezily upscale, drawing a clientele of worldly residents who work in the financial-services industries. Lunches are lighter and less formal than dinners, with a medley of salads, about a dozen pastas (including a version with crayfish and crabmeat), unusual pizzas (including an "Austrian" version with brie cheese and smoked Parma ham), and elegant platters of mostly white-meat and fish dishes such as chicken scaloppine with Marsala-and-mushroom sauce, and sautéed peppered yellowfin tuna with a red-bell-pepper sauce. Dinners range from a blue-crab spring roll and lobster quesadillas to rosemary-marinated duck breast with an orange demi-glace, and pan-seared sea bass served with capers and black olives.

Buckingham Sq., West Bay Rd. ✆ **345/945-3484.** www.ragazzi.ky. Reservations recommended Fri–Sat dinner. Lunch CI$12–CI$19; dinner CI$22–CI$35. AE, DC, MC, V. Daily 11:30am–11pm.

Thai Orchid THAI   This is the only spot on Grand Cayman that serves the intricately flavored and sometimes fiery cuisine of Thailand. The interior is graceful, elegant, and rather formal, with black lacquer furniture and lots of Thai paintings; the waitresses are beautifully outfitted in formal Thai costumes. Favorite dishes include divine Thai-style lobster and squid with red-curry sauce, pad thai, stir-fried chicken with cashews and bell peppers, curries, Thai-style spring rolls, and a deep-fried whole red snapper topped with Thai-style chili sauce (the best dish, in our opinion). A lunch buffet is served on Tuesday and Thursday.

In the Queen's Court Shopping Plaza, West Bay Rd. ✆ **345/949-7955.** www. thaiorchid.ky. Lunch CI$12–CI$18; dinner CI$14–CI$34. AE, DC, MC, V. Mon–Sat 11:30am–2:30pm; daily 6–10pm.

INEXPENSIVE

Al la Kebab MIDDLE EASTERN   If you're in the mood for a convivial outdoor snack with the young, the restless, and the wasted, consider driving over to this late-night kabob joint, open after most other restaurants have closed for the night. The setting is a vividly painted clapboard shack plunked down in a parking lot adjacent to the island's biggest theater. There's no dining room here, but the dashboard of your car works quite nicely as a table. The tasty, juicy kabobs—lamb, chicken, or beef—are seasoned with fresh herbs and grilled to perfection. They can be doused with any of a half-dozen varieties of sauce. Your hosts are Alan Silverman and Laura Wintermut (both from Canada) and their Caymanian partner, Frank McCoy.

In the Marquee Plaza, Lawrence Blvd. (adjacent to the cinema, across from World's Gym). (C) **345/943-4343.** www.kebab.ky. Kabobs CI$4–CI$8.90. No credit cards. Mon–Fri 11am–4am; Sat 11am–2am; Sun 11am–8pm.

Chicken! Chicken! ☺ AMERICAN   This venue completely lacks glamour, but within its cheerful and unpretentious premises (it looks like the interior of a brightly painted Creole cottage), you can feed a family for less money than at virtually any other restaurant on the island. The specialty, and the only available main course, is tender, richly seasoned, perfectly cooked chicken. As many as 32 chickens at a time rotate enticingly in the glare of the island's biggest and most theatrical rotisserie, prominently positioned near the restaurant's entrance. Each chicken is flavored with herbs and a touch of garlic. After placing your order at the stand-up counter, you can opt to dine in the restaurant, or you can haul your chicken away for consumption somewhere else. The chicken (breast, thigh, or whole roasted birds, depending on your order) is accompanied by cornbread and your choice of coleslaw, rice, or beans.

In the West Shore Shopping Plaza, West Bay Rd. (C) **345/945-2290.** www.chicken2.com. Lunch CI$7.30–CI$8.20; dinner CI$9–CI$12. AE, MC, V. Daily 11am–10pm.

Cimboco Caribbean Cafe INTERNATIONAL   Whimsical and tongue-in-cheek, this charming spot occupies a modern building very close to Grand Cayman's only movie theater. The venue is deceptively simple: At first glance, you might imagine you're in a cafe that just serves coffee and drinks, but a quick peek at the menu reveals a sophisticated medley of pizzas, salads, Caribbean-style roti (pancake-type bread with various fillings), and a full bar serving the fiesta-colored drinks you might expect at a breezy beachside joint. The caramelized scallops served with mango-flavored salsa are an excellent starter. Caesar salads can be garnished with grilled chicken or grilled shrimp. Pizzas can be livened up with all sorts of toppings, including slices of jerk chicken and lamb sausage. Other dishes include pastas (such as a three-cheese chicken fettuccine) and an oft-changing array of daily specials and soups. Canada-born Tom and Meg Lasley are your charming and hardworking hosts, whose culinary philosophy directs them to create all their food "from scratch," using only the finest and healthiest ingredients.

In the Marquee Shopping Center, near the corner of the Harquail Bypass and West Bay Rd. ✆ **345/947-2782.** www.cimboco.com. Reservations recommended for parties of 6 or more. Pizzas, burgers, and platters CI$8–CI$16. AE, MC, V. Sat–Thurs 7am–10pm; Fri 7am–11pm.

Corita's Copper Kettle ★ 🏷 CARIBBEAN/AMERICAN This place is generally packed in the mornings, when you can enjoy a full American breakfast or a wide selection of West Indian breakfast specialties, like green bananas served with fried dumplings, fried flying fish, and Corita's Special (ham, melted cheese, egg, and fruit jelly all presented on a fried fritter). For lunch, the menu varies from salads to chicken and beef along with conch, turtle, or lobster prepared as burgers or in a hearty stew.

Edward St., George Town. ✆ **345/949-2696.** Reservations required. Main courses CI$8–CI$16; lunch CI$9–CI$11. No credit cards. Mon–Fri 7am–3pm; Sat 7am–noon.

Eats Café ☺ AMERICAN/INTERNATIONAL   From early breakfasts to late-night dinners, this landmark cafe and restaurant is in its second decade, drawing families with its good food and affordable prices. In a shopping center across from the Westin, it

4

WHERE TO EAT ON GRAND CAYMAN

Inexpensive

kicks off the day serving hearty breakfasts, followed by a busy, bustling lunch hour. Diners order the super sandwich combos or freshly made soups and salads (the blackened chicken Caesar is a particular favorite).

The chef's main feature is a choice of 15 charbroiled burgers that range from a Cajun peppercorn burger to a crispy fish burger of North Atlantic cod. Burgers weigh 6 ounces and come with home-cut fries. At night you might feast on such appetizers as island conch fritters, coconut shrimp, and nachos, followed by one of the charbroiled chicken combo sandwiches such as Jamaican jerk chicken. Curry dishes and pizzas round out the menu.

Falls Plaza, West Bay Rd., Seven Mile Beach. ℰ **345/943-3287.** www.eats.ky. Reservations not required. Burgers CI$6.95–CI$9.95; sandwiches CI$5.95–CI$7.95. MC, V. Daily 6:30am–11pm.

Hard Rock Cafe Cayman Islands AMERICAN   In terms of the dollar amount of business it generates, this restaurant blows every other eatery in George Town way out of the water. Most of the restaurant's business is conducted at lunchtime, when long lines of hungry cruise ship passengers are handled efficiently, and vast quantities of party-colored drinks, commemorative T-shirts, and American-derived comfort food are sold at speeds and quantities that would make any restaurant deeply envious. On the street level, you'll find a faux-Victorian bar, a T-shirt boutique, and a waiting area for diners. The dining room lies at the top of a wide staircase on the building's second floor. You'll spot framed photographs of Mick Jagger and Bob Marley, outfits worn by Madonna and Buddy Holly, and more. Suspended from the ceiling, just above the stairwell that leads up to the dining room, is part of a 1959 pink Cadillac.

The most popular drink is the Hurricane, made from three kinds of rum and three kinds of fruit juice. Menu items include burgers, Reuben sandwiches, meal-size salads, steaks, pastas, Pig Sandwiches (barbecued pork with french fries), fish and chips, and a particularly comforting version of meatloaf. If you're looking to avoid the crowds, come in the evening, after the departure of the cruise ships, rather than at lunchtime.

43 S. Church St., George Town. ℰ **345/945-2020.** www.hardrock.com. Reservations accepted only for parties of 10 or more. Main courses CI$8.95–CI$28. AE, DISC, MC, V. Daily 10am–1am.

Harry's Caribbean Bar & Grill CARIBBEAN   This little hole-in-the-wall restaurant gives off a Caribbean home-style vibe. The pink-and-blue walls are cliché, but who cares? The distinctly local menu includes down-home favorites such as fried chicken, fish stew, curry goat, and ox ear. Harry Cupid, the owner, loves his little restaurant, and his staff is very welcoming. The adjacent bar serves tropical rum drinks.

Tropical Plaza, George Town. ☎ **345/945-2025.** Main courses CI$7–CI$15. MC, V. Mon–Fri 7am–1am; Sat 11am–11pm; Sun 7am–8pm.

Icoa Cafe ★ INTERNATIONAL   This is one of the most sophisticated cafe restaurants on the island. It is named after Icoa, the goddess of water to the indigenous people of the Paria Peninsula of Venezuela. The creative chef, Jurgen Wevers, from the Netherlands, draws inspiration for his dishes from various places in the world. The setting is minimalist, with mosaic tile floors, and simple tables and chairs in a bright, inviting atmosphere.

The appetizers are some of the best on the island, featuring such delights as a bruschetta of locally caught wahoo with an eggplant cream and a chorizo vinaigrette, and pan-fried Asian-style crab cakes with a warm asparagus bok choy salad flavored with a Szechuan pepper vinaigrette. One of the best salads consists of yellowfin tuna and fresh vegetables in a Creole mustard vinaigrette. Another salad contains pan-seared scallops with spinach, watermelon, and prosciutto.

For your main course, try the whole roasted Cornish game hen or the braised beef short rib osso buco flavored with a saffron garlic aioli. Pizzas are also a daily feature, including a hearty meat version made with prosciutto, chorizo, and mozzarella.

7 Mile Shops, No. 11, Seven Mile Beach Rd. ☎ **345/945-1915.** www.icoacafe.com. Sandwiches and salads CI$8.50–CI$15; dinner main courses CI$13–CI$18. AE, MC, V. Mon–Sat 7am–5pm; Sun 8am–1pm.

Mezza INTERNATIONAL   Hip, breezy, European-ized, and urban, this restaurant sits one floor above a landmark liquor store (Big Daddy's), immediately adjacent to the Treasure Island Hotel. This is an eatery that you might expect to find in South Beach, Miami. The lunch menu is simple, featuring steak sandwiches, burgers, Caesar salads, and seafood pasta. The dinner menu is more artful, with dishes that include bacon-wrapped mahimahi; basil-encrusted salmon steaks; sautéed shrimp with wine sauce and asparagus; steak au poivre with *pommes frites;* and fettuccine with jerk chicken. Caramel pecan fudge cake and crème brûlée comprise an enticing dessert menu.

233 West Bay Rd. ☎ **345/946-3992.** Reservations recommended. Main courses CI$12–CI$25. AE, DC, MC, V. Daily 11:30am–3pm and 5–10pm.

Inexpensive

Seaharvest Restaurant ★ INTERNATIONAL This place draws a pleasing mix of local residents and visitors, all enjoying a cuisine with origins reaching from Europe to India. You won't notice the restaurant from South Church Street because it's hidden behind rows of greenery and separated from the **Sunset House** (p. 67) by a parking lot. In a plush, high-ceilinged dining room accented with bubbling aquariums and elaborate draperies, you can enjoy a lunch of burgers, salads, pastas, coconut shrimp, salmon poached with orange slices—our favorite—and "calypso chicken," stuffed with ham and cheese, dredged in coconut flakes, and served with a raspberry-mango sauce. Dinners feature grilled shrimp wrapped in bacon and served with a honey-mustard sauce, roasted breast of duck with a Thai chili sauce, chicken *tikka masala*, and several different lobster options. Lamb *banjara*, slow-cooked with spices in the southern Indian tradition, is an excellent choice if you like Indian food.

At the Sunset House, 390 S. Church St. Ⓒ **345/945-1383.** Reservations recommended Fri–Sat dinner. Lunch CI$11–CI$25; dinner CI$14–CI$29. AE, DISC, MC, V. Daily 7am–10pm.

Seymour's Jerk Centre JAMAICAN In the parking lot of Roy's Boutique, Seymour Silburn runs this authentic joint, serving the best jerk chicken this side of Jamaica. Marinated according to a secret recipe, the chicken is cooked over a charcoal grill. His jerk pork is also a winner. Picnic tables are arranged out back, and the atmosphere couldn't be more casual. You come here for the tasty food, not the romantic ambience. If you really want to put hair on your chest, ask for "Manish water." There's also fried fresh fish, and you might begin with a conch soup.

Shedden Rd., George Town. Ⓒ **345/945-1931.** Main courses CI$9–CI$17. No credit cards. Mon–Thurs 11:30am–1am; Fri 11:30am–3am; Sat 11:30am–1am.

Triple Crown ENGLISH PUB FARE You know you're in a British territory when you eat here. The food of Henry VIII is served, more or less with success. Many locals patronize the joint on Sunday when "ye olde roast beef pudding" is served. It consists of a slab of roast beef, Yorkshire pudding, new potatoes, and fresh vegetables. At other times, you can feast on pub-grub favorites like shepherd's pie, beef-and-ale pie, and steak-and-kidney pie. These pies are justifiably the kitchen's most ordered items. The full English breakfast is a delight and served all day, and you can also order French toast and pancakes. Desserts are homemade and old-fashioned, including sticky toffee pudding or apple and blueberry crumble.

Marquee Plaza, Seven Mile Rd., Seven Mile Beach. (℗) **345/943-7821.** Main courses CI$9–CI$17. AE, MC, V. Mon–Fri 10:30am–1am; Sat–Sun 9am–midnight.

Vivine's Kitchen ★ 🎁 WEST INDIAN   Native Caymanian Vivine Watler runs this charming restaurant from a terrace beside her home on an isolated stretch of road in the East End. Identifiable by large signs in psychedelic colors, it beckons to motorists who appreciate a bit of local flavor in a landscape that's otherwise isolated and a bit lonely. You dine at plastic tables that are set either on a cement terrace surrounded by lattices or amid sea grapes, close to the edge of the sea. Don't underestimate Vivine's local fame within Caymanian society: When we were last here, an eminently respected, middle-aged hostess arrived from faraway West Bay, having driven almost 2 hours (each way) to retrieve a pot of conch stew, with the intention of serving it at a dinner party for old-time Caymanians who missed "cooking the way it used to be." Menu items are written on a blackboard, and change with the availability of ingredients. The tastiest offerings are fried fish, chicken and chips, cheeseburgers, tuna sandwiches, conch stew, turtle stew, whelk stew, barbecued ribs, and pork chops. Dessert choices almost always include "heavy cakes," made from raw grated cassava, yam, or breadfruit. Drinks include fresh juice made from mangos, tamarinds, and carrots, as well as old-fashioned lemonade.

Gun Bay, East End. (℗) **345/947-7435.** Main courses CI$5–CI$11. No credit cards. Daily 11am–7pm.

BEACHES & ACTIVE PURSUITS ON GRAND CAYMAN

The irresistible combination of almost-guaranteed sunshine, one of the world's most beautiful beaches, and the Caribbean's best scuba diving and snorkeling has permanently anchored Grand Cayman on the tourist map.

5

Grand Cayman has a number of smaller beaches, but its so-called **Seven Mile Beach** (actually 8.9km/5½ miles) is the major attraction, with its vast expanses of powdery white sand. Unlike the beaches on some islands to the south, such as Jamaica, Seven Mile Beach is litter-free and also relatively free of peddlers hawking souvenirs.

The beach is so big that there's always plenty of room for everybody, even in the midst of the winter tourist season and at the peak of the cruise ship arrivals. Most of Grand Cayman's hotels, restaurants, and shopping centers are found along this much-frequented strip of sand. Many scuba-diving and watersports outfitters are also based here.

Along with swimmers and beach buffs, scuba divers travel to the Cayman Islands in droves from around the world. As diver Bob Soto—who opened the first dive shop in the Caribbean back in 1957—puts it, "If there's any spot on the planet that God created just for divers, it is Grand Cayman." One-third of all visitors to the Cayman Islands come specifically to go scuba diving or snorkeling.

The Cayman Islands proudly boast more than 200 named and explored dive sites. Some of the most dramatic dive sites have not been thoroughly explored (and unfortunately aren't on the itineraries of most outfitters), owing to the massive coral reefs and drop-offs that surround all three Cayman Islands. Dive outfitters are familiar with the best of the accessible dive sites and will guide you to what interests you the most. The Cayman Islands have the most reliable outfitters in the Caribbean, complementing the Islands' reputation as one of the world's greatest scuba-diving destinations.

Even if you're not a scuba diver or snorkeler, you'll find many other attractions on the water, including fishing, boating, and windsurfing. If you're a landlubber, there's always golfing and horseback riding. But most landlubbers never seem to leave Seven Mile Beach.

Note: Some outfitters quote prices in both U.S. and Cayman dollars; others, especially those patronized largely by foreign visitors, quote their prices in U.S. dollars. We've quoted prices in this chapter according to the currency favored by each individual outfitter.

HITTING THE BEACHES

One of the finest beaches in the Caribbean, Grand Cayman's **Seven Mile Beach ★★★** (technically, the beach is named West Bay Beach, but everybody calls it Seven Mile Beach) is a haven of white, white sand, Australian pines, and palm trees, stretching all the way from George Town to Long Point. It tends to be crowded near the big resorts, but the beach is so big that you can always find room to spread out your towel.

Because the beach is on the more tranquil western side of Grand Cayman, the water is generally placid and inviting with no significant tide, making it ideal for families, even those with small children. A sandy bottom slopes gently to deep water. The water is great for snorkelers and swimmers of most ages and abilities, and it's so clear that you can easily see what's swimming around underwater.

Along the stretch of the beach, from one end to the other, are hotels and condos. The beach hotels have bars and restaurants open to nonguests, and most of these hotels also have watersports kiosks where you can book parasailing and windsurfing excursions or rent snorkeling equipment. Independent watersports concessions, including places to rent snorkeling gear, boats, windsurfers, WaveRunners, paddle cats (inflatable kayaks), and aqua trikes (floating tricycles), can also be easily found along the beach.

Of all the bars and restaurants strung along Seven Mile Beach, one of the friendliest is the **Beach Club Colony Hotel & Dive Resort,** West Bay Road (p. 62; ℂ **345/949-8100**), which welcomes nonguests. The modern Caribbean restaurant is open daily from 7:30am to 9pm and the beach bar is open Monday to Friday from 10am to 12:45pm and Saturday and Sunday from 11am to 11:45pm. A special offer here is a certified boat-diving package costing US$95 per person, which includes a two-tank boat dive. The on-site dive shop is open daily from 7am to 5pm.

Grand Cayman does have a number of minor beaches, although they pale in comparison to Seven Mile Beach. Visit these if you want to escape the crowds. Beaches on the east and north coasts of Grand Cayman are good—filled with white sand and protected by an offshore barrier reef, so waters are generally tranquil.

Just to the north of Seven Mile Beach, **Cemetery Reef** and its public beach are good spots for snorkeling. Cemetery Beach—at the southern tier of Boggy Sand Road—is reached by following the cemetery that's located opposite the fire station on the northern tip of West Bay Road.

Smith Cove Public Beach is located between Coconut Harbour and Cayman Coves, on the west side of George Town. Contrasting completely with the glitz and glitter of Seven Mile Beach, this attractive sandy strip is small but top-notch. It's a good spot for snorkeling and a nice venue for a picnic beneath the shade. Changing facilities and bathrooms are available on-site.

Rum Point lies 40km (25 miles) north of George Town, on North Sound along the northern coast. There's a fairly good beach here, though it happens to be one of the most remote. Calm, clear waters and tree shade make this an excellent spot for swimming. The beach has changing facilities, public toilets, and showers. On-site is the **Wreck Bar & Grill** (p. 157), in case you want a drink. Our favorite time to visit is Sunday, when locals stop by in their boats and bring a gregarious and animated atmosphere to the bar. On-site watersports activities are run by the reputable **Red Sail Sports** (see below).

One of our favorite beaches is on the north coast, bordering the **Cayman Kai Beach Resort,** directly to the southwest of Rum Point. This beach is a Caribbean cliché of charm, with palm trees and beautiful sands. You can snorkel along the reef to Rum Point. The beach is also an ideal spot for a Sunday-afternoon picnic. There are bathrooms and changing facilities.

The best windsurfing is found in the East End, at the beach near the settlement of **Colliers,** reached along Queen's Highway and lying near Morritt's Tortuga Club.

SCUBA DIVING & SNORKELING

What they lack in nightlife, the Cayman Islands make up for in watersports activities, especially scuba diving and snorkeling. Coral reefs and coral formations encircle each island and are filled with marine life, which scuba divers and snorkelers are forbidden by law to disturb (so enjoy the underwater views, but don't touch the coral). For our recommendations of the best scuba-diving and snorkeling sites, see p. 3 and 7, respectively.

The full diving scene in the Cayman Islands could fill a book, or several. If you're a serious diver, pick up one of the comprehensive divers' guidebooks. The best one we've seen is a paperback, *The Dive Sites of the Cayman Islands: Over 260 Top Dive and Snorkel Sites* by Lawson Wood.

It's easy to dive close to shore, so boats aren't necessary, although plenty of diving boats are available. For certain excursions, we recommend a trip with a qualified dive master. Many dive shops offer rentals, but they won't rent you scuba gear or supply air unless you have a card from one of the international diving schools, such as NAUI or PADI. Hotels also rent diving equipment to their guests who are certified divers, and will arrange snorkeling and scuba-diving trips.

Universally regarded as the most up-to-date and best-equipped watersports facility in the Cayman Islands, **Red Sail Sports** maintains its administrative headquarters at Coconut Place (PO Box 31473, Grand Cayman KY1-1206; ✆ **877/REDSAIL** [733-7245] in the U.S., or 345/945-5965; www.redsailcayman.com) and its largest, best-accessorized branch at the Grand Cayman Beach Suites, West Bay Road (✆ **345/949-8745**). Other locations are at the Westin Casuarina (✆ **345/949-8732**); at Rum Point (✆ **345/947-9203**); at the Marriott Beach Resort (✆ **345/949-6343**); at

On February 8, 1794, Captain William Martin was steering a lead ship, HMS *Convert,* when it hit a reef. The captain fired a cannon to signal a fleet of other merchant vessels about the treacherous reefs that lay ahead. The captains of the other ships mistook the signal for a warning of an impending pirate attack. One vessel after another in the convoy of 58 merchants ships, most of them square-rigged sailing vessels bound for Europe, met the same fate as the *Convert* in the rough, pitch-black seas.

In all, 10 ships were wrecked that disastrous night. By some miracle, villagers of the East End of Grand Cayman managed to save all 400 or so sailors and officers, bringing them ashore in canoes. Four of the ships were eventually salvaged, while the other vessels sank to the bottom of the sea. The ships' cannons were recovered and sent to England during World War II as scrap.

In the little community of Gun Bay in the East End, a monument can be seen commemorating that tragic maritime event. Queen Elizabeth II dedicated the statue on her visit to Grand Cayman in 1994. A local legend—untrue—claims that King George II gave the Caymanians tax-free status because of their heroic rescue. If you'd like to explore this shipwreck site, it is often included in the diving programs offered by **Ocean Frontiers** (p. 110).

the Courtyard by Marriott (© **345/946-5481**); and at Morritt's Tortuga Club (© **345/947-2097**).

Red Sail has the most comprehensive watersports program on the island, including all equipment rentals for everything from banana-boat tube rides to kayaking and water-skiing. Certified divers can choose from a variety of boat dives each day. A two-tank morning or afternoon dive goes for US$120, with a one-tank afternoon boat dive costing US$75. Special dives include a one-tank Stingray City dive for US$75 and a one-tank night dive for the same price. Full PADI open-water certification costs US$450 to US$550. All types of scuba gear can be rented.

The company also offers boat trips, including parasailing excursions. Catamaran sails are provided, the most popular being a 4½-hour jaunt to Stingray City, with lunch and snorkeling included, that goes for US$88 for adults or half-price for children 12 and under. Two-hour sunset sails along the North Sound cost

US$40 for adults or half-price for children 12 and under, and you can also book a dinner catamaran cruise for US$75 for adults or half-price for children 12 and under. Catamaran snorkeling trips cost US$55 or half-price for children.

Divetech, Cobalt Coast Resort & Suites, 18 Sea Fan Dr., Boatswains Bay (*©* **888/946-5656** or 345/946-5658; www.divetech. com), is one of the best organized and most attentive outfitters, with a fine reputation and a location near deep marine walls and drop-offs that divers find superb, if not the best shore-diving spot in the islands. The operation is headquartered in a clapboard-covered cottage on the grounds of the recommended **Cobalt Coast Resort and Suites** (p. 64), on Grand Cayman's most northwestern tip, far from the hubbub of Seven Mile Beach. The coastline is treacherously jagged, covered with bruising rocks that can puncture the side of any watercraft that ventures too close. Consequently, Divetech boats moor at a massive 36m (118-ft.) concrete pier that juts seaward. From here, within a relatively short distance, divers have access to a cornucopia of dive options that are difficult to duplicate anywhere else.

Many, but not all, of Divetech's clients opt to stay at its well-recommended associated hotel, Cobalt Coast Resort and Suites. Those who don't stay at Cobalt Coast must either drive or make

5

THE ISLAND'S NEWEST shipwreck ... AND NEWEST REEF

In January of 2011, the ex-**USS *Kittiwake,*** a 77m (253-ft.) World War II U.S. Navy submarine rescue ship, was sunk in 20m (66 ft.) of water off the northern end of Seven Mile Bridge. Its smokestack and bridge sit in a friendly 6m (20 ft.) of water, making this an ideal snorkeling site. The vessel was built in 1944 in the closing months of the war, and it has rested in mothballs for many years off the coast of Virginia. Now that it's an artificial reef, it has already attracted a great deal of marine life, including juvenile squirrel fish, goliath grouper, and even barracuda along with a school of horse-eye jacks.

Located across from the Great House next door to Governors Square, the site of the shipwreck is part of a private park managed by the Cayman Islands Tourism Association (*©* **345/949-8522;** www.kittiwakecayman.com). It is open only Monday to Friday 9am to 4pm, charging an admission of US$5 for snorkelers, or US$10 for scuba divers.

Further Outfitter Options

The **Cayman Islands Department of Tourism** website, www.caymanislands.ky, has a comprehensive list of all diving and snorkeling outfitters on the islands. We've listed our favorites, but the options don't end here.

special arrangements for transportation from hotels on other parts of the island. Activity prices are invariably cheaper when they're clustered within one of the resort's many dive packages. If you choose not to purchase a package, a two-tank dive for certified divers costs US$110, and a 3½-hour resort course for a first-timer goes for US$125. Open-water certification costs US$450. Guided shore dives are US$55.

Canadian-born Nancy Romanica is Divetech's founder and creative force. She's also an authority on the curious pastime known as free-diving, recommended only for very experienced divers, where aficionados reach alarming depths using only their carefully trained lung capacities (as in, without scuba tanks). The cost for a guided free-dive and a lesson (usually taught by Nancy herself) is US$110 per person for a half-day and US$220 per person for a full day.

Eden Rock Diving Center, 124 S. Church St., in George Town (© 345/949-7243; www.edenrockdive.com), specializes in dives to Eden Rock and Devil's Grotto, hailed as two of the best dive sites in the Caribbean. A full line of scuba and snorkeling equipment is available for rent, with a two-tank dive going for US$90 to US$100. Snorkeling trips cost US$30.

Ocean Frontiers Reef Resort, Austin Connelly Drive, East End (© 800/348-6096 or 345/947-7500; www.oceanfrontiers. com), is a well-run outfitter highlighting underwater attractions in the East End, where pristine reefs and easy access to wall diving are just offshore. This tends to be a less crowded dive center than around the West End. Its specialty is PADI-certified open-water dive instruction priced at US$399. A half-day program, which includes classroom instruction and pool practice, followed by a shallow reef dive, goes for US$149.

Oh Boy Charters (© 345/949-6341; www.ohboycharters. com) will pick you up and take you out on a motorboat to a sandbar where stingrays gather, and will also provide snorkeling equipment. The crew will help you on and off the boat on the sandbar, where

Scuba Diving & Snorkeling

BEACHES & ACTIVE PURSUITS

you'll be surrounded by these graceful creatures that look as if they are flying in the water. The stingrays will even "kiss" you. If you kiss one of them back, it will supposedly bring good luck. At least we hope so.

Although many guests "kiss" the stingrays, they are wild animals and you should do so at your own risk. In addition to allowing you to frolic with the rays, the boat also stops off at Coral Gardens, where you can snorkel and take in a preview of underwater life. Including the pickup, the whole trip costs US$40 for adults or US$28 for kids ages 4 to 11. From start to finish, the tour takes more than 3 hours. You can also book a full-day tour, including a beach lunch and snorkeling.

Don Foster's Dive, 218 S. Church St., George Town (© 345/ 949-5679; www.donfosters.com), operates from the waterfront at Casuarina Point in George Town. At its headquarters, there's also a pool with a shower. Boat dives are featured as well as offshore snorkeling. A two-tank dive costs US$95, and night dives go for US$55.

Seven Mile Watersports, West Bay Road (© 345/949-0332; www.7milediver.com), operates from the Seven Mile Beach Resort and Club and is particularly sensitive to the requests of individual divers. The outfitter takes out only 15 divers at a time in its 12m (39-ft.) boat. Most jaunts are to the north wall. A one-tank boat dive costs US$65, and a two-tank dive goes for US$100. A snorkel trip to Stingray City costs US$40 per person.

Off the Wall Divers, West Bay Road (© 345/945-7525; www.otwdivers.com), also caters to the individual diver as it specializes in custom dive trips for groups of 2 to 10, but no more. The outfitter offers resort training courses, as well as full and Nitrox certifications. A one-tank dive goes for US$70, two tanks for US$99. A PADI open-water certification course costs US$600 per person in a group of three or more. Resort scuba courses cost US$120, and equipment rentals, including dive computers, are available for rent.

Another good dive outfitter, **Tortuga Divers** (© 345/947-2097; www.tortugadivers.com), operates out of Morritt's Tortuga Club and Resort at East End, site of what are described as the best windsurfing conditions in the Cayman Islands, with easy access to the rich marine life. This outfitter caters to both experienced and novice divers, offering dives, whenever business justifies it, at 9am and 2pm. Half-day or full-day snorkeling adventures can also be arranged at the same time, and all types of gear are available for rent. The morning two-tank scuba dive costs US$120, and the afternoon one-tank dive goes for US$75. A half-day's snorkeling costs US$40.

Although nearly every scuba outfitter also offers snorkeling tours, the best outfitter just for snorkeling is **Captain Marvin's Watersports,** Cayman Falls Shopping Center, Seven Mile Beach (*©* 345/945-6975; www.captainmarvins.com). Captain Marvin, who launched his tours with a borrowed sailboat in the 1950s, is now one of the leading charter-boat operators in Grand Cayman. A 2½-hour trip, including stops at Stingray City and the Barrier Reef, costs US$35 for participants 12 and over, and US$27 for ages 4 to 11. A 3-hour trip goes for US$40 for ages 12 and over, and US$27 for ages 4 to 11. The full-day excursion, including lunch, costs US$65 for ages 12 and over, and US$45 for ages 4 to 11. All prices include snorkel gear and instruction if required and food for feeding the stingrays.

Watersports buffs use **Captain Bryan's,** North Church Street, George Town (*©* 345/949-0038; www.captainbryans.com), for snorkeling, fishing, and sailing trips on 15m (49-ft.) boats. Sunset sails and private snorkeling charters are also available. A half-day trip costs US$35, US$27 for children 9 and under.

Captain Crosby's Watersports, Coconut Place, West Bay Road (*©* 345/916-1725; www.cayman.org/crosby), was a pioneer of snorkeling trips to Stingray City. The outfitter still conducts 3-hour trips to the site on a 12m (39-ft.) trimaran for US$450. A freshly prepared seafood lunch is part of the package. Bonefishing and reef-fishing trips can also be arranged.

Ambassador Divers, located in the Comfort Suites Resort on West Bay Road, Seven Mile Beach (*©* 345/743-5513; www.ambassadordivers.com), is a small dive operation that usually takes out no more than eight passengers at a time. Trips feature the North and South Wall diving areas. PADI certification courses are offered, and dive packages are available, a 2-day deal going for US$200 per person.

Cayman Aggressor IV (*©* 800/348-2628 or 706/993-2531; www.aggressor.com) was designed by divers for divers. Participants are taken out for weeklong cruises aboard a 34m (110-ft.) boat. The living is simple, and the chow is basic. The boat has private cabins and an onboard cook. An inclusive package ranges from US$2,495 to US$2,995.

In addition to the outfitters listed above, you will easily find dozens of kiosks along Seven Mile Beach renting snorkeling gear.

YOUR TEMPORARY CAYMANIAN PET: a stingray

Grand Cayman is home to one of the most unusual underwater attractions in the world, **Stingray City ★★**. Set in the sun-flooded, 4m-deep (13-ft.) waters of North Sound, about 3km (1¾ miles) east of the island's northwestern tip, the site started to become popular in the mid-1980s when local fishermen would clean their catches and dump the offal overboard. They began to notice scores of stingrays (which usually eat marine crabs) feeding on the debris, a phenomenon that quickly attracted local divers and marine zoologists. Today, between 30 and 50 relatively tame stingrays hover around the site for daily hand-outs of squid and ballyhoo from increasing hordes of snorkelers and divers. About half a dozen entrepreneurs lead expeditions from points along Seven Mile Beach, traveling around the land-mass of Conch Point to the feeding grounds. The previously rec-ommended **Red Sail Sports** (p. 107) offers one-tank scuba dives to Stingray City, priced at US$75; snorkel excursions cost US$88 for adults and US$44 for children 3-11.

Warning: Stingrays possess deeply penetrating and viciously barbed stingers capable of inflicting painful damage to anyone who mistreats them. Need we mention the death in 2006 of Australian animal adventurer Steve Irwin, who received a barb from a stingray directly in his chest? A local spokesperson for Red Sail emphasizes that Irwin's stingray was of a more aggres-sive and larger breed than what you're likely to encounter in the Cayman Islands. She referred to the relatively tame beasts in Caymanian waters as equivalent to "big, sloppy puppy dogs," and the experience overall as "great fun." Nevertheless, we are not amused by this as a pastime, and simply cannot gush with any genuine thrill or enthusiasm. If you opt for an adventure with one of these underwater beasts "close up, touchy-feely, and personal," be alert, and don't make any fast moves (the rays can panic, we're told). And above all, as the divers say, never try to grab one by the tail.

MORE FUN IN THE SURF
Boat Rentals

Many travelers dream of sailing their own boat beneath an azure Caribbean sky, without the company of a crew. Alas, unless you're a very experienced sailor, and unless you can afford it, it might not be feasible to rent one of the very large sailing vessels that are the norm at most boat charter outfits (and often require a substantial cash deposit before a newcomer will be entrusted to take it out onto the deep blue sea). However, there are numerous ways for less experienced sailors to rent small boats.

Small (about 3.3m-long/11-ft.) sailing craft are the specialty at the **Cayman Islands Sailing Club,** Spinnaker Road, Red Bay, near the hamlet of North Sound (© **345/947-7913;** www.sailing. ky). On a sunbaked, gravel-covered compound, isolated from the traffic and congestion of West Bay, you'll find a two-story warehouse crafted from wood planks and corrugated metal panels, a clubhouse with its own trophy-filled bar, and an inventory of about 70 small-scale sailboats, usually Picos, Lasers, or (least high-tech of all) simple sailing dinghies, each suitable for one or two persons. Most boats rent for 2-hour periods, time enough to do some quality brisk sailing in Grand Cayman's North Sound. Boat rentals are CI$30 to CI$40 per hour. Rentals are available every day from 9am to 5pm and require at least a rudimentary level of sailing experience. If you don't feel completely proficient, you can sign up for an 8-hour sailing lesson for a fee of around CI$600.

Helmet Diving

Sea Trek (© **345/949-0008;** www.seatrekcayman.com) allows you the chance to experience helmet diving, walking and breathing 7.9m (26 ft.) underwater without getting your hair wet. The underwater experience lasts an hour, and is suitable for both swimmers and nonswimmers. This near-zero-gravity experience has been compared to a moonwalk, to borrow an expression from Michael Jackson.

The helmet dive is suitable for those 8 years and up. As you walk along, you get to experience the dramatic underwater life of the Caymans. This water-world adventure costs US$89 per person.

Sea Trek operates from a floating platform just north of George Town at Sotos Reef; its dive location lies over a 9.1m (30-ft.) "sand hole" (a sand patch surrounded by coral). You'll get to see living coral rising to a height of 7.6m (25 ft.) as well as thousands of rainbow-hued tropical fish. Sea Trek operates daily at half past the hour between 7:30am and 4:30pm.

Submarine Rides ★

Atlantis Adventures (© **800/887-8571** in the U.S., or 345/949-7700 from the Cayman Islands or other parts of the world, www.atlantisadventures.com) is the better established of two outfits on

Grand Cayman, both of which promise to take you, safely and panoramically, beneath the surface of the waves. The company provides underwater tours with views of the remarkable geology beneath the sea around Grand Cayman. Each trip departs from a clearly signposted building set directly on the waterfront of George Town, immediately south of the cruise ship piers.

The cheapest submarine experience, limited to relatively shallow waters, is offered within the **Seaworld Explorer** semisubmarine. Developed in Australia for viewing marine life from the surface of the Great Barrier Reef, this is a steel-hulled watercraft that only appears unusual beneath the waterline (it looks like a regular boat from above). In the ship's lowest level, in cramped proximity with up to 45 other passengers, you'll be seated next to windows that angle downward for panoramic views of the deep. Because the ship never descends beneath the surface of the sea, a ride is best suited for viewing sun-flooded reefs, shipwrecks, and objects lying no more than 7.6m (25 ft.) beneath the surface. Part of the attraction of this trip derives from the scuba divers who dispense scraps of fish to all manner of hungry marine life, including Bermuda chubs, sergeant majors, and angelfish. One-hour boat rides are priced at US$49 per adult, and US$24 per child age 2 to 12.

The second option is aboard the **Atlantis** submarine, a fully submersible craft holding 48 passengers. A 75-minute tour priced at US$99 per person descends to depths of 30m (98 ft.). Tickets for children ages 4 to 12 cost US$59, and teenagers (ages 13–17) are charged US$69 each. No children under 4 are permitted onboard. There's plenty to see underwater at this depth, as enough sunlight reaches down to allow for the growth of thousands of kinds of plant life, vital for the sustenance of an equally impressive number of species of fish. This is the most popular, and perhaps the most visually rewarding, of the submarine experiences.

The competitor is the 60-passenger **Nautilus,** Bush Centre, George Town (© **345/945-1355;** www.nautilus.ky), a semisubmarine with a protected glass hull that cruises only 1.5m (5 ft.) below the sea's surface—not exactly the full submarine experience. The craft, named after Jules Verne's futuristic vessel, departs from Rackham's Dock behind Rackham's pub in George Town. The trips take visitors to the *Cali* and *Balboa* shipwrecks and on to Cheeseburger Reef, where passengers can view divers feeding the fish. Departures are daily at 11am and 3pm, with the afternoon tour allowing passengers 30 minutes of snorkel time. The morning tour takes 1 hour, and costs CI$31 for adults and CI$15 for children 3 to 12; the afternoon tour takes 1½ hours and costs CI$36 for adults and CI$20 for children 3 to 12. Children 2 and under are free.

Windsurfing

Avid windsurfers rate the 6.4km (4 miles) of reef-protected shallows off East End the best location for windsurfing. Prevailing winds reach 24 to 40kmph (15–25 mph) from November through March, with 6- to 10-knot southeasterly breezes in summer months.

The best outfitter for windsurfing gear and lessons is **Cayman Windsurfing,** which operates as a subdivision of Red Sail Sports, at Morritt's Tortuga Club (*(C)* **345-947-7449**), in the East End of the island, an hour's drive from George Town. Open daily from 8:30am to 5pm, it charges US$45 per hour or US$120 for 3 hours for windsurfing gear. If your stamina demands 5 hours, gear rental costs US$180. Windsurfing lesson packages are also offered, beginning at US$65 for 1 hour and rising to US$300 for 10 hours, including training classes. Snorkeling equipment can also be rented here for US$15 for 24 hours. Or you can opt for a snorkeling trip farther afield on a WaveRunner. The 30-minute excursion costs US$75 for two people, or US$95 for one person.

OTHER OUTDOOR PURSUITS
Fishing

Grouper and snapper are the most common catches for those who bottom-fish along the reef. Deeper waters turn up barracuda and bonito. Sport fishermen from all over the world come to the Caymans with hopes of hooking one of the big ones: tuna, wahoo, or marlin. Most hotels can make arrangements for charter boats. Otherwise, contact **Bayside Watersports** (*(C)* **345/949-3200;** www.baysidewatersports.com), offering deep-sea-fishing excursions in search of tuna, marlin, and wahoo on a variety of air-conditioned vessels with experienced crew. Tours depart at 7am and 1pm, and are priced according to how many people join the tour. A half-day tour for up to four people costs US$600, while a full day for the same group is US$1,100. Bonefishing and reef-fishing tours are also available at US$500 for a half-day and US$900 for a full day for four people.

Golf

Golf courses on Grand Cayman are open daily from 8am to 6pm. Many golfers prefer to avoid the intense noonday sun.

The best course on the island is the **Britannia Golf Club** (*(C)* **345/745-4653;** www.britannia-golf.com), a well-respected, open-to-the-public 9-hole course designed by Jack Nicklaus, positioned across the avenue from the **Grand Cayman Beach Suites** (p. 59) on West Bay Road. Greens fees are US$65 to US$90 for 9

Other Outdoor Pursuits

BEACHES & ACTIVE PURSUITS

About 200 species of birds make their home in the Caymans, and some 50 species are known to breed here, ranging from the famous Cayman parrots to the elegant frigate birds with their 2.1m (7-ft.) wingspan. This magnificent bird with its forked tail has the ability to glide on its wings.

The islands are also home to the West Indian whistling duck, called the world's most endangered duck.

Sailors named a red-footed bird "booby," Spanish for "fool," because it was so easy to catch. This bird mostly nests on Little Cayman.

You can also spot two species of woodpecker, along with tangers, ibis, mockingbirds, and several species of egrets and herons.

The Cayman parrot is, in fact, the national bird of the islands. Cayman Brac is the best island for parrot viewing, as a large reserve is protected for these colorful birds, which are mostly green with a red throat, cheeks, and neck.

On Grand Cayman, bird-watchers flock to **Queen Elizabeth II Botanic Park,** the **Meagre Bay Pond,** and the **Michael Gore Bird Sanctuary,** among other sites, to see these birds in all their glory. The Michael Gore Bird Sanctuary lies on 1.4 hectares (3½ acres) of pristine wetland in the Spotts Newlands area.

holes, or US$90 to US$140 if you opt to play the course twice, thereby playing 18 holes. (Guests at the resort pay the lower rates.) Cart rentals are included, but club rentals cost US$20 for 9 holes or US$40 for 18. Incidentally, there's a charming restaurant associated with this golf course, the **Britannia Restaurant** (© 345/745-4653). Open daily for lunch and dinner, it offers a view of the lake accompanied by stiff drinks, excellent salads, and juicy burgers, in an atmosphere vaguely akin to that of a game lodge in Kenya.

Often swept by trade winds, **North Sound Club,** Seven Mile Beach, off West Bay Road (© 345/947-4653; www.northsound club.com), is a par-71, 6,011m (6,574-yd.) course designed by Roy Case, who factored the strong gusts into his design. The course is filled with water and sand traps, but attracts hundreds of golfers who want an extra degree of challenge. Case set the course into what is essentially a botanical garden. On-site are a clubhouse and pro shop, as well as a restaurant. Management requires that you wear collared shirts, not T-shirts. Greens fees are US$105 for 9 holes or US$175 for 18 holes, including the cart.

A final course, the 9-hole **Blue Tip,** West Bay Road (© **345/ 815-6500**), is reserved for guests of the **Ritz-Carlton** (p. 60), charging greens fees of US$200 per player. Designed by Greg Norman, Blue Tip also has the best pro shop on island.

Horseback Riding

Coral Stone Stables, at Bodden Town and Savannah (© **345/ 916-4799;** www.csstables.com) features 1½-hour horseback rides along the white sandy beaches at Bodden Town and across inland trails at Savannah. As a special feature, the outfit allows you to swim with the horses. Another special feature are its moonlit rides along the beach. Tour guides are provided for each horseback ride, and souvenir photos are taken. Coral Stone accepts both the novice and experienced rider. On the inland forest trail ride, you can view the natural wildlife of the island, including the sighting of land turtles.

A variety of rides are offered daily beginning at 8am, costing $80 per rider. A swim with the horses goes for $120 per rider. The stables also offer free pickup and drop-off, including from the cruise ship terminals. Of course, you must call to make arrangements.

Horse Back in Paradise with Nicki (© **345/945-5839;** www.caymanhorseriding.com) collects riders anywhere in the vicinity of Seven Mile Beach and takes them on early-morning or late-afternoon beach rides, with some inland trail riding. Nicole "Nicki" Eldemire has a wealth of information about life in Grand Cayman, and is full of anecdotes about island life, flora, and fauna. You're in the saddle for 75 minutes for US$100 per person. Sunset rides can also be arranged for a minimum of six riders.

Honey Suckle Trail Rides, Savannah (© **345/916-5420**), will also arrange to pick you up if you're staying in the vicinity of Seven Mile Beach. This outfitter offers morning and sunset rides lasting 1½ hours at a cost of US$60 per rider. Both Western and English tack are offered.

The magnificent horses of **Pampered Ponies** (© **345/945- 2262;** www.ponies.ky) carry you across stretches of sandy beaches or trails slightly inland. Sunset and full-moon rides are also a feature. The exploration is along the north coast beaches of West Bay. You'll have the beachfront almost to yourself along the stretch from Conch Point to Morgan's Harbour on the north tip beyond West Bay. Depending on what you book, prices begin at around $80 per rider.

Kayaking

Surfside Aquasports (📞 345/916-2820; www.caymankayakand
snorkelsafari.com) provides you with the Cayman Islands' finest
kayak and snorkeling safaris. In only a few minutes' drive from the
center of George Town, you arrive at the kayak staging area lying
on the shore of a tranquil lagoon protected from the open sea by a
coral reef. The safari takes you through the island's protected mangrove wetlands, where you're introduced to the "locals"—that is,
the indigenous animals including the nonstinging Cassiopeia jel-
lyfish and plant life.

Tours are in the shallow water of a protected bay on the southern coastline, lasting 3 hours. You get an overview of the local
ecosystem. At a secluded reef you can enjoy an underwater landscape on a snorkeling tour. The cost is $77 per adult or $39 for
children 11 and under. Of course, you call in advance to reserve
and make pickup arrangements.

Skating

Black Pearl Skate & Surf Park, Red Bay Road, Grand Harbour
(📞 345/947-4161; www.blackpearl.ky), is the size of a football
field, measuring some 5,760 sq. m (62,000 sq. ft.), making it the
world's second-largest such facility. It also boasts the world's largest
freestanding wave, and is the largest outdoor concrete park in the
world. It features three main courses—expert, intermediate, and
beginner, with both a flow and a street course for each level. Here
you can practice your tailslides, wheelies, grinds, and kickflips.
Skateboards and mandatory protective gear can be rented at the
on-site Black Pearl Board Shop.

Instructors offer classes in skateboarding and in-line skating at
all levels. The park also boasts one of the world's largest professional competition vert ramps, measuring 18m (60 ft.) wide.

Surfing here is just as popular as the skating, with an artificial
surf machine. You can ride under and over blue curls of water.
Water flow varies from 10,000 gallons per minute to 150,000 gallons per minute. Waves rise to a height of 3.4m (11 ft.), and surfers
try, often in vain, to stay on the wave.

In the outdoor patio of the Brick House Restaurant, you can
order some of the island's best pizzas. This is also an ideal seat to
watch local island daredevil surfers perform daring feats on Saturday nights. The show runs from 7 to 8pm costing CI$20.

The park is open Monday to Saturday 10am to dusk and on
Sunday from noon to dusk. Admission to the park costs CI$17.

5

Other Outdoor Pursuits

Tennis

Many of the big resorts have their own tennis courts available to guests. However, a total of nine courts are available to the public at the **Cayman Islands Tennis Club,** Ann Bonney Crescent, South Sound (© **345/949-9464;** www.tennis.ky). The fee for up to 2 hours on either asphalt or "classic clay" surfaced courts is CI$15 per person. Hours can vary according to the season and the weather, so call ahead.

INDOOR ACTIVITIES FOR INCLEMENT WEATHER

If it's raining or too hot outside but you're desperate to put your body in motion, try the World Gym, West Bay Road (© **345/949-5132;** www.worldgym.com/grandcayman). You'll find it behind a branch of Wendy's on Seven Mile Beach. As the original fitness center on the island, it's still going strong with state-of-the-art equipment like Nautilus and cardiovascular machines, plus activities such as aerobics, bodybuilding, jujitsu, karate, massages, weight lifting, and the like, with five personal trainers on call. A 1-day pass costs US$25; personal training costs an additional US$65 per half-hour training session. The gym is open Monday to Thursday 5am to 10pm, Friday 5am to 8pm, Saturday 8am to 6pm, and Sunday 8am to 4pm.

A competitor is **Fitness Connection,** Glen Eden Road, South Sound (© **345/949-8485;** www.fitness.ky), which is a full-service facility with a lot of extras—even belly dancing and tap-dancing classes. Regular gym workouts are offered, along with personal training and yoga. Admission is CI$30 per day for everybody (aerobics and dance classes are included in this fee), plus an additional CI$15 for use of special facilities and special programs. The complex is open Monday to Friday from 8am to 6pm and Saturday 9am to 1am.

EXPLORING GRAND CAYMAN

What attractions does Grand Cayman have other than Seven Mile Beach? Admittedly, this strip of shore is its most fabled lure, but if you can tear yourself from the surf and sand, you may be pleasantly surprised by all there is to see and do on the Caymans' largest island. As one villa owner, who had been living on Grand Cayman for 3 years, told us, "There is more to see and more diversity here than my wife and I ever realized."

The most interesting sections of George Town can be explored on foot in an hour or so, although you could easily spend hours shopping in town. Explore the island in greater depth on a guided tour, or rent a car or scooter and set out on your own.

Most visitors drive north of George Town along West Bay Road and Seven Mile Beach, which is the most heavily developed part of Grand Cayman. Those seeking a more in-depth look at the less touristy areas can take our guided tour of the East End, going all the way from George Town to Rum Point in the north.

In the East End, you'll find such attractions as blowholes (rock formations that produce huge spouts of water when waves hit) and botanical gardens, plus remains of Grand Cayman's earliest settlements. Of course, it's always fun to break up a drive across the island with a swim in the Caymans' warm waters or a picnic on a secluded beach.

THE TOP ATTRACTIONS

Boatswain's Beach/Cayman Turtle Farm ★★ You won't find another green-sea-turtle farm like this anywhere else in the world. Once the islands had a multitude of turtles in the surrounding waters (which is why Columbus called the islands "Las Tortugas"), but today these creatures are sadly few in number, and the green sea turtle has been designated an endangered species (you cannot bring turtle products into the United States). The main functions of the farm are to provide the local market with edible turtle meat, thus preventing the need to hunt turtles in the wild, and to replenish the waters with hatchling and yearling turtles. Visitors today can observe about 100 circular concrete tanks in which these sea creatures exist in every stage of development; the hope is that one day their population in the sea will regain its former status.

Turtles here range in size from 6 ounces to 600 pounds. Specific tanks give guests the opportunity to touch hatchling and baby turtles. Aside from turtles, the farm also has sharks, fish, and birds on display. You can expect to spend about an hour touring the turtle farm. At the snack bar and restaurant, you can sample turtle dishes. There's a well-stocked gift shop on-site. Choose from two tour options: Take the "dry tour," and visit the facilities only, or take the "wet tour," which includes the opportunity to snorkel in the artificial lagoon stocked with fish. The lagoon shares a glass wall with a shark tank, allowing snorkelers to swim "with" the sharks. During Pirates Week, baby turtles are released from the farm into the open ocean. *Note:* Many countries ban the importation of sea-turtle products, according to the Convention of International Trade in Endangered Species. More than likely, you won't be able to take home any souvenirs made out of sea turtles. For more information on the ban, see "What You Can Take Home from the Cayman Islands," in chapter 2.

825 Northwest Point Rd., West Bay. ⓒ **345/949-3894.** www.boatswainsbeach. ky. Admission dry tour US$30 adults, US$20 children 4–12; wet tour US$45 adults, US$25 children 4–12; free for children 3 and under. Daily 8am–5:30pm.

Cayman Islands National Museum ★ Set directly on the waterfront, in a George Town neighborhood that's more densely packed with cruise ship passengers than any other area on the island, this museum is housed in a dignified clapboard building that's one of the island's oldest and one of few to survive the disastrous hurricane of 1932. The 557-sq.-m (5,995-sq.-ft.) interior is a repository for the lore, history, and memorabilia of the Cayman Islands. Many older islanders feel that the importance of local

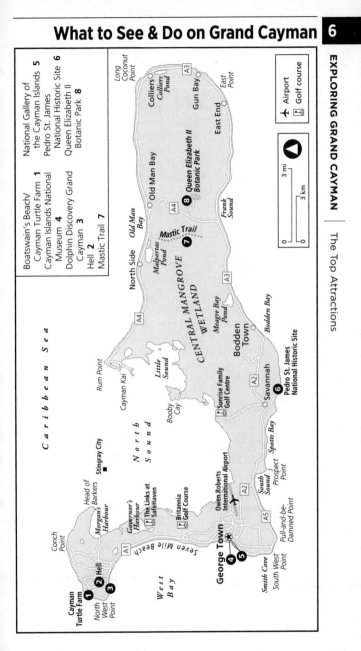

Boatswain's Beach/
Cayman Turtle Farm **1**
Cayman Islands National
Museum **4**
Dolphin Discovery Grand
Cayman **3**
Hell **2**
Mastic Trail **7**

National Gallery of
the Cayman Islands **5**
Pedro St. James
National Historic Site **6**
Queen Elizabeth II
Botanic Park **8**

✈ Airport
⛳ Golf course

0   3 mi
0   3 km

Caribbean Sea

Conch Point

Head of
Barkers

Morgan's
Harbour

Governor's
Harbour

🏌 The Links at
Safehaven

🏌 Britannia
Golf Course

Stingray City ■

*North
Sound*

Little
Sound

Booby
Cay

Rum Point

Cayman Kai

*West
Bay*

North
West
Point

**Cayman
Turtle Farm** **1**

Hell **2**
3

Seven Mile Beach

A1

A5

Owen Roberts
International Airport

George Town

4
5

Smith Cove

South West
Point

Pull-and-be-
Damned Point

Prospect Point

*South
Sound*

Spotts Bay

A2

🏌 Sunrise Family
Golf Centre

Savannah

A2

Pedro St. James
National Historic Site **6**

*CENTRAL MANGROVE
WETLAND*

Meagre Bay
Pond

Bodden
Town

Bodden Bay

Malportas
Pond

A3

North Side

Mastic Trail **7**

*Old Man
Bay*

Old Man Bay ○

A4

Frank
Sound

8 Queen Elizabeth II
Botanic Park

East End

Gun Bay

Colliers ○
Colliers
Pond

A3

Long
Coconut
Point

East
Point

history is being ignored by the younger generations of Caymanians. Thus, you might find more passion and ferocious national pride associated with the exhibits inside this museum than you might have expected. Exhibits focus on the sociological, archaeological, and mercantile history of the Caymans, with a heavy emphasis on the hardships suffered by the Caymanians prior to the advent of tourism and the modern-day financial-services industries. The formal exhibits feature more than 2,000 items depicting the natural, social, and cultural history of the Caymans, including an assortment of Caymanian artifacts that were collected by islander Ira Thompson beginning in the 1930s. The museum also incorporates a gift shop, theater, and cafe. Call ahead to make sure it's open when you visit. The museum can be seen in about 45 minutes.

S. Church St. (Harbour Dr.), George Town. ✆ **345/949-8368.** www.museum.ky. Admission US$5 adults, US$3 children 6–12, free for children 5 and under. Mon– Fri 9am–5pm; Sat 10am–2pm.

Dolphin Discovery Grand Cayman This dolphinarium is one of the latest attractions on Grand Cayman. It has three different programs for swimming with the dolphins. (Although some surveys have revealed that dolphins may not like such intimate contact with humans, nobody talks about that here.)

The least expensive program, for ages 8 and above, is the "Dolphin Lovers Swim," during which a dolphin might sing to you, or even give you a hug and a kiss. The second program, "Dolphin Swim Adventure," allows you to go for a belly ride with this sea creature. Participants stroke and pet the dolphins.

The final and most expensive program, "Dolphin Royal Swim," allows for even more intimate contact with the dolphins. They'll not only give you a kiss and a hug, but will pull you with their dorsal tows, giving a speedy ride. After that, the dolphins will push your feet to raise you up to the water surface. Visitors to the Dolphin Discovery can spend an hour or 3 hours, depending on what they want to do.

Northwest Rd., West Bay. ✆ **866/393-5158** in the U.S., 866/793-1905 in Canada. www.dolphindiscovery.com. Reserve in advance. Dolphin Lovers' Swim US$99 adults, US$79 children 8–11; Dolphin Swim Adventure US$119 adults, US$99 children 8–11; Dolphin Royal Swim US$159 adults, US$119 children 8–11. Daily 9am, 11am, and 1pm.

Pedro St. James National Historic Site ★ This is a restored great house dating from 1780, when only 400 people lived on Grand Cayman. It outlasted all of the island's major hurricanes,

STROLL THROUGH historic GEORGE TOWN

Arm yourself with a map (the tourist office will help you plot a route) and start at the **Old Courts Building,** now the Cayman Islands National Museum, on Harbour Drive. It has exhibits of the natural and cultural history of the island. To your left as you leave is **Panton Square,** with three old Cayman houses distinguished by pitched gables and ornate fretwork. On Harbour Drive, past the cruise dock, is **Elmslie Memorial Church,** built by Captain Rayal Bodden, a well-known shipwright. To the right, by the parking lot, are old grave markers shaped like houses, with small ones for children. In the churchyard is the **War Memorial** (for World Wars I and II), and across the street, the **Seamen's Memorial,** with names of 153 Caymanians lost at sea. Next to it are the remains of **Fort George,** built in 1790 for defense against the Spaniards who raided the islands, carrying captured inhabitants to Cuba.

but was destroyed by fire in 1970. It has been rebuilt and is now the centerpiece of a heritage park with a visitor center and an audiovisual theater that presents laser light shows. Because of its size, the great house was called "the Castle" by generations of Caymanians. Its primary historical importance dates from December 5, 1831, when residents met here to elect the Caymans' first legislative assembly, making the house the cradle of the island's democracy. The great house sits atop a limestone bluff with a panoramic view of the sea. Guests enter via a US$1.5-million visitor center with a multimedia theater (shows are presented on the hour 10am–4pm), a landscaped courtyard, a gift shop, and a cafe. Self-guided tours are possible. Check out the house's wide verandas, rough-hewn timber beams, gabled framework, mahogany floors and staircases, and wide-beam wooden ceilings. Guides (in 18th-c. costumes, no less) are on hand to answer questions. You can spend 30 minutes or 2 hours at this historic site, depending on whether you want to see a show in the theater.

Savannah. ℭ **345/947-3329.** www.pedrostjames.ky. Admission CI$8 adults, free for children 12 and under. Daily 9am–5pm.

Queen Elizabeth II Botanic Park ★★   On 24 hectares (59 acres) of rugged wooded land off Frank Sound Road, North Side,

✋ TRY TO avoid GOING TO HELL

This is the most overblown and fundamentally most irritating attraction on Grand Cayman. Hell is a tiny village in a desolate area, lying just under a kilometer (about ⅔ mile) from the sea. Covering about a quarter-hectare (⅔ acre) of jagged limestone in West Bay, near the island's most northwesterly point, Grand Cayman's earliest settlers (who wisely avoided this area) labeled this inhospitable location as "hellish" . . . ergo, Hell.

Don't even think of walking on the terrain: First of all, it's restricted. If you defy the signs and take a walk, you have a good chance of spraining your ankles or gashing your shins. A jagged lunar landscape of somber-toned gray rock, it evokes a treacherous coral formation—the kind that could easily tear open the hull of the sturdiest watercraft—that happens to be above the surface of the water. Except for birds, most animals tend to avoid the place.

The big "attraction" here is a little post office where you can get your cards and letters postmarked from Hell.

this park allows visitors to take a short walk through wetland, swamp, dry thicket, mahogany-tree stands, and patches of orchids and bromeliads. Hurricane Ivan destroyed some of the vegetation, but since then, the park has grown back. The trail is 1km (⅔ mile) long. You'll likely see chickatees, which are freshwater turtles found only on the Caymans and in Cuba. Occasionally you'll spot the rare Grand Cayman parrot, or perhaps the anole lizard, with its cobalt-blue throat pouch. Even rarer is the endangered blue iguana. The visitor center features changing exhibitions, plus a canteen for food and refreshments. It's set adjacent to the woodland trail and includes a heritage garden with a re-creation of a traditional Cayman home, garden, and farm; a floral garden with flowering plants; and a lake with three islands, home to many native birds. About 1 hour is sufficient time for visiting the botanic park.

Off Frank Sound Rd., North Side. ✆ **345/947-9462.** www.botanic-park.ky. Admission CI$8 adults, free for children 12 and under. Daily Apr–Sept 9am–6:30pm; Oct–Mar 9am–5:30pm.

OTHER ATTRACTIONS

Mastic Trail ★ 🎁 The trail is a restored 200-year-old footpath through a 2-million-year-old woodland area at the heart of the island. Lying west of Frank Sound Road, about a 45-minute drive from the heart of George Town, the trail showcases the Mastic Reserve's natural attractions, including a native mangrove swamp, traditional agriculture, and an ancient woodland area, home to the largest variety of native plant and animal life in the Cayman Islands.

The trail is supervised and maintained in safe and unobstructed repair by a government-appointed field agent, but during periods of heavy rain, the southern end is likely to be flooded. The government therefore recommends that during periods of prolonged rainfall, hikers approach the trail from the northern end, off Further Road, North Side, as opposed to via the southern end, off Frank Sound Road.

Guided tours of the trail, organized by the Cayman Islands National Trust, are scheduled every Wednesday at 9am, and every fourth Saturday, also at 9am. Tours last 2 to 3 hours each, and are limited to a maximum of 15 participants. Reservations are strongly recommended, and the cost is US$25 per person. The hike is not recommended for children 5 and under, the elderly, or persons

THE NATIONAL flower & THE NATIONAL tree

The Caymans are home to almost 30 indigenous orchid species, but islanders selected the wild banana orchid as their national flower. It blooms on all three islands in April and May, and is spectacular to behold. The wild banana orchid on Grand Cayman has white blossoms and purple lips, whereas those on Little Cayman and Cayman Brac are yellow in color.

The national tree, the silver thatch palm, has even figured into the economy of the islands. The underside of the palm leaves is silvery, with a lightish green upper frond. Locals call this palm "the money tree." Islanders used to go into the interior and crop the leaves from the top of the silver thatch palm. In turn, they would trade them for goods at the local shops. Merchants would then exchange them for goods imported from Jamaica.

The silver thatch palm has very tough leaves, and the early islanders also used these fronds to create thatch roofs over their homes. These roofs made the houses cool and rainproof. Sometimes they were used to create small kitchens away from the main house. This reduced the risk of fire. In the case of the kitchens, the palm leaves were also used for walls.

Except in rare instances, the silver thatch palm is no longer used for roofs, but it is still used for such items as belts, rope, and baskets.

A Master-Plan Community Blossoming into Life

Set on 202 hectares (500 acres) between Seven Mile Beach and the North Sound, **Camana Bay** (www.camanabay.com) is a new town in the making. Shops, offices, cafes, restaurants, and a six-screen cinema, along with new residences, are either nearing completion or are on the drawing boards. One of the focal points is the Cayman International School with more than 300 students. The eco-friendly community is geared toward the pedestrian, not the automobile. The whole village is filled with Caribbean architecture and lush, indigenous landscaping.

with physical disabilities. The trail is flat, and alternately gravelly and sandy. If you're in relatively good shape, you should not find it particularly challenging. Be sure to wear comfortable and sturdy shoes and carry water and insect repellent. For tour reservations, call the **National Trust** (© 345-949-0121; www.nationaltrust. org.ky). If the scheduled times for these organized tours aren't convenient for you, you can stop into the headquarters of the National Trust on South Church Street, Monday to Friday from 9am to 5pm, for a self-guided walking tour/map of the trail. The map, which costs CI$5, describes the botanical and geological features you're likely to see en route.

National Gallery of the Cayman Islands This gallery is the Cayman Islands' only noncommercial venue for the exhibition of art. The compact museum mounts about six fine-art exhibitions per year, each containing about 60 works. About 30% of the art is by local artists.

Harbour Place, S. Church St., George Town. © 345/945-8111. www.national gallery.org.ky. Free admission, though donations are welcome. Mon–Fri 9am–5pm; Sat 11am–4pm.

DRIVING TOUR 1: GEORGE TOWN TO RUM POINT

Start:	George Town.
Finish:	Rum Point.
Time:	2 to 2½ hours.
Best Time:	Daylight hours from 9am to 5pm.
Worst Time:	When rains have been, or are, heavy.

Leaving George Town heading along the coast, on South Church Street (A5), you will follow this route until you see **Grand Old**

Driving Tour 1: George Town to Rum Point

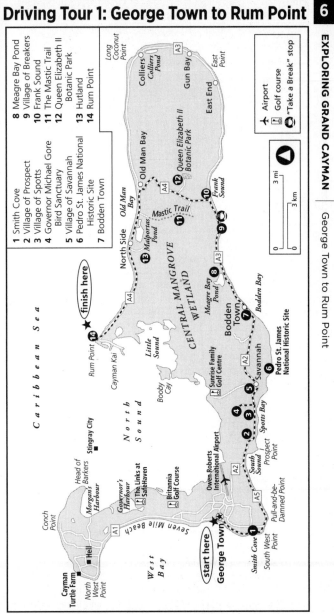

1 Smith Cove
2 Village of Prospect
3 Village of Spotts
4 Governor Michael Gore Bird Sanctuary
5 Village of Savannah
6 Pedro St. James National Historic Site
7 Bodden Town
8 Meagre Bay Pond
9 Village of Breakers
10 Frank Sound
11 The Mastic Trail
12 Queen Elizabeth II Botanic Park
13 Hutland
14 Rum Point

✈ Airport
⛳ Golf course
☕ "Take a Break" stop

House (p. 86), a landmark and one of Grand Cayman's leading restaurants. To begin your tour swimmingly, and to take in a scenic view, stop off at Smith Cove, signposted directly south of Grand Old House.

1 Smith Cove

This is one of the best spots for snorkeling among rainbow-hued fish and for swimming in calm waters. Local weddings on the beach often take place here. On one occasion, we glimpsed a couple getting married in their bathing suits. The beach is a bit rock-strewn. There is a parking lot, and bathrooms are available on-site.

After a stopover, continue south along South Church Street as it becomes South Sound Road (still the A5). This road runs along the south coast of Grand Cayman and is perhaps the most scenic on the island. Eventually at Red Bay, the A5 merges into the A2, also called Red Bay Road. Follow it directly east into the:

2 Village of Prospect

You are now passing through what is thought to be the site of the first settlement on Grand Cayman, although there is little to see today. Settlers established a fort and an outpost here sometime in the latter half of the 1700s—"ancient history" in Caymanian terms. You can see a little monument marking the site of Prospect Fort, the oldest fort on the island. The village, which lies to the immediate east of Red Bay Road along Prospect Point Road, has been mostly abandoned since 1932. The village's church, opening onto the coast, was left to decay. Nearby, the Watler Family Cemetery dates from the 1800s and is under the protection of the National Trust. The cemetery is open to the public and you can still see the gravestones—some curiously shaped like small homes. Caymanians called these family plots "Gardens of Memories." Of interest to most visitors is the good sandy beach lying just around the point at Prospect. Both divers and snorkelers are drawn to the beach and sea here. Beach shelters and public toilets are available.

Red Bay Road turns into Jack Road at the Village of Prospect. As you continue east along Jack Road (A2), you'll pass through the:

3 Village of Spotts

Like Prospect, Spotts is a historic village. It is currently a private residential area, although the government has plans to turn the coast into a public seaside park and to develop the area as a cruise ship docking space should the waters at

George Town be too rough for smooth landings. A sandy public beach is nestled between the rocks and is good for swimming. You can also visit an old cemetery, with 18th-century grave markers painted white.

From Spotts, you can take a short detour to the north along Governor Spotts Newlands Road to reach the:

4 Governor Michael Gore Bird Sanctuary

This bird sanctuary is open all day and is particularly interesting to visit from April to June, when it is at its most beautiful and shelters the most birds. At various times of the year, more than 60 species—both land and water birds—inhabit the sanctuary. It is a birder's delight. At least a quarter of the native birds of the Caymans can be seen here, and many of them use the freshwater pool at the center of the .8-hectare (2-acre) refuge. Birds can be viewed from an observation platform and from the walkways that lace the sanctuary. Admission is free.

Double back to the main road (A2) and continue east to the:

5 Village of Savannah

This village contains a 1940s schoolhouse that was restored by the National Trust. It's open to the public only by reservation, so call ✆ 345/949-0121 if you're interested. Frankly, we don't think it's worth the bother. We recommend you simply drive through the village, as there is little of interest here. After you've left town, a crossroads to the left, called Hirst Road, takes you to the Sunrise Family Golf Centre, a 9-hole, par-3 course that's open to the public.

At the golf course, turn right onto Pedro Castle Road, which leads to the historic 18th-century plantation great house:

6 Pedro St. James National Historic Site

This national historic site is one of the major attractions of Grand Cayman. For a detailed review, see p. 124. You can either visit Pedro St. James now or return at some point later if you don't want to get out of the car.

Back on the main road, A2 continues east and is called Poinciana Road before becoming Shamrock Drive. Shamrock Drive leads to:

7 Bodden Town

This is more of a village than a town, where single-story homes with corrugated-iron roofs and wooden verandas evoke British colonial architecture. Once called "South Side," Bodden Town was the first capital of Grand Cayman. "Respectable settlers" (or so the history books tell us) made the town their home back in the 1700s. Over time, Bodden Town's power and prestige were transferred to George Town in the west.

Because it doesn't have the commercial interest of George Town or the tourist frenzy of Seven Mile Beach, Bodden Town still retains some of its traditional aura.

Bodden Town is named for Gov. William Bodden, who was chief magistrate (which is virtually the same title as governor) of the island from 1776 to 1823. Because he did much to improve the life of the islanders, Governor Bodden is known today as "the Grand Old Man of Grand Cayman."

You can visit Guard House Park, opposite Manse Road, where an old guardhouse once stood. The guardhouse protected the western approach to town, with its cannons pointed down a rocky gorge toward the sea. The two cannons that stand here today are from the ships involved in Cayman's most famous disaster, the **Wreck of the Ten Sails** (p. 108). In a patriotic gesture, the Caymanians sent their antique cannons to England in the darkest days of World War II to be melted down and rebuilt into modern weapons.

Another small battery of cannons once stood on Gun Square, Bodden Town's second defense point, guarding the eastern approach to the town. Two of the original cannons are still in place. Behind Gun Square is Mission House. Its first floor was constructed in the 1840s, making it one of the oldest buildings in the Caymans.

Leaving Bodden, drive along A2 1.6km (1 mile) east to:

8 Meagre Bay Pond

This small wildlife sanctuary was once frequented by hunters seeking mallard and teal ducks. Today, the government protects the area. The freshwater pond dries out in the winter months and fills up again in the summer. Early morning or late afternoon is the best time to view this waterfowl breeding area, with its various flocks of shore birds and migratory wading birds, including willets, stilts, ibis, herons, grebes, egrets, and cormorants. Though the government owns this mangrove-fringed lagoon, the land around it is private; no public footpath leads to the sanctuary. You'll have to park off the side of the road and watch the birds from a distance.

Continue following the same road to the east. The road now changes its designation from A2 to A3. Follow A3 east to the:

9 Village of Breakers

The village of Breakers would hardly merit your attention were it not for the **Lighthouse Restaurant at Breakers** (p. 88).

TAKE A BREAK ☕

The **Lighthouse Restaurant at Breakers** (📞 345/947-2047; www. lighthouse.ky) is the ideal luncheon spot for those traveling the southern coast. Its combination of Caribbean and Italian food, with an emphasis on the catch of the day, is delicious. The lighthouse was built with the intention of housing a restaurant, with a terrace opening onto views of the sea.

From here, continue east on A3, which winds its way to the beautiful:

10 Frank Sound

The sound can be seen to your right as you drive. You might want to stop off and go for a swim along the narrow sands that are ideal for beachcombing, swimming, or even bonefishing. Part of the beach is set against a backdrop of Australian pines. A boat-launch ramp leads into the shallow and calm waters, which are protected by a reef.

Near the boat ramp, a road turns north, cutting down considerably on the driving time. This road, Frank Sound Drive, takes you to two of the major attractions of Grand Cayman: the **Mastic Trail** (p. 126) and **Queen Elizabeth II Botanic Park** (p. 125).

It's also possible to continue to the East End following A3 all around the coast. This is an interesting drive, although it's devoid of specific attractions, except for the **blowholes** near the hamlet of High Rock, where onshore sprays of water shoot up like geysers, creating a roar like a lion.

If you want to stick to the main tour, take Frank Sound Drive immediately north until you come to:

11 The Mastic Trail

These 400 hectares (988 acres) and their beautiful walking trail are adventures unto themselves (p. 126). If you want to finish the driving tour and get back to George Town in the late afternoon, you might skip the Mastic Trail for the moment and continue on your way. If you have time to negotiate the trail, you can find it just off Mastic Road, which is located to the left of Frank Sound Drive near the little fire station.

After leaving the entrance to the trail, you can continue north on Frank Sound Drive for 2.6km (1⅔ miles) to the entrance of:

12 Queen Elizabeth II Botanic Park

Named in honor of Her Majesty, this park and botanical garden is fully described on p. 125. If you're pressed for time and want to complete the driving tour, you may want to plan a leisurely visit to the park on another day.

After passing the entrance to the park, Frank Sound Drive continues north to the northern coast. Turn left on A4. With the sea on your right and the marshy interior on your left, you can drive along to the west, enjoying the fresh air and the scenery. A4 at this point is also known as Ralph Drive.

13 Hutland

This community takes its name from the huts that were constructed in the area by early British settlers who farmed the land. This is one of the last havens for the endangered whistling duck, the only duck that breeds in the Caymans. Count yourself lucky, though, if you see one.

From Hutland, A4 runs all the way west to:

14 Rum Point

This area has a good beach and is a fine place to end your island tour. Rum Point got its name from the barrels of rum that once washed ashore here after a shipwreck. Today, it is surrounded by towering casuarina trees blowing in the trade winds. Most of these trees have hammocks suspended from their trunks. Hop into one and enjoy the surroundings in a leisurely manner. Featuring cays, reefs, mangroves, and shallows, Rum Point is a refuge that extends west and south for 11km (6¾ miles). It divides the two "arms" of Grand Cayman. If you get hungry, drop in to the **Wreck Bar & Grill,** Rum Point (p. 157; ✆ **345/947-9412**), for a juicy burger.

After visiting Rum Point, you can head back to George Town by backtracking along the route that you took to get here.

DRIVING TOUR 2: GEORGE TOWN TO WEST BAY

Start:	**George Town.**
Finish:	**Batabano.**
Time:	**2½ hours.**
Best Time:	**Daily between 10am and 4pm (traffic is less heavy during these hours).**
Worst Time:	**When many cruise ships are docked (Seven Mile Beach roads are the most crowded at this time). You can ask when cruise ships are coming in at the tourist bureau.**

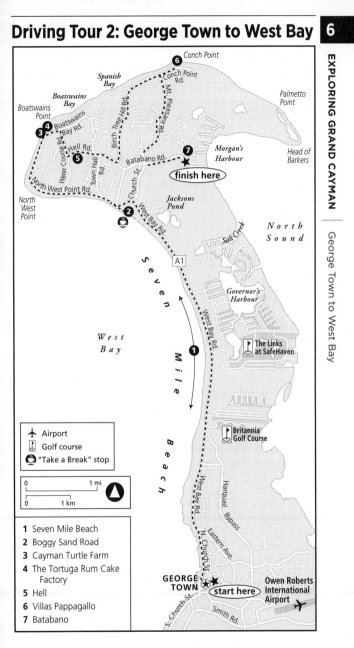

Legend

✈ Airport
⛳ Golf course
☕ "Take a Break" stop

0 _____ 1 mi
0 _____ 1 km

1 Seven Mile Beach
2 Boggy Sand Road
3 Cayman Turtle Farm
4 The Tortuga Rum Cake
  Factory
5 Hell
6 Villas Pappagallo
7 Batabano

This second driving tour is shorter than the previous one and takes you north of George Town to West Bay, one of the oldest and most colorful districts in the Caymans, inhabited for 2 centuries.

From the center of George Town, follow North Church Street north to the intersection with A1 coming up from the south. Hug left and continue on West Bay Road north, which will take you along:

1 Seven Mile Beach

This is the beach that put Grand Cayman on the tourist maps of the world. True, it doesn't really stretch for 7 miles (11km). Most locals claim it's only 5½ miles (8.9km) long, but that's still a whole lot of beach.

More than likely, at least part of your Grand Cayman vacation will be spent swimming and sunning here, and enjoying the many fine restaurants that line the beach. The southern part of the sandy stretch is heavily developed, saturated with condos, villas, restaurants, hotels, apartment buildings, a number of shopping centers, and fast-food joints.

This is the most congested part of Grand Cayman and the speed limit here is only 40kmph (25 mph). Joggers, motorists, cyclists, and pedestrians clog the streets throughout the day and for most of the evening.

There are no specific attractions along the beach itself, so you can continue your drive without making stops.

West Bay Road (also called A1) eventually leads to North West Point Road. With Jackson's Pond on your right, you'll approach Cemetery Road and a fire station. At this junction, turn left along:

2 Boggy Sand Road

This scenic coastal road contains some of the most traditional historic Cayman houses and churches. Many visitors miss it if they drive along the main road, and this route is well worth exploring.

Vibrant tropical plants surround many of the old gingerbread-style fisherman's cottages, which date from the first 2 decades of the 20th century. You can stop at Grandma Julia's Beach if you'd like to go for a swim. The beach is raked by hand every morning.

At the end of Boggy Sand Road, you will connect once more to West Bay Road, which you can continue to follow by heading west and then north, bypassing such geographic landmarks as Dolphin Point and North West Point. North West Point Road will lead you by the:

3 Cayman Turtle Farm
This is one of the major sights on Grand Cayman. Established in 1968, it's the world's only commercial green-sea-turtle farm, where you can observe turtles in all stages of development. See p. 122 for a complete review.

Right next door to the turtle farm is:

4 The Tortuga Rum Cake Factory
Many of the rum cakes that visitors purchase as souvenirs in George Town stores are made on-site at this large bakery. You can watch the process of making rum cake through glass windows and sample some of the various flavors of rum before making your purchase. The factory charges no admission and receives guests Monday to Friday from 8am to 5pm, and Saturday from 8am to 2:30pm.

If you'd like to stop for lunch nearby, drop in at the **Cracked Conch,** West Bay Road (© **345/945-5217**), near the turtle farm. For a complete review of the restaurant, see p. 84.

After leaving the factory or the Cracked Conch, follow North West Point Road to the junction with Water Course Road, and head south. At the junction with Hell Road, continue east on Hell Road to:

5 Hell
Did we already mention that this is the biggest tourist trap in the Cayman Islands? Hell is said to be the setting for a few scenes in Defoe's *Robinson Crusoe,* but some biographers dispute this claim. It's a rugged outcropping of iron shore with a bleak lunar landscape that does indeed look like the charred remains of hellfire. Granted, the landscape is completely unique. Grab some souvenirs if you must, and then press on to the greater charms planned below.

Leave Hell by traveling east along Reverend Blackman Road until you reach the junction with Birch Tree Hill Road. Take Birch Tree Hill Road north until you reach the northern coastline at Spanish Bay. Continue east along this road (whose name changes from Birch Tree Hill Rd. to Conch Point Rd.), bypassing Spanish Bay Reef Hotel. At the end of the road you come to:

6 Villas Pappagallo
Here, you'll find a complex of private villas and **Ristorante Pappagallo** (p. 91), a good choice for dinner, but closed at lunch. You can get out of your car and head toward Barkers, the site of a 5.6-hectare (14-acre) bird sanctuary, which the restaurant overlooks. This tidal lagoon is home to numerous

💬 Did You Know?

- The green sea turtle can survive underwater for days at a time.
- The Cayman Trough, between the Caymans and Jamaica, contains the deepest waters in the Caribbean, reaching depths of 6.4km (4 miles) or more.
- Fire coral will actually defend itself and attack you. You'll feel like a match has been put to your body. (Outfitters will issue warnings on how to avoid this and other dangers while snorkeling and scuba diving.)
- A peg-legged, swashbuckling turtle is the national symbol of the Cayman Islands, seen as a sort of mascot.
- Caymanians refused to become a protectorate of Jamaica when the latter island country achieved independence in 1962.
- Agouti, rabbit-size rodents, still live on the island. Cayman residents once hunted them for meat.
- Only one egg out of 10,000 laid by the green sea turtle reaches maturity.
- More than 100 nationalities live on the Cayman Islands. One-fifth of Caymanians are Jamaican.
- The first settlers on the Caymans may have been deserters from the British army in Jamaica.
- According to numerous surveys, Caymanians have one of the highest standards of living in the Caribbean.
- The root cassava was used by the Taíno Indians to make flour, and Caymanians use it today to make a local dessert called "heavy cake." But don't try this yourself—it is poisonous until processed to remove its prussic acid.
- In the summer months, Texans and many travelers from the southern U.S. flee to the Caymans, where the cooling trade winds provide a (relative) respite from the heat.

migrant birds, including ducks and white egrets. You'll see more birds in winter than in summer.

For your final look at West Bay, double back along Conch Point Road, heading west. When you reach the junction with Mount Pleasant Road, take Mount Pleasant Road south to the junction with Batabano Road. Turn left on Batabano Road and take it east to the settlement at:

7 Batabano

At Morgan's Harbour Marina, on the North Sound in the little backwater of Batabano, fishermen tie up their catch of the day, much to the delight of photographers. You can often buy fresh lobster, fish, and conch here. A large barrier reef protects the sound on three sides, and is a mecca for diving and sport fishing.

To head back to George Town or Seven Mile Beach, drive west along Batabano Road until you come to the junction with Willie Farrington Drive. Take this drive south to the junction with North West Point Road and turn onto North West Point Road. This road will carry you south along Seven Mile Beach and eventually back into George Town.

ORGANIZED TOURS

Since getting around Grand Cayman can be difficult, even if you have a car, many visitors opt for an organized tour. These tours are

💬 THE PIRATES OF THE caribbean

Have you heard of the Teach the Rover
And his knavery on the Main,
How of gold he was a lover,
How he loved all ill-got gain?

Arguably, the most notorious temporary resident of Grand Cayman was the notorious Edward Teach, more famously known as "Blackbeard" (1680–1718). The archetypal icon of all Caribbean pirates, he sailed his vessel, *Queen Anne's Revenge,* to loot and plunder.

He wore a big feathered tricorn and carried multiple pistols, knives, and swords. To intimidate his enemies, he placed lit matches into his enormous black beard. His beard was twisted into Rastafarian-style locks. He was said to have had 14 so-called wives, and he often buried his treasure. He would take a lone sailor with him on a small boat and return alone. The sailor's corpse was placed atop the chest of gold to discourage excavation.

Legend has it that Blackbeard shot and lamed Israel Hands on Grand Cayman in an attempt to show how fierce he could be if opposed. Crippled for life, Hands was immortalized as the blind Pew in Robert Louis Stevenson's *Treasure Island.*

Blackbeard met with a bloody demise in a duel off the Carolina coast. He was said to have suffered 25 wounds, five of them by gunshot, before finally collapsing and dying. Blackbeard's ghastly head ended up dangling from the bowsprit end of the conquering ship captained by Lt. Robert Maynard.

The death of this particular pirate more or less ended piracy along the American coast.

especially helpful if you want to see more than just the standard sights.

Many visitors prefer a private taxi tour that includes such destinations as the **Cayman Turtle Farm** (p. 122) or **Queen Elizabeth II Botanic Park** (p. 125). One to four people can create their own tour at a cost of CI$45 for one to three persons or CI$60 for four passengers. Call **Cayman Cab Team** (*℃* **345/926-8294**) or **Holiday Taxi** (*℃* **345/945-4491**) for these options.

Tropicana Tours (*℃* **345/949-0944;** www.tropicana-tours. com) is the original tour operator on Grand Cayman. Its best offering is a 6½-hour sightseeing tour of the island, which costs US$75 for adults and US$53 for kids 12 and under. On this tour, you'll visit George Town, points along Seven Mile Beach, **Pedro St. James National Historic Site** (p. 124), the East End, and the blowholes. If you'd like to spend less time touring, a 2½-hour sightseeing tour of the island's highlights, including the Cayman Turtle Farm and George Town, costs US$31 for adults and US$22 for children 12 and under.

Janet and Geddes Hislop are the chief promoters of eco-tourism on the island, operating **Silver Thatch Excursions** (*℃* **345/945-6588;** www.earthfoot.org). They provide the best tours of Mastic Trail, costing around US$50 per person. Early-morning birdwatching trips can also be arranged.

SHOPPING ON GRAND CAYMAN

S hopping in the Cayman Islands has improved drastically because of all the new business generated by cruise ship arrivals. Although the Cayman Islands are definitely not a shopping destination in the league of St. Thomas and St. Maarten, they do offer a vast array of merchandise, most of it imported. Because there's no sales tax, you'll find duty-free shopping galore, ranging from jewelry and toys to coral and rum cakes.

THE SHOPPING SCENE

You can get good deals here on island-made art, crafts, and other products. Many local souvenirs tend to be a bit cheesy, but some handicrafts are artistic statements in their own right and have more lasting value. Jewelry fashioned from caymanite, a hard, marble-like stone harvested in the cliffs of Cayman Brac, is especially popular. In recent years, local art has made increasing strides, finding a ready market among the constantly arriving cruise ship passengers and expat villa owners who want to brighten up their surroundings.

Many products, including jewelry, are fashioned from black coral. Eco-sensitive visitors urge other travelers not to purchase these products. Much of the black coral comes from Central American countries such as Honduras and Belize. The Cayman Islands themselves have strong marine laws to protect their reefs, but countries to the south often do not, and the coral reefs can be seriously harmed or damaged when harvested. Since black coral is known to grow at a rate of only 7.6cm (3 in.) per decade, it qualifies as an endangered species.

Because the Cayman Islands are under the rule of Great Britain, you can sometimes get good deals on British imports. You'll find an array of top-quality jewelry, some of it comparable in quality to jewelry in the stores of London, Paris, and New York.

Grand Cayman, especially around George Town, abounds with imported luxury items. For example, you might find French and American perfumes; Spanish, French, and Swedish crystal; Swiss watches; premium liquor; Japanese cameras; and English china. However, the prices for some of these items are often on par with what you might find in your hometown. Know the average cost of a desired item before you head to the Caymans, so you'll know whether or not you're getting a bargain. Some of the best deals we've discovered have been on native crafts, watches, jewelry, rum, designer sunglasses and clothing, art, cameras, crystal, and cosmetics. Cuban products such as cigars are sold, but you can't bring them back into the United States. The carefully packaged Cayman rum cake is the most popular purchase.

U.S. citizens (including children) can return with up to US$1,000 worth of goods duty-free. Since the amounts are collective, a family of three has a duty-free allowance of US$3,000. No duty is imposed on handicrafts, art, food (including those famous Cayman rum cakes), or books.

Make sure you know which dollar a merchant is quoting in before you step up to the cashier. The U.S. dollar is valued approximately 20% less than the Caymanian dollar.

There is no local sales tax in the Cayman Islands.

Most stores keep regular business hours of 9am to 5 or 6pm Monday to Saturday.

SHOPPING: A TO Z
Art Galleries

Art is very important on the Cayman Islands and local talent is abundant. As you peruse the island's galleries, you might want to remember the names of painters (described below) who define the Cayman Islands as their home and, often, as the source of their inspiration.

Canadian-born, silver-haired, and elegant, **Joanne Sibley** lived for 25 years in Jamaica, and has dwelled for the same length of time on Grand Cayman. She's noted for her luminous portrayals of light on West Indian landscapes, creating canvases that seem to glow. Although her works are for sale at some galleries, she welcomes interested visitors into her studio for private showings if they phone in advance. Contact her at ℂ **345/947-7273** before heading out to see her at 1342 Bodden Town Rd., 3.2km (2 miles) east of Bodden Town, 21km (13 miles) east of George Town.

Charles Long (ℂ **345/917-5741;** www.charleslong.ky) is another well-known Caymanian painter, celebrated for his use of solid, bright colors in paintings that often depict Cayman flora and fauna. He is happy to give tours of his studio to art lovers who call in advance. His home is at 114 West Lane, off Pedro Castle Road, in the hamlet of Savannah, about a 15-minute drive southeast of George Town.

Al Ebanks Studio (ℂ **345/945-8278**) gives you a chance to visit the atelier and studio of this talented artist, Luelan Bodden. His studio is a flamboyant display of paintings, sculpture, and mosaics in a riot of color and form. He's a master of painting everything from an island iguana, to carnival time when locals don their most colorful apparel. He can brilliantly depict the plants and flowers that make the Caymans so vivid. Call for an appointment to visit his studio at 186B Shedden Rd., George Town.

Cathy Church's Underwater Photo Centre & Gallery
Exploding with underwater images, this is the best place to visit for stunning photos of the underwater world surrounding the Cayman Islands. The collection ranges from spectacular color shots to black-and-white photographs. Cathy is as intriguing as her pictures, especially when she speaks of her underwater adventures across the globe. You can also purchase an autographed copy of her coffee-table book of photos. She will also arrange for you to have instruction in underwater photography, or perhaps a trip on her own dive boat, which contains special graphic-oriented computers. 390 S. Church St., George Town. ℂ **345/949-7415.** www.cathychurch.com.

Kennedy Gallery ★ This art gallery—the most important, visible, and influential in the Cayman Islands—showcases works by each of the nation's recognized artists, including local masters Joanne Sibley and Charles Long. Works by less widely recognized artists are also featured. Our favorite among these lesser-known artists is Petrina Wright, who once taught art in a high school on Cayman Brac, and whose works seem to incorporate reggae, soca, Caymanian nationalism, racial pride, sexual liberation, and adolescent trauma, all at the same time. In the artwork here, expect to find an excellent selection of seascapes and tropical landscapes, bronze castings of Caymanian sea turtles by artists in California,

Caymanian Artist Miss Lassie

No retrospective of Caymanian art would be complete without the artfully naive paintings of **Gladwyn Bush,** known to most of Grand Cayman by her affectionate nickname, **Miss Lassie.** Born on Grand Cayman in 1914, she left the Cayman Islands only once in her life: to attend an exhibition of her works in Curaçao. Displayed in galleries as far away as Baltimore and Paris, her paintings depict, among other subjects, God talking with Elijah and Nicodemus chatting with Jesus. She once described her paintings as visions that came to her "in the state between sleeping and awakening." She died in 2003, at age 89, and since then her works have become increasingly difficult to find in the public domain. Count yourself lucky if you see her work on display in a local gallery, but don't count on buying one. Miss Lassie's paintings would sell for upward of CI$8,000—when she was alive.

and absolutely brilliant sculptures by emerging artists in nearby Cuba. Works of art range from CI$8 to CI$50,000. Members of the Hill family, who are extremely articulate spokespersons for the art scene on Grand Cayman, manage this fine gallery. West Shore Center, West Bay Rd., Seven Mile Beach. ✆ **345/949-8077.** www. kennedygallerycayman.com.

Beachwear

Brazilian Point Indulge fashion-plate tendencies at this stylish and whimsical shop where all the garments (for women only) are imported from Brazil. Each "minimalist" item here evokes a beach-front venue in Bahia. Bikinis average around CI$35. There's also an inventory of belts, bags, shoes, and flesh-revealing "flirtware." In the Queen's Court Shopping Center, West Bay Rd., Seven Mile Beach. ✆ **345/945-5679.**

Latitude 19 Set close to the cruise ship piers in downtown George Town, this shop sells everything you'll need for a sun-flooded day on the beach. All kinds of beachwear, including sun-glasses, beach batiks, straw hats, sandals, sunblock, and suntan lotion are for sale. There's also a collection of undergarments with "Cayman Islands" emblazoned on the seat. N. Church St., George Town. ✆ **345/946-6178.**

Books

The Book Nook Here, at one of the largest bookstores on Grand Cayman, you'll find novels, travel guides, cookbooks, diet

---

Lighting Up a Stogie for the Castro Brothers

Although you can buy Cuban cigars in the Cayman Islands, it is still illegal to bring them (or any Cuban products) back to the United States. If you want to enjoy one of these prized stogies, you'll have to smoke it on the islands.

---

books, and dictionaries. You can also peruse the rambling, somewhat disorganized inventory of souvenirs, children's toys, porcelain, and gift items. A smaller branch of this outfit is in the Anchorage Shopping Centre, on Harbour Drive, directly opposite the cruise ship terminal (🕻 **345/949-7392**). In the Galleria Plaza Shopping Centre, West Bay Rd., Seven Mile Beach. 🕻 **345/945-4686.**

Cameras

Cayman Camera Ltd.   This top outlet for all of your photographic needs is also the best shop at which to purchase duty-free cameras and binoculars. In addition to its regular cameras, compacts, and SLRs, the store also sells video cameras and offers 1-hour processing. It can also make prints and enlargements from negatives, slides, prints, and digital sources, and it is the local distributor for Fuji and Hasselblad. 32 S. Goring Ave., George Town. 🕻 **345/ 949-8359.** www.caymancamera.com.

Cuban Products

La Casa del Habano   Tucked into an inner courtyard and accessible via a narrow alleyway from the busy sidewalk outside, this is a small-scale but charming emporium of Cuban cigars, Cuban coffees, and Cuban art objects. (U.S. travelers should be aware that they will not be allowed to bring Cuban products back to the States.) In the Cayside Building, Shedden Rd., at the corner of N. Church St., George Town. 🕻 **345/946-4666.**

Diving/Snorkeling Gear

Divers World/Aqua-Fit/The Beach Boutique   If you're even remotely interested in watersports, this trio of shops—each owned by the same entrepreneur and within the same shopping center—has virtually everything you'd need to play on or below the surface of the sea. The largest and most impressive of the stores is **Divers World Ltd. of Cayman** (🕻 **345/949-8128**), which has probably the Caribbean's largest collection of diving and snorkeling equipment. Expect an impressive inventory of underwater digital cameras, film, watches, scuba-tank regulators, swim masks and fins, wetsuits, weight belts, lighting devices, and scooters that propel scuba enthusiasts either above or beneath the surface of the water. If you're in the market for sports clothes, bathing suits, gift items, protective wading shoes, sunglasses, suntan oil, candles shaped like shells, or rash guards (a Lycra or latex shirt that protects you from being stung or scraped by a coral reef), head for the **Beach Boutique** (© **345/949-8128**), immediately next door. In the Seven Mile Shopping Centre (The Yellow Plaza), West Bay Rd., George Town.

Fashion

Arabus Clothiers ★   Some of the mostly European clothing here costs less than it would in the U.S., partly because of the duty-free status of natural fibers such as cashmere, silk, linen, and wool in the Cayman Islands. You may find a few over-the-top items, such as slinky, scarlet women's evening dresses, complementing merchandise that is for the most part restrained, subdued, and in very good taste. 8 Fort St., George Town. © **345/949-4620.**

Food

Foster's Food Fair   If you're renting a private condo or villa and want to do light cooking "at home," Foster's is the best pit stop. Just off Seven Mile Beach, it's a huge emporium of food products. This is the most visible of five branches scattered widely across Grand Cayman Island. Since nearly everything has to be imported, food is much more expensive in the Caymans than it is likely to be in your hometown. Expect to be shocked by the bill. Strand Shopping Centre, West Bay Rd., George Town. © **345/945-4748.** www.fosters-iga.com.

Gifts & Souvenirs

Also see the "Handicrafts" and "Jewelry" sections below for other great gift and souvenir ideas.

Beyond the Horizon   This emporium—loaded with excellent Asian handicrafts—is one of the most exotic gift shops on Grand Cayman. Tara Parker operates the store and travels twice a year to Indonesia, India, and Southeast Asia to find the tables, armoires, Indian temple drawings, jewelry, and textiles that transform her shop into something akin to a bazaar. Expect depictions of Buddha and the Hindu gods, wrought iron in a style known throughout India as the *jali* school, and furniture carved from Asian hardwoods. In the Galleria Plaza Shopping Centre, West Bay Rd., Seven Mile Beach. © **345/946-1498.** www.bthcayman.com.

Harley-Davidson of Grand Cayman   At this official outlet of the motorcycle and lifestyle purveyor, expect commemorative T-shirts, gift items, and the kind of clothing that can protect you from windburn during your real or imagined roadfest with the Hell's Angels. In the words of the staff, they sell "the yada yada" (souvenirs), but no actual motorcycles. In the Aquaworld Mall, N. Church St., George Town. ✆ **345/949-4464.** www.harley-davidson.com.

Pure Art   This is the most imaginative and innovative gift shop in the Cayman Islands. Located within an unpretentious and low-slung wood-frame house about a mile south of George Town proper, it has reached its present level of creativity under the stewardship of Debbie Chase, a U.S.-born artist. She has friendly relations with craftspeople throughout the Cayman Islands, which has resulted in a treasure-trove of gift items that are a lot more interesting than what's available at many nearby competitors. Expect a densely packed space loaded with paintings, artifacts, books, and clever handcrafted items from the Caymans, Cuba, Jamaica, Key West, and Central America. The common link between all the items offered here is good taste, good humor, and an appreciation for detail-intensive labor. The collection of island-inspired jewelry is particularly comprehensive. 5 S. Church St. at Denham-Thompson Way, George Town. ✆ **345/949-9133.** www.pureart.ky.

Shellections   Few other shops on Grand Cayman sell seashells in such an imaginative way. Look for boxes covered with seashells, delicate shells accented with gold trim, and—best of all—some of the most artful Christmas decorations we've ever seen, including angels, cherubs, and infants in swaddling clothes, all of them crafted from fish bone, shells, gauze, shiny gilt ribbons, and gilt paint. You'll also find T-shirts, black coral jewelry, and blown-glass paperweights. This is the largest of three branches of this store. The other two are found at the Waterfront Center and across from the Bayshore Mall. Harbour St. at the corner of Shedden Rd., George Town. ✆ **345/946-4590.**

Handicrafts

For more handicrafts, see also **Beyond the Horizon, Pure Art,** and **Shellections** under "Gifts & Souvenirs," above; and **Mitzi's Fine Jewelry** under "Jewelry," below.

Guy Harvey's Gallery & Shoppe ★★   For the serious shopper, this is one of the best bets in George Town. Guy, of course, is among the world's most celebrated biologists, and a fish and marine conservationist. He is also a marine-animal artist, and his best works are on sale here. This outlet contains the biggest array of Guy's merchandise ever assembled under one roof. You can purchase original art or limited-edition prints, as well as nautical clothing for both men and women and the usual T-shirts, gifts, and souvenirs. Other items include logo tableware, sculpture, tile art, and photographs taken on his fascinating research trips. After a shopping spree, you can grab a bite next door at Guy Harvey's Island Grill. 49 S. Church St., George Town. ✆ **345/943-4891.** www.guy harveyinc.com.

Pirate's Grotto Another outlet for Cayman souvenirs is this very touristy shop on the lower level of the Landmark Shopping Center. Check carefully or you might find an island souvenir made in Asia. The shop also sells Cuban cigars, but you must smoke them on-island, as they are as of press time still banned in the United States. Duty-free liquor is also sold at this outlet. Harbour Dr., George Town. ✆ **345/945-0244.**

Jewelry

Bernard K. Passman Gallery ★★★ At two locations in George Town, this shop is a rare treasure, selling stunning black coral creations, including jewelry, of internationally acclaimed sculptor Bernard K. Passman. Connoisseurs of unusual fine jewelry and unique objets d'art are drawn to these outlets. Passman produced the Cayman Islands' wedding gift to Prince Charles and Lady Diana: a 97-piece cutlery set of sterling silver with black coral handles. Another commission for the Cayman Islands was the creation of a black coral horse and corgi dogs for Queen Elizabeth and Prince Philip. Signed, limited-edition pieces are excellent investments.

Bernard K. Passman accumulated a vast collection of black coral before the Cayman ban went into effect. His shop is very popular, but those offended by the harvesting of coral might want to select items not made from this protected species. Cardinal Plaza Bldg., Cardinal Ave., George Town (✆ **345/949-0123**); Port St., George Town (✆ **345/949-0170**). www.passman.com.

Boutique Cartier ★★ This store is targeted at big spenders and connoisseurs of such timeless pieces as the Trinity ring and the Tank ring and watch, along with classic Cartier watches, including the Tank Française. The La Dona Jewelry and Watch Collection is stunning, bringing a touch of Paris's Place Vendôme to Grand Cayman. You can also buy pens and fashionable leather goods, all highly stylized, along with elegant silk scarves and deluxe perfumes. Cardinal Ave., George Town. ✆ **345/949-7477.**

> ## The Diamonds of the Sea
>
> It is said that even the simplest meal tastes better with just a pinch of Cayman Sea Salt. With this in mind, mother-and-daughter team Monique and Vanessa Polack came up with an idea for a cottage industry. They started harvesting sea salt and using it as a cooking spice. Eventually they began to use these chunky crystals, which they call "diamonds of the sea," to make skin-softening, scented bath salts. Prices range from US$5 to US$30. For information, call *②* **345/943-7258;** www.caymanseasalt.com. These salt products are available at the Cayman Sea Salt Booth at the Craft Market on the waterfront in George Town, at the Ritz-Carlton and Westin hotels, and at various other outlets around the island.

Colombian Emeralds International   Splashy, elegant, and glittery, this is one of the largest jewelry stores on Grand Cayman, almost directly across the street from the cruise ship terminal. As its name implies, a lot of the emphasis here is on colored stones, including emerald and topaz. You'll find a wide selection of diamonds and timepieces as well. Corner of Cardinal Ave. and Harbour Dr., George Town. *②* **345/949-8808.** www.colombianemeralds.com.

Mitzi's Fine Jewelry   This plush, elegant jewelry store and art gallery was established by Mitzi Callan, the most famous and celebrated craftsperson in the Cayman Islands and winner of dozens of local and international art contests. Set just north of the Grand Cayman Beach Suites, on the opposite side of West Bay Road, it's a showcase of work imported by Ms. Callan, including Italian porcelain, Carrera & Carrera sculptures, and work she has designed herself from black coral, gold, platinum, and gemstones. Simple pieces of jewelry begin at around CI$30, ascending to prices as high as CI$50,000. 5 Bay Harbour Centre, West Bay Rd., Seven Mile Beach. *②* **345/945-5014.**

Lingerie

Passions Boutique   The merchandise sold here is similar to the sexy and erotic lingerie marketed by Victoria's Secret. Brand names include Casa Bello, La Perla, and Jezebel. Come here with a credit card, a sense of humor, and a lot of imagination. In the Galleria Plaza, West Bay Rd., Seven Mile Beach. *②* **345/945-5571.**

Perfumes

La Perfumerie I and II   These stores, set directly across the street from one another on Cardinal Avenue, contain the largest selection of perfumes and cosmetics on the island. If you're especially interested in cosmetics and makeup, head for Perfumerie I, the branch on the north side of the street; if perfume is your weakness, head for Perfumerie II, on the avenue's south side. Cardinal Ave., George Town. ☎ **345/949-7477.**

Rum & Liquers

Tortuga Rum Company   Founded in 1984, this company pioneered the first locally labeled rums in the Caymans, developing into the largest retail and duty-free liquor business in the little archipelago. Its most famous brands are Tortuga Gold, Rum Cream, Coffee Liqueur, Orange Rum Liqueur, and the 12-year-old Tortuga Gold Rum. Many people visit to purchase a carefully sealed rum cake, based on a century-old family recipe. The cake is the Cayman's number-one export and souvenir item. Tortuga Rum Ave., Industrial Park, George Town. ☎ **345/949-7701.** www.tortugarumcakes.com.

Shopping Malls

Many visitors, especially cruise ship passengers, don't go to the independent stores, but do one-stop shopping at Grand Cayman's heavily patronized malls. Lying south of the cruise ship docks on Harbour Drive, **Harbour Place** is the newest of them. Stores here range from the chic, such as Natalie Bishop Designer Clothes, to the sophisticated, including the Winery.

In George Town, at Carnival Avenue, stands the long-enduring **Kirk Freeport Plaza,** which carries all types of luxury items ranging from Gucci leather to duty-free china. Lots of designer labels are found here, including Rolex, Patek Philippe, Cartier, TAG Heuer, Omega, Roberto Coin, and Mikimoto. Near the Grand Cayman Beach Suites on West Bay Road is **Galleria Plaza,** opening onto Seven Mile Beach. Outlets here sell books, liquor, mobile phones, lingerie, sports equipment, and even cosmetics. Also opening onto Seven Mile Beach, **West Shore Shopping Centre** is known for its artwork and casual sports clothing. The Centre also has a pharmacy, candle shop, and diving equipment store. Finally, consider **Queen's Court Shopping Centre,** another mall opening onto Seven Mile Beach. It boasts an eclectic collection of shops that sell everything from T-shirts with your favorite dogs printed on them to beauty products. Handicrafts and gifts are also sold at outlets here.

Stamps

For the philatelist in the family, Grand Cayman's main post office in George Town, at Edward Street and Cardinal Avenue (☎ **345/ 949-2474**), sells the Cayman Islands' beautiful stamps at the on-site philatelic bureau, open Monday to Friday 8:30am to 5:30pm and Saturday 8:30am to 1pm.

Artifacts Ltd.   This is the premier outlet for some of the rare stamps issued by the Caymanian government. In U.S. coinage, stamps range in price from about US20¢ to US$900, and the inventory includes the rare War Tax Stamp issued during World War I. Other items for sale include antique Dutch and Spanish coins unearthed from shipwrecks, enameled boxes, and antique prints and maps. Harbour Dr. (across from the cruise ship dock), George Town. ✆ **345/949-2442.** www.artifacts.com.ky.

Toys

Hobbies and Books   This store sells toys "for all ages." The range of merchandise covers everything from the latest electronic toys to traditional board games. Special children's events are presented on Saturdays. Piccadilly Centre, George Town. ✆ **345/949-0707.**

GRAND CAYMAN AFTER DARK

A "full" day on Grand Cayman generally means spending most of your time on Seven Mile Beach, perhaps doing a little shopping, and then sipping sunset drinks, followed by a long, leisurely dinner. Yet, lately, the choice of after-dark diversions has been slowly but steadily growing. Weekends are sacred in the Cayman Islands, and the locals party hard; relaxation is taken very seriously. Of course, Grand Cayman hardly rivals Puerto Rico or Aruba for nightlife supremacy in the Caribbean, and unlike those two other islands, there's no gambling in the Caymans. The party-till-dawn crowd should travel elsewhere, since most venues are shut tight by 1am, and liquor licensing laws are strict in the Cayman Islands.

Often, some of the best bars on the island are attached to restaurants, so you can dine, drink, and party all in the same place.

The live-entertainment scene changes on a nightly basis. One club might be jumping with a live band one night, and then be calm and devoid of live entertainment the following evening. Someone at your hotel's reception desk can usually tell you what the hot spots are on any given evening. Otherwise, grab a copy of the **Caymanian Compass** (www.caycompass.com), available at most hotels, which runs a comprehensive list on Fridays of entertainment choices for the weekend. If you want to see where the locals go, don't dismiss some of our more offbeat and low-key recommendations, including **Antica Gelateria** (p. 159).

CLUBS

Club Jet Opposite the Marriott Resort is a club that's hot every night of the week. The clientele is young and the parties get wild. If you want a more relaxed atmosphere, call ahead and try to reserve a private VIP lounge. One lounge is quieter than the rest; request it specifically if you plan to have in-depth conversations. The state-of-the-art lighting and sound systems make this club a perfect place for avid clubgoers visiting the island. The disco ball gives the dance floor a Studio 54 look, but make no mistake, you won't see anyone doing the Hustle here.

Monday is all-you-can-drink night, and the night when all your favorite top-40 hits are sure to be played. Women drink for CI$15, and men pay CI$25. If hip-hop is your thing, go to Tuesday night's Strictly Hip Hop Party. Wednesday features local musicians and is by far the most popular night. Visitors and locals come in herds to hear DJs Keith Tibbetts and Linbern Eden, who started their group, Coalition, in 1995. If you like Latin music, check out Thursday's Caliente Night, which is also especially popular for its CI$3.50 vodka–Red Bulls served all night. DJ Jeremie Voillot, aka Deliverance, is a young Canadian DJ who's been spinning for more than 5 years and is a Cayman favorite. Crowd requests are taken on Friday night, and Saturday is a mixed night with dance hits from the 1970s to today. The club is open Monday to Friday from 10pm to 3am, and Saturday and Sunday 8pm to midnight. Seven Mile Beach. ✆ 345/946-6398. www.jet.ky. Cover CI$5–CI$10.

O Bar In a two-story shopping plaza off West Bay Road, this nightclub is located immediately adjacent to the Attic Billiard Lounge (p. 158). It's a large, glossy, terra-cotta-and-black space with an industrial-looking steel staircase that leads to a hideaway lounge. There's been a concerted effort here to appeal to the island's hip, urbanized, and trend-conscious yuppies, with DJs imported from faraway New York, and a focus on bringing in cutting-edge music. Look for lots of circle motifs in the decor (hence the name "O Bar"). Beer costs around CI$5 a mug, and cocktails go for CI$7 each. The club is open Monday to Friday from 11:30am to 1am, Saturday and Sunday 11am to midnight. In the Queen's Court Plaza, West Bay Rd. ✆ **345/943-6227.** www.obar.ky. Cover CI$5.

Royal Palms Beach Club Opening onto Seven Mile Beach, this is one of the premier live-music venues for islanders and visitors. The bar, open to the trade winds, is a great place to enjoy dancing in the moonlight. We recommend the on-site restaurant, the **Reef Grill** (p. 90), but many patrons choose to dine elsewhere before coming here for the rest of their evening out. On Thursday, Friday, and Saturday nights, live bands play calypso, light reggae, salsa, and merengue, among other music styles. The club caters to a wide age group, from those in their 20s and 30s to those over 50. The bar opens daily at 9am and stays open until 11pm, though the action doesn't get underway until 8:30pm. The club closes as late as 1am on Friday and Saturday and at 10pm throughout the week. West Bay Rd. ✆ **345/945-6358.** No cover.

BAR/RESTAURANT COMBOS

Aqua Beach Restaurant & Bar   Set across the road from the beach in a funky "beer, babes, and sports" venue, AquaBeach places high emphasis on the sporting events broadcast on its big-screen TVs, and on two-for-ones (margaritas, beers, rum punches), which come and go as quickly as your post-binge headaches. DJs spin on Fridays; live bands raise a ruckus on Saturdays. The restaurant specializes in burgers and steaks (p. 92). The kitchen is open daily from 11am to 11pm, and the bar closes at 1am Monday to Friday, and at midnight Saturday and Sunday. 426 West Bay Rd., Seven Mile Beach. ✆ **345/949-8498.**

Coconut Joe's Beach Bar & Grill   Something's always going on at this little hot spot. Located across from the Comfort Suites, this used to be a run-down and modest private house on the "wrong" side of the road. The young and hip staff comes from all over the world, including Italy, Australia, the U.S., and various parts of Canada. Some crazy event is always being planned. Past soirees include boat cruises, bikini parties, and the annual St. Patrick's Day party. The bartender will mix you almost any drink you can think of and the cocktails are reasonably priced. Try a "beergarita," a Corona and margarita hybrid. Main courses range from CI$8 to CI$28, and include juicy burgers and chicken, beef, and shrimp rice bowls. Coconut Joe's is open Monday to Saturday, the grill from 6:30am to 1am, and the beach bar from 10am to 1am. 362 West Bay Rd., Seven Mile Beach. ✆ **345/943-JOES** (5637).

Kaibo Beach Bar & Grill   This fun, relaxed, hip, counterculture spot—collectively called "the Kaibo Yacht Club"—contains both a bar and a special dining area (p. 88). Far from the maddening crowd of tourists and touristy infrastructure closer to George Town, it's perched on the island's distant corner, and the raffish beach-level bar is a major stop on the Grand Cayman nightlife circuit. Clients are fun and free-spirited. In many cases, customers are American and Canadian expats and visitors, who mingle gracefully with local Caymanians and boat owners. In the downstairs bar, you can enjoy a menu of sandwiches, burgers, and salads.

Drinks of choice, served in copious quantities throughout the day and evening, include Mudslides, Bloody Caesars, and Sex on the Beach, priced between CI$5.50 and CI$10 each. The entire place is fun, romantic, and appealingly permissive. The bar and grill are open daily from 11am to 11pm. In the Kaibo Yacht Club, 858 Water Bay Rd., North Side. ✆ 345/947-9975. www.kaibo.ky.

Morgan's Harbour Marina   Thanks to the charm of its Austrian-born owner, Richard Schweiger, this bar enjoys a reputation for mixing millionaires from New York with local roustabouts and marina crew members. Shoehorned between gas pumps at the nearby marina and stocks of provisions for outfitting boats, there's a battered bar area serving stiff drinks, fresh lobster, and platters of burgers, salads, and steaks priced at CI$19 to CI$32. It's open daily from 7am to 1am. Morgan's Harbour. ✆ 345/949-3948.

BARS

Bamboo Lounge   Few other bars in Grand Cayman have as aggressively (and successfully) tapped into a market of young, attractive, trend-conscious, and upwardly mobile singles as this one. Be prepared to deal with local hipsters and/or hipster wannabes here, along with a strong dose of food-and-beverage marketing hype. Also expect to spend more than you would at an everyday pub.

Amid tones of red, black, and bamboo, you'll find a bustling, intimate bar area on one side, a state-of-the-art sushi kitchen on the other, and a stylishly minimalist lounge with tables at the top of a short flight of steps. Dining takes place in an ultramodern, Asian-influenced setting with full-grained wood detailing. A long list of light dishes—including sushi, sashimi, and artfully prepared appetizers—can be combined to make a full meal. Live jazz is presented every Tuesday night beginning around 8pm. The ambience is fun and flirtatious.

Drinks run the gamut from the standard and conventional to the "students-on-spring-break-getting-bombed" variety. A Wiki Waki Woo is an example of the latter. According to the menu, its blend of vodka, tequila, rum, three kinds of sweet liqueurs, and two kinds of fruit juice is guaranteed "to make you crazy." Another spring-break-style drink is the Samurai Sunset, made from raspberry-flavored sake, vodka, and peach schnapps. A list of martinis reveals headache-inducing combinations of ingredients with names that you might find a bit corny. The bar and restaurant are open Monday to Friday from 5:30pm to 1am and Saturday 5:30pm to midnight. On the ground floor of the Grand Cayman Beach Suites (p. 59). ✆ 345/947-8744. www.grand-cayman-beach-suites.com.

My Bar ★ 🎁   Located on the premises of the **Sunset House** (p. 67), this is one of Grand Cayman's most dramatically designed bars. Set on a smooth cement platform near the coastline, it's about 1.2km (¾ mile) south of George Town. Because its two predecessors were swept away by hurricanes, its designers sank its foundations deep into the bedrock and capped it with the highest and most elaborate Polynesian-style thatched roof on Grand Cayman (it contains an estimated 36,000 palm fronds). Come here for a grandly proportioned and very relaxing indoor-outdoor venue. Many local residents, including lots of Caymanian lawyers, have adopted this bar as their regular hangout and engage in spirited games of dominoes that are observed intently by many of the bar's patrons. My Bar is especially busy on Friday nights, when the energy level is high. It's open Monday to Friday from 10am to 1am, Saturday 10am to midnight, and Sunday 11:30am to midnight. At the Sunset House Hotel, 390 S. Church St., George Town. ℂ **345/949-7111.** www. sunsethouse.com.

PUBS

Fidel Murphy's ★   This is the unofficial Irish headquarters of Grand Cayman. Large gatherings of drinkers avidly follow the pub's live broadcasts of Gaelic soccer, rugby, and hurling matches. The pub offers Irish wit, charm, and nostalgia with a Caribbean twist, as the owners tried to convey by adding "Fidel" to the name of the pub.

The place originated in 1999 when the mostly Irish staff of a Cuban restaurant (La Habana) called in a team of architectural designers from the Guinness brewery in Ireland. Within a few months, the Guinness team had built and shipped, from Dublin, a dark-paneled, prefabricated, late-Victorian pub, complete with brass trim and ornate railings. The place is so authentic that after about an hour and a few drinks, even the Spanish-language speakers seem to develop a brogue. Expect a winning combination of bar and dining space. Seven kinds of beer, plus cider, are on tap, and Irish breakfasts (bacon, sausage, tomato, black-and-white pudding, baked beans, and two fried eggs) are available at all hours. Other menu items include shepherd's pie, steak and Guinness pie, grilled lamb cutlets, shrimp and chips, and such island food as Fidel's chicken curry and Cuban-style pork tenderloin. An Irish breakfast costs CI$11; sandwiches and salads range from CI$9.50 to CI$12. Main-course platters range from CI$10 to CI$17. The bar is open Monday to Friday from 10am to 1am, Saturday and Sunday 7am to midnight. The kitchen closes at 11pm. In the Queens Court Shopping Plaza. ℂ **345/949-5189.**

Lone Star Bar & Grill You can enjoy juicy burgers in the dining room or head for the bar in back at this transplanted corner of the Texas Panhandle. Here, beneath murals of Lone Star beauties, you can sip lime or strawberry margaritas and watch several sports events simultaneously on 14 TV screens. Monday and Thursday are fajita nights, all-you-can-eat affairs, at CI$13, and Tuesday is all-you-can-eat spicy tacos, for CI$10; Wednesday is all-you-can-eat surf and turf, at CI$27. The bar and grill are open Monday to Friday from 11am to 1am, Saturday and Sunday 11am to midnight. West Bay Rd. ✆ **345/945-5175.**

Rackham's Waterfront ★ Because of the hip, hospitable, and well-informed locals who congregate within its appealingly casual premises, Rackham's is the first pub we visit every time we come to Grand Cayman. The pub is set on an open-air pier jutting seaward, just south of the center of George Town, and is protected from the sun and rain by an overhanging roof. As you gaze seaward from your perch here, notice the schools of tarpon swimming beneath the pier. The pub was named after "Calico Jack" Rackham, an 18th-century pirate who seemed to delight in terrorizing the shipping lanes offshore.

The friendly local crowd at Rackham's includes paralegals, financiers, and office workers from throughout Canada, Britain, and the U.S.; about a half-dozen watersports professionals; and a large crowd of West Indian locals. Come here for a glimpse of who's living and working on Grand Cayman these days. Everyone seems to get along swimmingly well, thanks in part to the party-colored cocktails served. Shots of Jack Daniel's cost CI$5 each, and a head-spinning version of Cayman Islands lemonade (vodka, peach schnapps, triple sec, cranberry juice, and whiskey sour mix) goes for CI$6. American and international fare is served at the restaurant, including burgers, fries, conch salad, and filet of beef with french fries. Salads and sandwiches cost CI$9 to CI$12, with main courses priced from CI$13 to CI$28. It's open Monday to Friday from 10am to midnight, Saturday and Sunday 11am to 11pm. N. Church St. ✆ **345/945-3860.**

Wreck Bar & Grill One of our favorite watering holes is at Rum Point, which can be reached by boat. Divers and snorkelers, some arriving with stingray "hickeys," join expats and occasional cruise ship passengers to form a varied age group, and all appreciate the charms of this laid-back joint. It's the latest reincarnation of an old thatched bar that stood here in the 1950s, during which time a bartender dubbed "Old Judd" is said to have invented the world's first frozen Mudslide. Sunday is the most popular time to visit, when locals arrive in their private boats. In addition to two-fisted drinks, enjoy West Indian food, ranging from conch (fritters or chowder) to jerk-pork sandwiches and juicy burgers. You can eat outside at a picnic table under a casuarina tree. The bartender's special is the Attlee Mudslide. Saturday afternoons from 2 to 5pm is also a big time here, with a barbecue and live entertainment right on the beach. The bar and grill is open daily from 10am to 5pm. Rum Point. ℭ **345/947-9412.**

POOL HALL BARS

The Attic Billiard Lounge   On the upper floor of a building in a shopping center off West Bay Road, this pool hall attracts a higher percentage of visitors than the larger, noisier, more raucous, and admittedly more interesting **Corner Pocket Pool Hall** (see below). Here at the Attic, you'll pay a fee of CI$13 per hour for use of one of eight pool tables or one snooker table. Old Dutch beer (brewed locally and priced at CI$3 per pint) is the drink of choice for many of the players here, most of whom wouldn't dream of congregating until after 8 or 9pm. If you're hungry, burgers and sandwiches can be prepared in the tiny kitchen for CI$5 to CI$11. The lounge is open Monday to Friday from 5pm to 1am, Saturday and Sunday 1pm to midnight. In the Queen's Court Plaza, West Bay Rd. ℭ **345/949-7665.**

Corner Pocket Pool Hall ★   Locals crowd this trendy pool hall in Grand Cayman to drink, flirt, gossip, and, in many cases, actually play some intense games of pool. It lies on the second floor of an industrial-looking, all-concrete building in a commercial zone about 2.4km (1½ miles) north of the center of George Town. If you can handle the transition from the glittery tourist-oriented world of West Bay Road to the dark, permissive, and distinctly insider atmosphere here, this venue can be a whole lot of fun—we prefer it over the Attic Billiard Lounge. There is a very real possibility that you'll be invited to join some off-the-record wagers (we don't advise this unless you really know what you're doing). You pay CI$6 per half-hour for a pool table, regardless of how many people are playing. With only six pool tables, you will most likely put your name on the waiting list. Have a drink and relax in the meantime. Besides pool, you'll also find a steady diet of either country-western or rap music, friendly dart competitions, and welcoming patrons and staff. Corner Pocket Pool Hall is open Monday to Thursday from 4pm to 1am, Friday 3pm to 1am, and Saturday and Sunday 4pm to midnight. 139 Allister Towers, N. Sound Rd., George Town. ℭ **345/946-8080.**

OTHER DIVERSIONS

Antica Gelateria   The variety of ice cream flavors sold here surpasses the selection at any other outlet in the Cayman Islands. Tucked away in a shopping center off West Bay Road, just behind the also-recommended Cimboco Caribbean Cafe (p. 98), it was established in 2002 by the Casteldello family, an Italian family who knows a lot about gelato and how a *gelateria* should be run. You'll find about two dozen varieties of ice cream here, including all the flavors you might find in an ice-cream parlor in Rome or Palermo, as well as such Caribbean-influenced selections as mango, pineapple, apricot, almond and rum, and chocolate and rum. Servings cost from CI$3.50 to CI$6, and ice-cream cones go for CI$3.50 each. Takeout ice cream costs CI$6 per pint. It's open Tuesday to Sunday from 2 to 10pm. In the Marquee Shopping Center, Harquail Bypass near West Bay Rd. ☎ **345/946-1400.**

The Harquail Theatre   Mrs. Helen Harquail donated this US$4-million theater in memory of her late husband, F. J. Harquail. Musicals, dramas, and comedies featuring local performers are regularly produced on the Harquail stage. Seating 330, the theater is also the venue for classical concerts, operas, dance performances, art exhibitions, fashion shows, and other events. Tickets usually run between CI$5 and CI$45. The theater also hosts the **International Scuba Diving Hall of Fame** ceremony in early November (p. 20). Harquail Dr. (a bypass heading north from George Town). ☎ **345/949-5477.** www.artscayman.org.

CAYMAN BRAC

A 17th-century Scottish fisherman dubbed this 19km-long (12-mile) island Brac (Gaelic for "bluff"). The Bluff is a towering limestone plateau rising 42m (138 ft.) above the sea, covering the eastern half of Cayman Brac. Caymanians refer to the island simply as Brac, and its 1,400 inhabitants, a hospitable bunch of people, are called Brackers. Pirates occupied the Caymans in the early 18th century, and Edward Teach, the infamous Blackbeard, supposedly spent quite a bit of time on Cayman Brac. The island is about 143km (89 miles) east of Grand Cayman.

More than 170 caves honeycomb the limestone heights of the island. Some of the caves are at the Bluff's foot; others can be reached only by climbing over jagged limestone rock. One of the biggest is Great Cave, which has a number of chambers. Harmless fruit bats cling to the roofs of the caverns.

You won't see many people on the south side of the Bluff, and the only sound is the sea crashing against the lavalike shore. You'll find the island's herons and wild green parrots here. Most Brackers live on the north side, in traditional wooden seaside cottages, some of which were built by the island's first settlers in the 1700s. Looking at the variety of flowers, shrubs, and fruit trees in many of the Brackers' yards, it is clear that many of the islanders have green thumbs. You'll see poinciana trees, bougainvillea, Cayman orchids, croton, hibiscus, aloe, sea grapes, cactuses, and coconut and cabbage palms. Gardeners grow cassava, pumpkins, breadfruit, yams, and sweet potatoes.

There are no actual towns on the island, only settlements—among them Stake Bay (the "capital"), Spot Bay, the Creek, Tibbetts Turn, the Bight, and West End, all of which are clustered by the airport.

Hotels quote their rates in U.S. dollars. Restaurant menus vary in which currency they list, so ask if you're not sure. Most restaurants give you a choice of paying in U.S. or local Caymanian currency.

ESSENTIALS
Visitor Information

The **Cayman Brac Tourist Office,** West End Road, North Side (℃ **345/948-1649**), is open Monday to Friday 8:30am to noon and 1 to 5pm. It's located to the east of the little airport.

Getting There

Cayman Airways (℃ **800/422-9626** in the U.S., or 345/949-8200; www.caymanairways.com) offers seven flights a week to and from Cayman Brac on Boeing 737s. The flights leave from Miami and make a short stop on Grand Cayman.

The cost of a one-way ticket ranges from US$67 to US$106 per person. Note that the larger planes that fly this route—such as the 737s, which have 122 seats—allow twice the luggage allotment per passenger, without payment of the additional surcharge required by the 18-seaters. If you have a lot of luggage, it's wise to book a flight on a larger plane.

Getting Around

For getting around Cayman Brac, you have a choice between taking taxis, renting a bike, renting a car, or relying on your trusty feet. Renting a car is easiest, especially if you don't like getting stuck in the hot sun.

CAR RENTALS   Car rental agencies will meet your incoming flight if you make reservations in advance. You won't find many rental places here, so reserve as far in advance as possible during the winter season.

B & S Motor Ventures, 422 Channel Rd., South Side (℃ **345/948-1646;** www.bandsmv.com), is run by Steve and Nola Bodden, who will supply you with plenty of insider information about Cayman Brac. Cars and jeeps cost US$40 per day. The best deal is their weekly rate, beginning at US$240 for 6 to 7 days. SUVs can be rented for US$46 per day. Off-season rates are generally about 10% lower. They also rent bikes and scooters (see below). You must be at least 25 years old to rent a car.

Four D's Car Rental, Kidco Building, South Side (℃ **345/948-1599**), offers car rentals for US$35 a day and up, and vans for US$45 a day. If you rent for 6 days, the seventh day is free. You must be 21 years old to rent a car.

Essentials

TAXIS   Taxi service on Cayman Brac is slow and not particularly organized, but it is available. Be prepared, however, to wait. Taxis do not always meet incoming planes unless arrangements are made in advance. Most taxi companies will take you on a 2-hour tour for CI$24 per person. All the taxi companies charge the same rates. The first mile costs CI$4; each additional mile costs CI$1.75. Traveling from the airport to one of the resorts or villas on Stake Bay along the north side of the island costs about CI$8 to CI$40 per person, depending on the distance of the resort or villa from the airport.

The major taxi services are **D&M** (☎ **345/948-2307**) and **Elo's Taxi** (☎ **345/948-0220**).

BIKES & SCOOTERS   You can explore almost all of Cayman Brac by bike or scooter, except for the area around the Bluff, which is too rugged. Most roads along the coast are flat and easy to traverse by bike. The main road across the west of Cayman Brac is also a relatively easy cycle route.

Many hotels either lend or rent bikes to guests. If yours doesn't, you can rent both bicycles and scooters from **B & S Motor Ventures** (☎ 345/948-1646; www.bandsmv.com). Scooters here cost US$30 per day or US$180 for 6 to 7 days. Bikes go for US$13 per day or US$75 for a week. If you find that the bike your hotel lends or rents is too simple, you can get a bike with gears and good brakes from B & S. The company will deliver a bike or scooter to you at any location on the island.

[FastFACTS] CAYMAN BRAC

Banks The local branch of **Cayman National Bank** is at 14 West End, Cross Roads (☎ **345/948-1451**). It's open Monday to Thursday 9am to 4pm and Friday 9am to 4:30pm. It has the only **ATM** on the island.

Dentist For dental service, call ☎ **345/948-2618**.

Emergencies The main safety issues here are related to climbing the Bluff. In the event of an accident, the only rescue agency is the fire department. Dial ☎ **911** to reach them.

Hospitals & Clinics The government-run **Faith Hospital** is at Stake Bay (☎ **345/948-2225**). The hospital is open daily 24 hours. For a nonemergency consultation with a doctor, you can visit the hospital daily from 8:30am to 5pm. The **Cayman Brac Clinic** at Tibbetts Square, West End (☎ **345/948-1777**) is open Monday to Friday 8am to noon and 3 to 6pm, and Saturday 9am to noon. For clinic treatment outside opening hours, call ☎ **345/948-2363**.

Fast Facts: Cayman Brac

CAYMAN BRAC

Internet Access You can access the Internet at **Brac Reef Beach Resort,** South Side (📞 **345/948-1323**), which provides Wi-Fi in the lobby daily from 7am to 9pm. Internet access is also available at the post office (see below) for CI$6 per hour.

Pharmacies The hospital and clinic mentioned under "Hospitals & Clinics" have small pharmacies, which generally share the same opening hours as the hospital or clinic.

Post Office The **Cayman Brac Post Office,** West End (📞 **345/948-1422**), is open Monday to Friday from 8:30am to 5pm and Saturday from 9 to 11:30am. There are also branch post offices near Tibbetts Square in Stake Bay, at Watering Place, and at Spot Bay. These are all open Monday to Friday 9 to 11:30am and 1:30 to 3pm.

Water Tap water is distilled seawater and is perfectly safe to drink.

WHERE TO STAY
The Major Resorts

Alexander Hotel ★ This intimate boutique hotel is the first choice for business travelers, and quite serviceable for the vacationer as well. It lies about a 2-minute walk from a pebble-strewn white sandy beach, although there's an on-site swimming pool that most guests prefer. The Alexander is conveniently located next door to a little shopping mall. The well-decorated, very contemporary bedrooms come in a variety of options, ranging from a standard double to a suite with two large bedrooms, a sitting room, and a kitchenette. The well-appointed accommodations evoke a Caribbean summerhouse. A family restaurant, serving three meals a day, is on-site, and occasional live entertainment is offered.

West End Cayman Brac, B.W.I. 📞 **800/381-5094** or 345/948-8222. www.alexanderhotelcayman.com. 29 units. Year-round US$156–US$181 double; US$218 suite. MC, V. **Amenities:** Restaurant; bar; outdoor pool. *In room:* A/C, TV, DVD (in some), MP3 docking station, Wi-Fi (free).

Brac Caribbean Beach Village ★ The largest condo structure on the island offers 16 bright, spacious two-bedroom/two-bathroom or two-bedroom/three-bathroom condos on a white sand beach, along with a pool and a scuba-diving program. Each unit has a full-size refrigerator with an icemaker and a microwave, and 12 units open onto private balconies. A variety of items, including breakfast food, are already stocked in the units upon your arrival, though be warned that you'll be charged for their use. The master bedroom is furnished with a queen-size bed, the guest bedrooms with twin beds. The units are rather simply furnished in a Caribbean tropical motif. The hotel provides some of the best dining on the island, at the **Captain's Table** (p. 169).

Stake Bay (PO Box 4), Cayman Brac, B.W.I. ☏ **866/843-2722** or 345/948-2265. Fax 345/948-1111. www.866thebrac.com. 16 units. Winter US$185 apt for 2, US$245 apt for 4, weekly US$1,100 apt for 2, US$1,600 apt for 4; off season US$139 apt for 2, US$184 apt for 4, weekly US$825 apt for 2, US$1,200 apt for 4. Dive packages from US$888 per person double occupancy, including 7-night stay and 5 days of three 2-tank dives per day. AE, MC, V. **Amenities:** Restaurant; bar; outdoor pool; extensive watersports equipment/rentals. *In room:* A/C, ceiling fans, TV, kitchen.

Brac Reef Beach Resort ★   Located on a sandy plot of land on the south shore 3km (1¾ miles) east of the airport, near some of the best snorkeling in the region, this family-friendly, family-run resort contains motel-style units comfortably furnished with carpeting and ceiling fans. Durable and resilient, it's the most visible hotel on Cayman Brac. Once the location was little more than a maze of sea grapes, a few of whose venerable trunks still rise amid the picnic tables, hammocks, and boardwalks. There are still lots of nature trails surrounding the resort, good for bird-watching. A dive shop is on the premises. Don't expect grandeur or anything approaching urban style or poshness, though: It simply isn't part of the equation here.

PO Box 56, KY2-2001 Cayman Brac, B.W.I. ☏ **800/594-0843** or 727/369-2507 for reservations in the U.S. and Canada, or 345/948-1323. www.bracreef.com. 40 units. Year-round US$145–US$177 double, US$172–US$205 triple. Dive packages available. AE, MC, V. **Amenities:** Restaurant; bar; babysitting; exercise room; Internet facility; Jacuzzi; outdoor pool; tennis court (lit). *In room:* A/C, ceiling fans, TV.

A Guesthouse

Walton's Mango Manor ★★   This personalized, intimate B&B is more richly decorated, more elegant, and more appealing than you might have thought possible in such a remote spot. Originally the home of a sea captain, it was moved to a less exposed location and rebuilt from salvaged materials shortly after the disastrous hurricane of 1932. Set on 1.6 hectares (4 acres) on the island's north shore, within a lush garden, it contains intriguing touches such as a banister salvaged from the mast of a 19th-century schooner. The best accommodations are on the upper floor and have narrow balconies with sea views. There is also a two-bedroom, two-bathroom luxury villa, the perfect getaway for two to four guests. The villa contains a kitchen, washer/dryer, phone, TV, and both air-conditioning and ceiling fans. Your hosts are Brooklyn-born Lynne Walton and her husband, George, a former United States Air Force major who retired to his native Cayman Brac.

Stake Bay (PO Box 56), Cayman Brac, B.W.I. ☏ **888/866-5809,** tel/fax 345/948-0518. www.waltonsmangomanor.com. 6 units. Winter US$120–US$130 double; off season US$105–US$115 double; year-round villa for 1–2 people US$185

Hotels & Restaurants on Cayman Brac

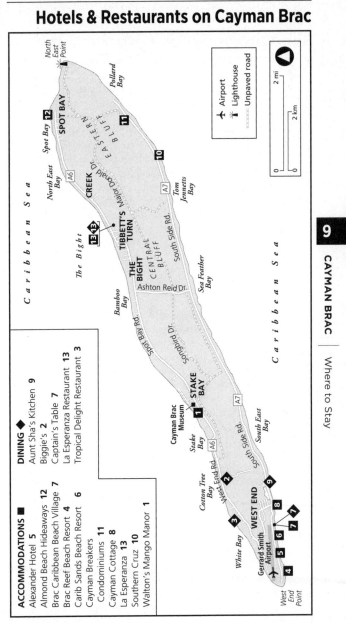

ACCOMMODATIONS ■

Alexander Hotel **5**
Almond Beach Hideaways **12**
Brac Caribbean Beach Village **7**
Brac Reef Beach Resort **4**
Carib Sands Beach Resort **6**
Cayman Breakers
  Condominiums **11**
Cayman Cottage **8**
La Esperanza **13**
Southern Cruz **10**
Walton's Mango Manor **1**

DINING ◆

Aunt Sha's Kitchen **9**
Biggie's **2**
Captain's Table **7**
La Esperanza Restaurant **13**
Tropical Delight Restaurant **3**

Airport ✈
Lighthouse ✴
Unpaved road ⋯⋯⋯

0 ━━ 2 mi
0 ━━ 2 km

Caribbean Sea

North East Point
Pollard Bay
Spot Bay
North East Bay
Tom Jennetts Bay
Sea Feather Bay
The Bight
Bamboo Bay
South East Bay
Stake Bay
Cotton Tree Bay
White Bay
West End Point

SPOT BAY
CREEK
TIBBETT'S TURN
THE BIGHT
CENTRAL BLUFF
EASTERN BLUFF
STAKE BAY
WEST END

Cayman Brac Museum
Gerrard Smith Airport

Major Donald Dr.
South Side Rd.
Ashton Reid Dr.
Songbird Dr.
Spot Bay Rd.
West End Rd.
South Side Rd.

A6
A7
A7
A6

daily, US$1,200 weekly; villa for 3–4 people US$210 daily, US$1,400 weekly. Rates for doubles include full breakfast. MC, V. *In room:* A/C, no phone.

Self-Catering Villas & Apartments

Almond Beach Hideaway ★ 🎁   The scene outside your door could be a picture postcard, with a beachfront of white sand against a backdrop of coconut palms. Think of these villas as get-away-from-it-all hideaways. The free-standing, air-conditioned, two-bedroom villas here offer much tranquillity and privacy. Each has its own patio, private bathrooms, and fully equipped kitchen including a large refrigerator. The master bedroom houses a queen-size bed; the guest bedroom has two twin beds; the living room includes a queen sofa bed. All bed and bathroom linens are supplied, and a member of the staff will meet you at the airport to transport you to the villa. In addition, maid service and a caretaker are on call 24 hours a day. Hammocks, chaise longues, a beach cabana, and a barbecue grill are available.

Spot Bay (PO Box 132), Cayman Brac, B.W.I. ⓒ **503/472-7628.** Fax 503/472-6394. www.almondbeachhideaways.com. 2 units. US$185 double, US$210 triple, US$240 quad; weekly US$1,150 double, US$1,300 triple, US$1,500 quad. Each additional person US$30. Children 8 and under stay free in parent's room. MC, V. **Amenities:** Babysitting. In room: A/C, TV/DVD, kitchen.

Carib Sands Beach Resort ★ ☺   This is one of the island's most modern oceanfront condo resorts. Attractively furnished one-to four-bedroom units all have fully equipped kitchens. The resort often attracts families. The first-class property opens onto one of the most beautiful strands of white sand on Cayman Brac and boasts an on-site dive center. The concrete condos are furnished with Navajo white wicker furniture, often set against dramatic tones of blue, burgundy, or sea green. Rooms have either a garden or ocean view. Rollaway beds can be requested for extra guests (US$25/night; cribs available for US$10/night). A bar and restaurant are a short stroll from the resort.

Stake Bay (PO Box 4), Cayman Brac, B.W.I. ⓒ **204/982-9680** or 345/926-1341. Fax 204/982-9687. www.caribsands.com. 52 units. Year-round US$148 1-bedroom, US$185 2-bedroom, US$220 3-bedroom, US$260 4-bedroom. Children 11 and under stay free in parent's room. AE, MC, V. **Amenities:** Restaurant; bar; babysitting; bikes; outdoor pool; watersports equipment/rentals. *In room:* A/C, TV, CD player, kitchen.

Cayman Breakers Condominiums   This condominium development lies on the secluded southeast end of the island. If you're interested in diving, rock climbing, cave exploring, or other adventure activities, this is the place for you. To help you get started, you'll find a book on Cayman Brac attractions in each unit.

Complimentary use of bikes makes it easier to get to activity spots. Guests also have access to a private shore dive entrance.

The units all have two bedrooms and two bathrooms, a living room, a kitchen, and a utility room complete with a washer and dryer. You can relax in a well-kept courtyard with picnic tables and barbecue grills. The congenial managers, Robert and Nina Banks, live on-site and are more than happy to assist you with any of your needs.

Southeast End, Cayman Brac, B.W.I. ℰ **345/948-1463.** Fax 345/948-1407. www. caymancondosonline.com. 18 units. Year-round US$157–US$172 per night for up to 2 people, US$228 per night for 3–4 people. 7-night minimum stay. MC, V. **Amenities:** Bikes; outdoor pool. *In room:* A/C, TV/DVD, kitchen, Wi-Fi (free).

Cayman Cottage ★ 🎁 If your dream is to retreat to a little West Indian cottage hideaway with a loved one, here's your chance. Seclusion and privacy prevail at this cottage, lying just 23m (75 ft.) from a white sand beach. The fully furnished cottage is on the grounds of the owner's home in the West End, on the south side of the island. The cottage provides 183 sq. m (1,970 sq. ft.) of living space, including a private bedroom, a large living and dining area, a bathroom with a tub/shower combo, a fully equipped kitchen, and a washer/dryer.

South Side, Cayman Brac, B.W.I. ℰ **505/898-6854** in the U.S., or 345/948-1617. Fax 345/948-1350. www.caymancottage.com. 1 unit. Year-round US$130–US$150 for up to 4 people. Children 9 and under stay free in parent's room. No credit cards. *In room:* A/C, TV, kitchen.

La Esperanza ★ 🎁 This modern complex consists of a series of apartment and cottage rentals, with easy access to a private beach on the south side. The complex lies midway along the north shore. Launched in 1986 when it was a small gathering place for four friends and the only spot in the area for people to come and relax in the "cool, cool, cool of the evening," as the popular '50s song goes, the complex grew, but even today is still relatively small and casual. It's better known for its restaurant and bar (p. 169) than for its accommodations.

Each well-furnished and comfortable apartment, decorated in a typical light, breezy West Indian style, consists of two bedrooms with 1½ bathrooms, a full kitchen, and a living/dining room. Each cottage has two or three bedrooms and two bathrooms with showers, plus a full kitchen, a living room, a dining room, and an open-air deck. Under large trees or other open shelters on the grounds, you'll find a lot of extras, including laundry facilities, an outside shower, gas grills, and hammocks. Sometimes the rare blue iguana will stroll onto the grounds looking for a tasty treat (they don't eat people, so don't worry).

Cars can also be rented here for US$40 per day. Free transportation can be arranged between the lodgings and the beach.

Stake Bay (PO Box 216), Cayman Brac, B.W.I. © **345/948-0591.** Fax 345/948-0525. www.laesperanza.net. 11 units. Year-round US$94 double in apt, US$125–US$138 double in cottage. Extra person US$15. AE, MC, V. **Amenities:** Restaurant; bar; babysitting. *In room:* A/C, TV, kitchen.

Southern Cruz Although the setting is a bit bleak—no lush landscaping except for a buffer grove of sea grapes—this is one of the most comfortable small-house rentals on the island. For many visitors, it would make an ideal "second home" in the Caribbean.

The concrete units are decorated in a typical West Indian style, with pastels, whitewashed woods, and tiles. The rentals each have a well-maintained, medium-size private bathroom. The sofa bed in the living room can be converted to receive additional guests. Each of the bedrooms has a king-size bed and a walk-in closet. You can enjoy the ocean view with a cup of coffee in the morning from your private patio, or a cocktail at night from the covered porch. The kitchen is generously equipped with utensils and hardware. There's also a laundry room adjacent to the kitchen, and an outside shower to wash off sand after a day at the beach. This oceanfront house accommodates up to six, making it an ideal space for families, or a small group of friends who can appreciate its casual, laid-back style. Hammocks are strung up on the covered porch for lazy enjoyment of the surroundings. Other features include a barbecue grill and covered parking.

South Side, Cayman Brac, B.W.I. © **877/229-6637** in the U.S. www.mcginley vacationcabins.com/caymanbrac.html. 2 units. Winter US$215; off season US$200. MC, V. *In room:* A/C, TV, kitchen.

WHERE TO EAT
Moderate

Biggie's AMERICAN/CONTINENTAL The newest restaurant on the island, this place generated a lot of buzz when it first opened. It faces a traffic roundabout on the island's West End, occupying a peachy-white-painted dining room with clean white napery and glass-topped tables. The staff and owner (Kent Rankin) work hard to keep clients happy. Lunches focus on an all-you-can-eat American-style buffet of salads and hot foods; dinners are more elaborate, more formal, and permeated with Continental flair, with lots of emphasis on seafood, chicken, beef, and pastas, some of them vegetarian.

West End. © **345/948-2449.** Reservations recommended. Lunch buffet CI$8–CI$13; dinner main courses CI$13–CI$25. MC, V. Daily 11am–2:30pm and 5:30–9pm.

Captain's Table ★ AMERICAN   The decor here is vaguely nautical, with oars over and around the bar and pieces of boats forming the restaurant's entryway. The restaurant has both indoor, air-conditioned seating and outdoor, poolside dining. Every Saturday night, its karaoke party draws more business than any other bar on the island. Begin a meal here with shrimp and lobster cocktail or a conch fritter; then try one of the soups, such as black bean or a tomato-based conch chowder. Main dishes include everything from the catch of the day, often served pan-fried, to barbecue ribs. Lunch features burgers, salads, and sandwiches.

In Brac Caribbean Beach Village, Stake Bay. ℂ **345/948-1418.** Reservations recommended. Main courses lunch CI$8–CI$12, dinner CI$16–CI$34. AE, MC, V. Daily 11am–3pm and 6–9:30pm. Bar daily 11:30am–midnight.

Inexpensive

Aunt Sha's Kitchen ★ 🍴 CAYMANIAN/CHINESE   This bright pink building beckons from its isolated location on the south side of Cayman Brac. While relaxing on the patio at high tide, you can often see turtles, squid, lobsters, dolphins, and several shapes of rays in the water, and the very occasional shark. A local favorite, this place serves the food that islanders have eaten for decades. Try such classic dishes as turtle stew with rice and beans, homemade conch fritters, and Key lime pie. Other favorites include sweet-and-sour chicken with fried rice, and chicken or shrimp chop suey. We gravitate toward the catch of the day, often kingfish or mahimahi, which is usually grilled or fried and topped with buttery onions and pepper. The prices are among the most affordable on the island. There's also a lively bar with a pool table (p. 175).

South Side. ℂ **345/948-1581.** Main courses CI$8.80–CI$12. AE, MC, V. Daily 11:30am–11pm.

La Esperanza Restaurant ★ 🍴 CAYMANIAN   Islanders flock here, referring to this place as "Bussy's" in honor of its likable owner, Bussy Dilbert, who is the island's most popular and beloved innkeeper. For a drink, a room, or a meal, many devotees of this place wouldn't go anywhere else. You're offered a choice of indoor or outdoor dining, and the restaurant is decorated with wood furnishings and pictures of nautical life and island memorabilia.

Bussy's jerk chicken is the best on the island and as zesty as any in Jamaica. Most dishes come with corn bread, rice, red beans, or fried plantains. Fresh and locally caught mahimahi, kingfish, or snapper appear frequently on the menu, and these catches of the day are served in a lemon sauce with sautéed vegetables. One of the island's best T-bones is served here, with side dishes of your choice. Other delights include savory conch fritters; shrimp, lobster, or turtle dishes; and fish and chips. The Key lime pie is the eternal favorite.

In La Esperanza hotel (p. 167), Stake Bay. ✆ **345/984-0591.** www.laesperanza. net. Main courses CI$10–CI$19. AE, MC, V. Daily noon–2pm and 6–10pm.

Tropical Delight Restaurant CAYMANIAN One of the island's most authentic old restaurants, this place is popular with locals and draws an occasional visitor. It's most festive on Sunday when church groups in their Sunday meeting clothes pour in for a "fill-up." The restaurant is housed in a wooden structure decorated with ship carvings and pictures of Caymanian life. The cooks make the island's most savory kettle of turtle stew, served with rice, beans, potato salad, and coleslaw. You can also order such hearty fare as braised oxtail or roast beef in gravy with vegetables and rice. The choice selection is always the catch of the day—usually mahimahi, snapper, or kingfish—served fried or grilled.

West End. ✆ **345/948-1272.** Main courses CI$9–CI$12. No credit cards. Mon–Fri 7am–7pm; Sat–Sun 7am–10pm.

BEACHES & ACTIVE PURSUITS

Come to Cayman Brac for spectacular outdoor activities rather than man-made attractions. Scuba divers flock here in droves, and everyone—from singles to families—loves the beaches.

The Beaches

Though Cayman Brac can hardly compete with Grand Cayman and its Seven Mile Beach, the beaches on Brac will satisfy most tastes, even if they're on a smaller scale.

Most of the beaches lie in the southwest, the northeast, and the northwest. The East End, where the cliffs of the Bluff meet the sea, is definitely not beach country.

The majority of visitors choose the small beaches along the southwest coast because this is the site of the major resorts where they're likely to be staying, such as **Brac Reef Beach Resort** (p. 164). We've also found that these beaches are better for sunning than snorkeling because of the huge outgrowth of turtle grass in the water.

Directly east of these resorts is the public beach, reached by heading east along South Side Road West. You'll find it to the immediate south of the marshes and wetlands. With its gentle rollers, the beach itself is quite beautiful, though the wire enclosure

> ### In Case of Inclement Weather: An Indoor Attraction
>
> If it's raining outside (and even if it's not), history buffs might want to check out the **Cayman Brac Museum,** in the former Government Administration Building, Stake Bay (© **345/948-2622**), which has an interesting collection of Caymanian antiques, including pieces rescued from shipwrecks and objects from the 18th century. Hours are Monday to Friday from 9am to noon and 1 to 4pm, Saturday from 9am to noon. Admission is free, but donations are accepted.

enveloping the picnic area is somewhat unappealing. There are public showers here, but we've never known them to be in order (plus the water in the bathrooms has an unpleasant odor), and the toilets are foul. We suggest you do your showering elsewhere.

Many visitors opt to find their own small stretch of sand, particularly in the southwest area beyond Salt Water Pond. Another stretch of coastline is to the east at Hawksbill Bay.

Along the northern tier, the only stretch of coastline with a reef is to the west of Spot Bay, though strong currents on both the eastern and western tips of Cayman Brac make snorkeling a bit hazardous. It is also possible to snorkel at the wreck of the *Captain Keith Tibbetts* to the northwest (see below).

Scuba Diving

Because diving on Cayman Brac is lauded as some of the best in the Caribbean, divers from all over the world, both experienced and beginner, come here. Seas are usually calm and the best dive sites lie only a 5- to 20-minute boat ride offshore.

In all, there are about 50 prime dive sites, geared to all levels of divers. The most dramatic is the wreck of the frigate **Captain Keith Tibbetts** ★, which was deliberately sunk in September 1996 after being brought over from Cuba. This 99m (325-ft.) former Russian frigate lies 180m (591 ft.) offshore in northwest Cayman Brac, its bow resting in 34m (112 ft.) of water, the stern just 17m (56 ft.) below the surface. During the Cold War era, this ship was part of the old Soviet fleet sent to Cuba. After the fall of the Soviet Republic, the ship was abandoned for 3 years before it was purchased by the Cayman Islands to turn it into a site of marine conservation. Today it has become a habitat for abundant marine life. Divers can swim through its trio of upper decks, keeping company with everything from four-eyed butterflyfish to batfish.

Reef Divers, South Side (© **800/594-0843** or 345/948-1642; www.bracreef.com), is affiliated with the previously recommended **Brac Reef Beach Resort** (p. 164) and is the island's most visible and recommended dive operator. Divers' magazines consistently rate this outfitter as offering the best wall diving and wreck diving on Cayman Brac. Reef Divers' fleet of dive boats, with a complete inventory of tanks and scuba gear, ranges from 13 to 14m (43–46 ft.). A one-tank dive costs US$65, a two-tank dive US$95, and a three-tank dive US$125. Snorkeling trips are also possible for US$25 for a half-day and US$35 for a full day. Rentals of wetsuits, masks, fins, and snorkeling equipment, among other gear, are available. After discussing your interests, the dive operator will guide you to dozens of different sites.

Exploring by Car

The Bluff ★ is the island's most distinctive geographic feature. As mentioned before, the Bluff is a soaring limestone plateau rising 42m (138 ft.) above the sea, covering much of the easternmost point of the island. To drive up the Bluff, take Ashton Reid Drive, the one paved road that leads to the summit. The panoramic view over the south side of the Bluff is well worth the journey. If you suffer from vertigo, know that it is a sheer drop to the sea below. Many people choose to hike up the Bluff (see "Hiking," below).

To become fully acquainted with the Brac's natural wonders, take one of the **guided nature tours** run by Cantrell Scott and Keino Daley, the government's tour guides. What they don't know about Cayman Brac isn't worth knowing. They can, for example, name all 50 to 60 species of birds that, at least for part of the year, land on Cayman Brac. Tours last about 3 hours and are free. Mr. Scott and Mr. Daley will join you in your car for the tour. Call © **345/948-2651** to establish a meeting time and place.

Fishing

Fishing is another reason many visitors come to Cayman Brac: The fishing here rivals that of the waters surrounding Little Cayman. Bonefishing inside the reef along the coast to the southwest is especially rewarding. Catches around the island include wahoo, sailfish, marlin, tuna, grouper, and snapper.

Indepth Watersports (© **866/396-8704** or 345/948-8037; www.indepthwatersports.com) has fishing charters for US$600 per half-day or US$1,000 for a full day for up to eight fishermen.

Hiking

Hiking is becoming more and more popular on Cayman Brac, enough so that the **Cayman Brac Tourist Office** (p. 161) now has free printed guides to the best hikes on the island. Trails, though not always well maintained, are indicated by white "heritage markers." In all, some three dozen marked trails wind their way across the island. Some are easy to reach and hike, while others require more skill and experience. The following recommended hikes are moderately difficult.

Some of our favorite trails include **West End Point Overlook,** starting on South Side Road, west of the Brac Reef Beach Resort. The ideal hike for bird-watching is at the far western point of Brac. Islanders also claim, and with good reason, that you have the best view of sunsets here. Locals watch for the "green flash" of light as the sun goes down.

Another good trail to follow is **Westerly Ponds,** South Side Road, across from the Brac Reef Beach Resort (p. 164). The two ponds along this trail are the best spots for observing the life of wetland fowl. Boardwalks cut across the marshes, with small viewing sections.

The Lighthouse Trail ★, taking 3 hours, starts at Spot Bay in the East End of the island. You'll approach the beginning of the trail by walking along Spot Bay Road, then follow the trail up the northeast face of the Bluff. On the way, you'll pass the entrance to Peter's Cave, used in olden days as a hurricane shelter. As you continue hiking, you will come to a spot dubbed Peter's Outlook by locals, with a panoramic sweep across Spot Bay. There are two lighthouses in this area, one modern and the other from the 1930s.

The best nature trail on Brac is the **Parrot Reserve ★★** in the center of the island, which is perfect for self-guided tours. The trail meanders for 1.6km (1 mile), taking hikers through the heart of the reserve, which is a visitor's best chance to see the endangered Cayman Brac parrot. Trails are always open and there's no fee to enter. You must, of course, bring your own provisions, including plenty of water. This preserve is reached along Major Donald Drive (sometimes called Lighthouse Rd.), a 9.7km (6-mile) dirt road leading to cliffs. From this vantage point on the Bluff, the best view of North East Point is spread before you. Many hikers come here to take in the most dramatic sunrise in the Cayman Islands.

Spelunking

Cayman Brac has a series of caves that are open for exploring. While the island does not offer organized spelunking excursions, you might seek advice at the tourist office at the time of your visit to see if any spelunking excursions are being organized, if you wish to explore the caves with a group.

Peter's Cave, on the Lighthouse Trail in the East End, is mammoth, with tunnels leading off in several directions. **Rebecca's Cave** lies off South Side Road, near the **Carib Sands Beach Resort** (p. 166), and is well marked. It's the best known of Brac's caves, and takes its name from a young child who died here during the disastrous hurricane of 1932 that destroyed the island. Rebecca's tomb can still be seen in the middle of the cave.

Bat Cave takes its name from its inhabitants, several species of which can be seen hanging from above if you shine your flashlight up to the roof. Most of the bats you'll see here are Jamaican fruit bats. The bats emerge in the evening to fly about, usually after 9pm. Bat Cave is on the south side of the island and is marked by signs.

A final cave, **Great Cave,** stands 1.6km (a mile) or so from the lighthouse that designates the easternmost point of the island, at the top of the Bluff. Filled with stalagmites and stalactites, it is one of the most interesting caves to explore, although a bit eerie. The terrain is dry and rocky, with plenty of sharp, loose rocks. Wear long pants and sturdy shoes, preferably with ankle supports, for scrambling around underground.

Tennis

The best tennis court on the island is found at the previously recommended **Brac Reef Beach Resort,** South Side (p. 164; ℂ **345/ 948-1323**). The court is open to nonguests at the cost of CI$6.25 per day. The court is open daily and is also lit for night play.

SHOPPING

There isn't much here in the way of shopping on Cayman Brac. The best shop for souvenirs is **Treasure Chest,** Tibbetts Square (ℂ **345/948-1333**), which is a relatively easy walk from the airport landing strip. It's open Monday to Saturday from 9am to 5pm.

If you're staying at one of the resorts along the north shore, the **Bayside Grocery,** at La Esperanza, Stake Bay (ℂ **345/948-0531**), is sure to come in handy, especially if you're in a self-catering villa. There's a grocery store on-site at La Esperanza, plus a general merchandise mart, an electronics store, and a souvenir section.

Kirk Freeport, Kirk Freeport Plaza, Stake Bay (☎ **345/948-2612**), is a small shop with a surprisingly wide range of merchandise, featuring everything from elegant coral items to china, jewelry, glassware, silver, and gold items, along with T-shirts and casual sports clothing. It's the best place for upmarket gifts on the island. It's open Monday to Saturday from 10am to 6pm.

The best place on the island to purchase liquor is **Brac Freeport,** West End (☎ **345/948-1332**), which is open Monday to Saturday from 10am to 7pm.

Sharon's Hair Clinic, Tibbetts Square (☎ **345/948-1387**), is the place to go for hair care. The salon is especially adept at braiding and is open Monday to Saturday from 10am to 7pm.

CAYMAN BRAC AFTER DARK

Most visitors and islanders view hanging out at a bar and having dinner as an evening unto itself. Most travelers hit the sack early, preparing for their next day's adventure early in the morning. Don't expect allegedly "late-night" festivities to go much past midnight.

Except on the slowest of evenings, there's usually one spot that's hotter than any other because it's featuring a DJ or live band. The venues vary, but your hotel staff will usually know where to direct you to find the evening's best entertainment.

On Friday and Saturday nights, **Aunt Sha's Kitchen,** South Side (p. 169; ☎ **345/948-1581**), turns into an island social center with music (mostly reggae and soca) supplied by a DJ, and an occasional happy hour.

Live music is often featured at the **Bar at Brac Reef Beach Resort,** South Side (p. 164; ☎ **345/948-1323**)—one of the island's most popular bars, especially with visitors. Monday night is the manager's party, Wednesday night is karaoke night, and Thursday is movie night. Nonguests are always welcome. It's open from 11am to 1am daily.

Coral Isle Club, South Side, east of Denis Point (☎ **345/948-1581**), is the island's top karaoke bar, with a DJ on Wednesday through Saturday nights. The bartender's specialty is a Blue Lagoon, made with tequila and vodka and costing CI$5. The bar is open daily from 7:30am to 11pm.

For a good time on Friday and Saturday nights, join the islanders filing into the previously recommended hotel, restaurant, and bar

La Esperanza, Stake Bay (p. 169; ✆ **345/948-0531**). Dig into mounds of barbecue or jerk chicken prepared by the owner himself, Bussy, and enjoy the island band that often plays on weekends. On other nights, a blaring jukebox is responsible for the music, which can range from top tunes of the 1940s to calypso. The inside lounge has a full bar, TV, pool tables, and a seaside ambience. It's open daily from 9am to 1am.

LITTLE CAYMAN

T he smallest of the Cayman Islands, cigar-shaped Little Cayman has only about 170 permanent inhabitants, so nearly everybody you'll see will be a visitor, most likely from the U.S. Little Cayman is 16km (10 miles) long and about 1.6km (a mile) wide at its broadest point. Electricity didn't make it here until 1990, and phone service didn't arrive until 1991. Little Cayman lies about 109km (68 miles) northeast of Grand Cayman and some 8km (5 miles) from Cayman Brac. The entire island is coral and sand. Blossom Village, the island's "capital," is on the southwest coast.

The Cayman Islands archipelago is made up of mountaintops of the long-submerged Sierra Maestra Range, which runs north into Cuba. Coral once formed in layers over the underwater peaks, eventually creating the islands. Beneath Little Cayman's Bloody Bay is one of the mountain's walls—a stunning sight for snorkelers and scuba divers.

Little Cayman seems to have come into its own now that fishing and diving have taken center stage; the island is a near-perfect place for these pursuits. Jacques Cousteau hailed the area around the little island as one of the three finest diving spots in the world. The flats on Little Cayman are said to have the best bonefishing in the world, and a brackish inland pool can be fished for tarpon. Even if you don't dive or fish, you can row 180m (591 ft.) off Little Cayman to isolated and uninhabited Owen Island, where you can swim at the sandy beach and picnic by a blue lagoon.

Pirate treasure may still be buried on the island, but it's in the dense interior of what is now the largest bird sanctuary in the Caribbean. Little Cayman also has the largest population of rock iguanas in the entire Caribbean (you will surely spot them) and is home to one of the oldest species of reptiles in the New World—the tree-climbing *Anulis maynardi* (which is not known by any other name). This rare lizard is difficult to spot because the females are green and the males are brown, and, as such, they blend into local vegetation. Keep your eyes open for them!

ESSENTIALS
Visitor Information
Little Cayman is too small to have a tourist office. Before you go, you can visit the tourist office in George Town (p. 195) and pick up what limited information on this island is available.

Getting There
Most visitors fly from Grand Cayman to Little Cayman aboard any of the several daily flights operated by Cayman Express, a subdivision of **Cayman Airways** (℗ **800/422-9626** in the U.S. and Canada, or 345/949-8200; www.caymanairways.com), the national carrier. The cost of one-way passage aboard any of its 18-seater planes is US$66 to US$91. Luggage is limited, without payment of an additional surcharge, to two suitcases per person, totaling no more than 55 pounds for both bags, so it's wise to pack light. Airplanes only land and take off on Little Cayman during daylight hours.

Getting Around
You can get around this small island in four ways: You can use your feet, rent a jeep, rent a bike, or go on an organized tour. If you make arrangements in advance, your hotel will often send a van to meet your plane.

CAR RENTALS
The island's only car rental outlet is **McLaughlin Enterprises,** Blossom Village (℗ **345/948-1000**). Its office, located in a small shopping strip, is clearly visible from the airstrip and within easy walking distance. You can also call the company through an airport courtesy phone and ask them to pick you up. Rates begin at CI$65 per day; adding a second driver costs CI$14. The insurance charge is CI$16 per day. McLaughlin is open Monday to Saturday 8am to 6pm, and Sunday 8am to noon and 3 to 5pm.

The speed limit for the entire island is 40kmph (25 mph). The only place to get fuel is at the gas station near McLaughlin. Since

> ### 💬 Road Rules: Iguanas Have Right of Way
>
> One local rule to remember is that the prehistoric-looking gray
> iguana is the king of the road and always has the right of way,
> should he want to make a leisurely crossing.

the cars McLaughlin rents are not four-wheel-drive, avoid driving
on soft sands.

BICYCLES

Little Cayman is too small to support a bike rental shop. The good
news is that most hotels and little guesthouses will either lend you
one (most often the case) or rent you one. There's little traffic, the
land is flat, and it's relatively easy to cycle along the paved roads.
Just avoid the East End; the unpaved roads here result in a very
bumpy, uncomfortable ride. Drifting sand is also a menace.

[FastFACTS] LITTLE CAYMAN

Banks Little Cayman has **no ATMs.** The **Cayman National Bank,**
Little Cayman Mall (📞 **345/948-1551**), is open Monday and Thursday only from 9am to 2:30pm.

Emergencies Dial 📞 **911.** There's only one police officer on the
island.

Hospitals & Clinics A nurse is based at the **Little Cayman
Clinic,** Blossom Avenue on Guy Banks Road, in Blossom Village
(📞 **345/948-0072**). Hours are Monday, Wednesday, and Friday
9am to 1pm; Tuesday and Thursday 1 to 5pm. In an emergency, the
nurse can be contacted off-hours at 📞 **345/948-1073.** The nearest
hospital is the **Faith Hospital** on Cayman Brac (📞 **345/948-2225**),
to which patients on Little Cayman are airlifted in an emergency.
Should there be a scuba-diving accident resulting in a patient need-
ing decompression, the patient is airlifted at once to Grand
Cayman.

Internet Access Your hotel may or may not have Internet
access; ask when booking.

Pharmacies A small pharmacy is located at **Little Cayman Clinic**
(see "Hospital & Clinics," above).

Post Office The **Little Cayman Post Office** (📞 **345/948-0016**) is
easily spotted near the airfield on the southwest side of Little Cayman. It's open Monday to Thursday 9 to 11:30am and 1 to 3pm, Friday 9 to 11:30am and 1 to 3:30pm.

Water If your hotel relies on rainwater collected in cisterns, it's best to drink bottled water. Ask about the water source when you book. Also, drink bottled water when dining out at restaurants.

WHERE TO STAY
Expensive

The Club at Little Cayman ★★   Set on lushly landscaped grounds, this complex affords the most luxurious living on Little Cayman. It's a pocket of posh, boasting elegantly furnished luxury villas that you'd expect to spot along Florida's Gold Coast. For this reason, we prefer this resort over the Conch Club. The Club at Little Cayman opens onto one of the most magnificent beaches on the island. Villas, which are located in a setting of coconut trees and flowering plants, boast oversize balconies or porches. The pool is our favorite on the island, custom-designed with bench seating and waterfalls. The one-, two-, and three-bedroom rentals have glamorous architectural touches, including crown-molding trim and ceramic tiles. High-quality furnishings and luxury fabrics add to the elegance. The in-room kitchens are the best on the island, with such features as a glass-top range. If you tire of cooking inside, you can take advantage of the barbecue area outside. Guests at the club can also use the amenities of the **Little Cayman Beach Resort** (see below).

Guy Banks Rd., Little Cayman, B.W.I. ✆ **888/756-7400** or 345/948-1033. Fax 345/948-1040. www.theclubatlittlecayman.com. 40 units. Winter US$310 1-bedroom, US$430 2-bedroom, US$500–US$550 3-bedroom; off season US$248 1-bedroom, US$330 2-bedroom, US$400–US$450 3-bedroom. AE, MC, V. **Amenities:** Jacuzzi; outdoor pool. *In room:* A/C, TV, kitchen.

Conch Club ★   Opening onto one of the island's best beaches, Conch Club is a condo complex that evokes a maritime development on Cape Cod except for the West Indian gingerbread trim. The accommodations, with their gables and dormers, offer a panoramic view of the ocean. A shuttle is available to transport guests to the Little Cayman Beach Resort for use of its more extensive facilities. Nestled on the island's secluded South Hole Sound, the complex is in a garden setting, offering two- and three-bedroom units. The accommodations are privately owned and comfortably furnished, and are rented when the owners are away. Guests can prepare meals in the modern, fully equipped kitchens, although many prefer to barbecue at night at their communal grill. The day is yours if you anchor in one of the hammocks under thatched cabanas, or else immerse yourself in the hot tub.

Guy Banks Rd., Little Cayman, B.W.I. ✆ **345/925-2875.** Fax 345/948-1028. www.conchclubcondos.com. 18 units. Winter US$385 2-bedroom condo, US$495

Hotels & Restaurants on Little Cayman

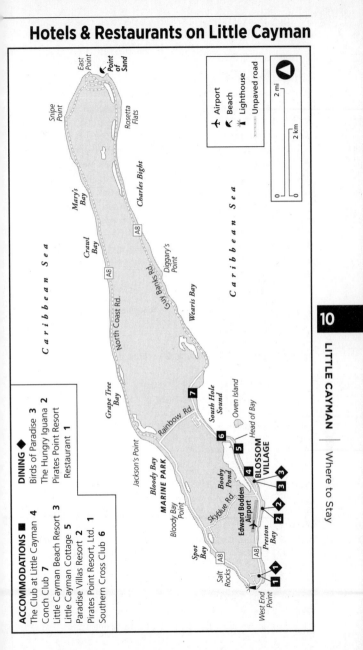

ACCOMMODATIONS ■

The Club at Little Cayman **4**
Conch Club **7**
Little Cayman Beach Resort **3**
Little Cayman Cottage **5**
Paradise Villas Resort **2**
Pirates Point Resort, Ltd. **1**
Southern Cross Club **6**

DINING ◆

Birds of Paradise **3**
The Hungry Iguana **2**
Pirates Point Resort
Restaurant **1**

10

LITTLE CAYMAN | Where to Stay

181

3-bedroom condo; off season US$275 2-bedroom condo, US$385 3-bedroom condo. Minimum 3-night stay. AE, MC, V. **Amenities:** Free airport transfers; bike rentals; 2 outdoor pools; scuba diving; spa; tennis court (lit). *In room:* A/C, TV, DVD, kitchen, Wi-Fi (free).

Little Cayman Beach Resort ★★

Set on the south coast, this resort is close to many of the island's diving and sporting attractions, including the South Hole Sound Lagoon's bonefishing. It's popular with anglers, divers, bird-watchers, and adventurous types. The hotel lies only 1.5km (1 mile) from the Edward Bodden Airport and has a white sand beach fringing a shallow, reef-protected bay. It is divided into three pastel, coral-colored, two-story buildings with gingerbread trim. The most desirable units are the 12 oceanfront rooms. Each unit has a harmonious color scheme and an inviting, airy atmosphere. The resort has been much improved, now boasting a superior dive shop and a collection of Hobie cats and kayaks.

Blossom Village, Little Cayman, B.W.I. © **800/327-3835** in the U.S. and Canada, or 345/948-1033. Fax 345/948-1040. www.littlecayman.com. 40 units. Winter US$585–US$701 for nondiver, US$809–US$981 for diver; off season US$474–US$612 for nondiver, US$688–US$879 for diver. Rates are per person and include a stay of 3 nights with breakfast and dinner; diver rates include 3 one-tank dives per day. Minimum 3-night stay. AE, MC, V. **Amenities:** Restaurant; bar; babysitting; bikes; health club & spa; watersports equipment/rentals. *In room:* A/C, ceiling fan, TV, kitchenette.

Little Cayman Cottage ★ 🎁

This cottage, located about 1.6km (1 mile) from the airport, is the type of hideaway where one would retreat to write a novel. The cottage is set among sea-grape and swaying palm trees, with a view of a white sand beach—a cliché of Caribbean charm and style. You can spend the entire day lying in a hammock or you can partake in various watersports. Six people are accommodated comfortably in this single one-floor villa, which has tiled floors and rattan furnishings. The two midsize bedrooms are furnished in a light, breezy style. In total, there are two twin beds, a king-size bed, and a convertible queen-size couch. The cottage also has a living and dining area and a fully equipped kitchen with a screened-in porch, plus a grill for barbecuing and two bicycles.

117 Airport Rd., Little Cayman, B.W.I. © **800/235-5888** or 345/945-4144. Fax 345/949-7471. www.caymanvillas.com. 1 unit. Winter US$325–US$430; off season US$225–US$330. MC, V. **Amenities:** Babysitting; bikes. *In room:* A/C, TV, kitchen, no phone.

Pirates Point Resort, Ltd. ★

For watersports or just relaxing, this resort near West End Point provides a family environment with gourmet cuisine, although it's a notch down from Little Cayman

Beach Resort. The place has remodeled rooms, and a non-air-conditioned family cottage with two large rooms. In addition, it has four seaside cottages, with balconies overlooking Preston Bay. The resort's packages include a room, three excellent meals per day with appropriate wines and all alcoholic beverages, and two-tank boat dives daily, featuring tours of the Bloody Bay Wall and Jackson Reef. Other activities include snorkeling, bird-watching, and exploring.

The food here is excellent. The owner and manager, Texas-born Gladys Howard, is an award-winning cookbook author and a graduate of Cordon Bleu in Paris. She has studied with such stars as Julia Child, Jacques Pepin, and James Beard. She uses fresh fruit and vegetables grown locally, as well as local seafood.

Preston Bay, Little Cayman, B.W.I. ⓒ **345/948-1010.** Fax 345/948-1011. www. piratespointresort.com. 11 units. Winter US$1,595 per person 7-day nondiver package, US$1,995 per person 7-day dive package; off season US$1,595 7-day nondiver package, US$1,895 per person 7-day dive package. Children 5–12 stay free in parent's room. MC, V. No children 4 or under. **Amenities:** Restaurant; bar; outdoor pool; watersports equipment/rentals. In room: A/C (in some), no phone.

Moderate

Paradise Villas Resort ★ ☺ On high-priced Little Cayman, this resort on the beach is the best deal—especially if you're traveling with your family, as babysitting can be arranged. The style is typically Caymanian, with gingerbread decoration, metal roofs, and porches in the front and back. The resort consists of six duplex cottages that border the sea; each cottage is divided into two one-bedroom units with small but comfortable rooms. Pullout couches in the living room easily accommodate extra guests. The compact bathrooms contain shower stalls. The units include kitchenettes where guests can prepare their own meals. The resort is on the island's south side, near the little airport, and pickup is provided at no extra charge. The resort also rents cars to guests, although a grocery store, boutique, and liquor store are all within walking distance, and the resort provides free bikes. On the premises is the best affordable restaurant on the island, the **Hungry Iguana** (p. 184).

At Edward Bodden Airport (PO Box 48), Little Cayman, B.W.I. ⓒ **877/3-CAY-MAN** (322-9626), or 345/948-0001. Fax 345/948-0002. www.paradisevillas. com. 12 units. Winter US$195 double, US$210 triple; off season US$175 double, US$190 triple. Children 11 and under stay free in parent's room. Dive packages available. AE, MC, V. **Amenities:** Restaurant; bar; free airport transfers; bikes. In room: A/C, ceiling fans, TV, Wi-Fi (free).

Southern Cross Club ★ Opened in 1959, this was the first resort on Little Cayman. The inn, which attracts divers and fishermen, must be doing something right, considering that two-thirds of the patrons are repeat customers—the highest such rate anywhere in the Cayman Islands. The resort is located on the southern side of Little Cayman, to the southeast of Booby Pond, opening onto Head O'Bay, with the offshore Owen Island clearly visible. The Southern Cross is named after the constellation, which can be seen here on a clear winter's night.

The rooms open onto 240m (787 ft.) of golden sands. Accommodations are in comfortably furnished one-bedroom cottages, with one unit containing two bedrooms. Bedrooms are decorated in a simple Caribbean style, and each has a sitting room and a small bathroom. This resort is among the very best for fishing, with two boats—one deep-sea, one flat—for deep-sea fishing or fishing in the lake. No more than 12 divers go out at one time in the resort's dive boat. Bikes and kayaks are provided free. Hotel guests, islanders, and visitors patronize the restaurant and bar, making this one of Little Cayman's few nightlife spots (p. 191).

South Hole Sound (PO Box 44), Little Cayman, B.W.I. ✆ **800/899-2582** in the U.S., or 619/563-0017. Fax 619/563-1665. www.southerncrossclub.com. 10 units. Winter US$1,645 per person; off season US$1,390 per person. Rates include room and all meals for 5 nights. Minimum 5-night stay. AE, DISC, MC, V. No children 4 or under. **Amenities:** Restaurant; bar; outdoor pool; watersports equipment/rentals; Wi-Fi (free in clubhouse). *In room:* A/C, no phone.

WHERE TO EAT

Birds of Paradise AMERICAN/CONTINENTAL   Part of the **Little Cayman Beach Resort** (p. 182), this restaurant caters primarily to guests, but it welcomes anyone. The specialty is buffet-style dinners—the kind your parents might have enjoyed back in the 1950s or 1960s. Saturday night features the island's most generous barbecue spread—all the ribs, fish, and Jamaican-style jerk chicken you could want. On other nights, try the prime rib, fresh fish Caribbean style (your best bet), or chicken (either Kiev or *cordon bleu*). There's a fresh salad bar, and the homemade desserts are yummy, especially the Key lime pie. At night, opt for an outdoor table under the stars.

At Little Cayman Beach Resort. ✆ **345/948-1033.** Reservations recommended for dinner for nonguests. Breakfast CI$12; lunch CI$17; dinner CI$35. AE, MC, V. Daily 7–8:30am, 12:30–1:30pm, and 6:30–8pm.

The Hungry Iguana AMERICAN/CARIBBEAN   At the beach, you'll spot the mammoth iguana mural that marks this place immediately. The island's tastiest dishes are served here, a winning combination of standard American fare and some zesty flavors from islands to the south. It's the rowdiest place on Little Cayman, especially the sports bar area with its satellite TV in the corner, which has a sort of T.G.I. Friday's atmosphere. The lunch menu consists of the usual burgers and fries along with some well-stuffed sandwiches. We prefer the grilled chicken salad. Dinner gets a little more elaborate—there's usually a special meat dish of the day, depending on the market (supplies are shipped in once a week by barge). The chef always seems willing to prepare a steak as you like it. Marinated conch with homemade chips is another tasty choice.

At Paradise Villas Resort (p. 183). ℂ **345/948-0007.** Reservations recommended. Main courses lunch CI$7–CI$16, dinner CI$15–CI$28. AE, MC, V. Daily noon-2:30pm and 5:30-9pm. Bar Mon-Fri noon-1am; Sat-Sun noon-midnight.

Pirates Point Resort Restaurant ★ INTERNATIONAL   The cuisine here is the island's best, as the owner and manager, Gladys Howard, is a graduate of Cordon Bleu in Paris and has studied with such culinary stars as Julia Child and James Beard. Howard has even written several cookbooks of her own. She uses fresh fruit and local vegetables, as well as seafood caught in local waters. She imports as little as possible. The menu changes, but some of its most memorable, creative options have included a zesty conch and a saffron scallop couscous. Two of the best dishes we've sampled here are the macadamia-crusted mahimahi in a lemon-dill sauce, and the herb-roasted leg of lamb with a burgundy demi-glace. Don't miss the smoked-salmon cheesecake with a green-onion coulis. Desserts are luscious, including a four-layer chocolate cake and a white-chocolate tropical torte.

At Pirates Point Resort (p. 185). ℂ **345/948-1010.** www.piratespointresort.com. Reservations required 24 hr. in advance for nonguests. 2-course fixed-price menu CI$50, including wine and pickup and return to your hotel. MC, V. Daily 1:45-2:30pm and 7:30pm (1 seating).

BEACHES & ACTIVE PURSUITS

Visit Little Cayman for the diving, fishing, and beaches, not for the sightseeing, although there are a few sights to see.

Little Cayman has long been popular with birders and anglers, but scuba diving is its main draw. Some 60 dive sites—marked with moorings—are found along this 16km (10-mile) island. The most celebrated site is Bloody Bay Wall (see below) on the northern tier of the island.

The Beaches

Point of Sand ★ is our favorite beach on the island, located at the southeastern tip of Little Cayman and accessible from Blossom Village by heading east along Guy Banks Road. Point of Sand is also great for snorkeling, and the sand here is luminescent pink. On most weekdays, you'll have the beach to yourself, although many visitors come over on Saturday and Sunday from Cayman Brac. Plan to take a picnic lunch and enjoy it at a covered picnic table. You'll find bathrooms and changing facilities here. It's dangerous to attempt to drive a jeep down to the beach because you might get stuck in the deep sands. Park it at the lot and walk down to the beach.

Owen Island ★ lies off the southwestern coast, east of Blossom Village and South Town, in South Hole Sound, which is between Booby Pond and Tarpon Lake. The island—which features a beautiful sand beach—is an easy 180m (590-ft.) rowboat ride off the coast. Pack a picnic lunch and make a day of it. Owen Island—locals call it "the Cay"—is the fourth-largest island in the Cayman archipelago, yet it has a land area of only 4.4 hectares (11 acres). It's a peaceful spot with trees and plenty of sand, plus gulls and migrant waders in its shallow waters and flats. Many resorts on Little Cayman schedule picnic trips to this secluded island. The snorkeling is especially good on the south side. Many visitors rent a kayak at **Little Cayman Beach Resort** (p. 182) and spend a day here, which could be as close as you'll come to experiencing a Robinson Crusoe existence in the Caymans.

Scuba Diving & Snorkeling

One of the most spectacular and most varied dive locations in the world is **Bloody Bay Marine Park** ★★★, reached along North Coast Road. To the east is Jackson Wall, with the Bloody Bay Wall lying to the west. A total of 22 listed dive sites are found in this park alone. The snorkeling here is also very rewarding.

The drop at Bloody Bay begins at only 6m (20 ft.), but soon plunges to more than 360m (1,181 ft.). At one point, the reefs plummet to 1,800m (5,906 ft.). *Note:* We strongly suggest that you explore the dive sites with one of the experienced dive operators recommended below.

Conch Club Divers is based at the previously recommended Conch Club condominiums, Guy Banks Road (p. 180; ℂ **888/ 756-7400** or 345/948-1033; www.conchclubdivers.com). These experts offer everything from relaxing snorkeling tours to advanced diving courses. The outfitter's 13m (42-ft.) boat, *Sea-esta,* takes customized dive excursions to the area's major dive sites, including Bloody Bay Wall. A one-tank dive costs CI$55, a two-tank dive is CI$85, and a three-tank dive goes for CI$120. Snorkeling gear costs CI$15 for a day's rental. The full PADI certification course costs CI$350, and a resort course is CI$150.

Paradise Divers is installed at another previously recommended resort, Paradise Villas Resort, at Edward Bodden Airport (p. 183; ✆ **345/948-0001;** www.paradise-divers.com). Like all the other dive outfitters, it provides PADI and NAUI certification courses. Prices are quoted in U.S. dollars, with a single dive going for US$45 or a two-tank dive for US$89. Night dives cost US$60, with snorkeling trips priced at US$25.

Reef Divers at Little Cayman Beach Resort, Guy Banks Road in Blossom Village (p. 188; ✆ **800/327-3835** or 345/948-1033; www.littlecayman.com), was established in 1993. It has a trio of 13m (43-ft.) boats and all the latest equipment. On-site is a dive shop, and the staff here gives PADI courses. Certified divers are charged CI$75 per tank dive. Kayak rentals are also available.

Southern Cross Club, South Hole Sound (p. 183; ✆ **345/ 948-1099;** www.southerncrossclub.com), is another one of the island's leading dive outfitters, providing an intimate dive with no more than a dozen divers per boat. This outfitter has all the latest equipment and is very experienced at directing divers to some of the most dramatic offshore dive sites. A two-tank dive costs CI$95, a three-tank dive CI$160, and night dives CI$75. Snorkeling trips cost CI$15.

Fishing

Little Cayman is recognized as the best island year-round for fishing tarpon, bonefish, and permit (a type of pompano fish).

Anglers can catch bonefish averaging 1.4 to 2.7kg (3–6 lb.) in the shallow areas of South Hole Sound near Owen Island. Bonefish can be spotted in areas known as "muds," or patches of water where the sea looks milky because of fish churning up the bottom while feeding. Muds are especially visible from the air on a flight to the island.

Many guides use fry (young fish) rather than flies for bonefish. Anglers who want to try fly-fishing should bring their own tackle. South Hole Sound offers the best fishing. Although these fish bite all day, local guides agree that finding bonefish depends on tides and weather conditions. They often prefer to fish from the beach rather than stalk fish in the mud of the lagoon.

Tarpon are plentiful in Tarpon Lake, the landlocked, brackish natural pond that offers excellent fly-fishing. These fish used to grow no larger than 1.8 to 3.6kg (4–8 lb.), but larger specimens (up to 9kg/20 lb.) are now caught frequently, especially in the early morning and late afternoon.

Permit of 6.8 to 15.9kg (15–35 lb.) frequent Little Cayman waters, and may be the Cayman Islands' best-kept secret. Schools are especially abundant on Little Cayman's southeastern end and in the flats of the northwestern coast.

Although Little Cayman has good deep-sea fishing, its main attraction is light tackle and fly-fishing, and the island is best prepared to accommodate anglers. The **Southern Cross Club** (p. 183) caters to both divers and light-tackle fishing enthusiasts. Anglers can also be accommodated on day trips with advance reservations. Light tackle gear is available, but anglers should bring their own fly-fishing equipment. Contact the hotels directly to arrange fishing excursions and to confirm the availability of experienced local guides during your visit.

In addition to the Southern Cross Club, we also recommend **LCB Tours (© 800/327-3835** in the U.S., or 345/948-1033) for fishing excursions. A full day of bonefishing costs CI$450 and a half-day is CI$260. A full day of deep-sea fishing costs CI$850 and a half-day is CI$450. The charters have a three-person maximum.

Kayaking

Several resorts rent kayaks, notably **Little Cayman Beach Resort** (p. 182). Nonguests can hire kayaks here for CI$16 per half-day for a single or CI$24 per half-day for a two-person kayak. Kayak rentals are especially useful for trips to Owen Island (see above).

Tennis

The best court on the island is at the **Little Cayman Beach Resort** (p. 182). It's open daily from 6am to 10pm to guests and nonguests. The charge is CI$5 per game. The sun is fierce here for most of the year, so the best times for games are in the early morning or after 4pm. The court is lit so you can play after dark.

EXPLORING LITTLE CAYMAN

The main settlement on island is the romantically named **Blossom Village,** lying directly to the east of the airport between South Hole Sound and Preston Bay. Use the village as a refueling stop, not only for gas (petrol), but also for groceries if your rental has a small kitchen. Be forewarned: Since everything has to be shipped in, prices are steep. Most of the rental units on island are found here, and there's a place or two to grab a bite.

Don't speed through the village. The sole cop uses a radar speed gun—and seems to enjoy it, so be careful.

Some of the best scuba diving on island is possible in the area. See "Scuba Diving & Snorkeling" (p. 186) for specific recommendations of dive outfitters who will direct you to the best sites, such as Bloody Bay Marine Park.

💬 BIKING ON water

Surf bikes—often called "floating bicycles"—are used together for two riders—that is, if the maximum weight of each rider does not exceed 225 pounds. The cost for this riding-on-water experience is US$35 per person in cash or US$38 per person if a credit card is used. These water bikes, often referred to as a "hydrobike," came onto the market in 1989, the creation of aeronautical engineers.

If you're only slightly athletic, you can cruise at 8kmph (5 mph) on these bikes, which can be ridden in windy conditions or when the waves are a bit high (not hurricane-force winds, of course). The bikes almost never tip over, and many visitors use them for fishing out in the water instead of on shore.

You create no pollution when you ride these bikes, which maneuver quite well in narrow, shallow channels. Surprisingly, they also perform well in the ocean's surf in swells up to 1.2m (4 ft.). The bikes are said to be safe for children, but parents should always exercise caution, of course. On occasion the bike is even used as a dive platform. Since you are the "motor" for this bike, a ride on it is like a workout in a gym.

Birders flock to the **Booby Pond Visitor's Centre** (© 345/ 948-1010; www.nationaltrust.org.ky/info/boobypond.html), which is operated by the National Trust. The visitor center is located in an 83-hectare (205-acre) nature reserve and has exhibits on Little Cayman's indigenous species, including the common crab and the seed shrimp. For a closer view of bird life, take a look through one of the two telescopes on the visitor center's porch. A gift shop here sells locally made crafts and island art. Admission is free and the center is open daily from 9am to 6pm.

Booby Pond ★★ itself is a 1.9km-long (1¼-mile) brackish mangrove pond, home to a breeding colony of splendid frigate birds. The red-footed boobies who live at this pond are the Caribbean's largest booby breeding colony. Estimates say that some 7,000 feathered creatures of different types call this pond home, including the black-necked stilt, the West Indian whistling duck, the graceful egret, the heron, and, of course, the booby.

Of minor interest is **Little Cayman Museum,** Guy Banks Road, Blossom Village (© 345/948-1033), open Monday to Friday 3 to 5pm. It's free, although the staff will request a donation. In a green-and-white building with a wood veranda, the museum contains relics from Little Cayman's past. Some of the memorabilia date back a century and a half. The collection stemmed from the private treasures of Linton Tibbetts, an islander who sailed to the United States with US$50 in his pocket and returned to Little Cayman a multimillionaire. Everything from the attics of Little Cayman is here, including grandmother's old sewing machine.

Since getting around Little Cayman can be difficult, you may want to take an organized tour. **LCB Tours,** Blossom Village (© **800/327-3835** in the U.S., or 345/948-1033), offers a guided tour that visits all of the island highlights for CI$20 per person, with lunch costing an extra CI$16. You can also rent snorkeling gear, kayaks, sailboats, pedal boats, and surf bikes (which are basically floating bicycles).

The previously recommended **Little Cayman Beach Resort** (p. 182) offers snorkeling and bus tours of the island for CI$25 per person. The best tours, however, are the guided nature hikes conducted by Gladys Howard, owner of **Pirates Point Resort** (p. 182). These tours are sponsored by the National Trust, and only a CI$1 donation is requested. These tours can only be arranged by appointment.

SHOPPING

Shopaholics be warned: It's slim pickings on Little Cayman. At some point, all visitors seem to stop in at **Village Square,** Guy Banks Road (© **345/948-1069**), which sells a little bit of everything. Villa owners come here for supplies, groceries, and hardware. You can purchase fishing gear, household goods, film, newspapers, and magazines. You can even rent movies. Prices are high because everything has to be shipped in by boat. It's open Monday to Saturday from 8:30am to 6pm.

Nature Spa Health & Beauty, at the Little Cayman Beach Resort (p. 182), provides a full range of services, including massage, pedicures, facials, manicures, and hairdressing, plus beauty supplies. The spa is open daily from 11am to 6pm and requires an appointment.

Reef Photo & Video Centre, also at the Little Cayman Beach Resort (p. 182), provides daily film processing, and underwater video and camera rentals cost CI$9.60 per half-day. It's open daily from 7:30am to 5pm.

LITTLE CAYMAN AFTER DARK

Nightlife in Little Cayman usually means hanging out in a bar and ordering dinner.

Locals, expats, and visitors gather daily at the bar at **Southern Cross Club,** South Hole Sound (p. 183), open from 11am to midnight. The best time to hit the bar is Friday night at 7pm, when it stages barbecues at the poolside deck near the beach, which cost CI$14 per person.

FAST FACTS

Business Hours Normally, banks are open Monday to Thursday from 9am to 4:30pm, and Friday 9am to 1pm and 2:30 to 4:30pm. Most shops are open Monday to Saturday from 9am to 5pm, but hours can vary greatly.

Country Code The country code for the Cayman Islands is **345.**

Drinking Laws The legal drinking age is 18. Beer, wine, and liquor are sold at most grocery and convenience stores Monday to Saturday. It is legal to have an open container on the beach. Do not carry open containers of alcohol in your car or any public area that isn't zoned for alcohol consumption. The police can fine you on the spot. Don't even think about driving while intoxicated.

Driving Rules See "Getting Around," p. 31.

Drugstores If you're traveling to Little Cayman or Cayman Brac, don't depend on local outlets there to have the drugs or medication you need. Stock up before you go. On Grand Cayman the most convenient pharmacies are **Fosters Food Fair Pharmacy** in the Strand Shopping Centre on West Bay Road, Seven Mile Beach (℡ **345/945-7759;** www.fosters-iga.com), open Monday to Saturday 7am to 10pm; and **Cayman Drug** in Kirk Freeport Centre, George Town (℡ **345/949-2597**), open Monday to Friday 9am to 5:30pm and Saturday 8:30am to 4pm.

Electricity Electricity on the Cayman Islands is 110-volt AC (60 cycles), so adapters or transformers are not required for U.S. and Canadian appliances. You will need to bring adapters and transformers if you're traveling with appliances from Europe, Australia, or New Zealand.

Embassies & Consulates No nations maintain an embassy or consulate in the Cayman Islands.

Emergencies On Grand Cayman dial ℡ **555** for an ambulance; ℡ **345/949-0241** for an air ambulance from Island Air; and ℡ **911** for police, fire, or medical emergencies. On Cayman Brac and Little Cayman, dial ℡ **911** in an emergency.

Etiquette & Customs You should pay attention to dress code etiquette in the Cayman Islands, as it remains a "proper" British crown colony and its residents are often conservative in dress and manners. Avoid wearing bathing suits or scanty beachwear outside of beach areas and cruise ships. Cover up in public areas, especially on the streets of George Town. There are no nude beaches, and public nudity, including topless bathing, is strictly prohibited by law. Visitors will want to wear smart casual tropical resort wear at most restaurants. When attending church, "Sunday dress" is appropriate—that is, no shorts or T-shirts. Men don't have to wear ties, however. Avoid profanity in public—it is very much frowned upon.

For business attire, concessions are made for the local climate. Open collars, white trousers, knit shirts, and blazers are, to an increasing degree, appropriate for business meetings. Punctuality is appreciated, even if the temptation exists to observe a more relaxed "island time." Don't be surprised if some of the meeting planners suggest a fishing or snorkeling trip on a private boat.

Gasoline (Petrol)   Stations charge about the same rates. Taxes are already included in the printed price. One U.S. gallon equals 3.8 liters or .85 imperial gallons. For information on driving in the Cayman Islands, see "Getting Around," p. 31.

Holidays   Caymanians observe New Year's Day (Jan 1), National Heroes' Day (Jan 27), Ash Wednesday (Feb or Mar), Good Friday (Mar or Apr), Easter (Mar or Apr), Discovery Day (third week in May), Whitsunday (May or June), the Queen's Birthday (June), Constitution Day (July 7), Remembrance Day (second Mon in Nov), Christmas Day (Dec 25), and Boxing Day (Dec 26). For more information on holidays, see "Calendar of Events," p. 18.

Hospitals   On Grand Cayman, **George Town Hospital** (🕐 **345/949-8600;** www.hsa.ky) lies south of George Town on Hospital Road (south of Smith Rd.). For hospitals and clinics on Cayman Brac and Little Cayman, see p. 162 and 179, respectively.

Insurance   For information on traveler's insurance, trip cancellation insurance, and medical insurance while traveling, visit **www.frommers.com/tips**. In general, we always recommend that visitors to the Cayman Islands purchase travel insurance if they can afford it. For the most part, the Caymans are a safe destination. However, in spite of safety precautions, accidents do occur, especially among snorkelers and scuba divers. Even if you're an adventurous traveler, any number of things can go wrong on a trip—lost luggage, trip cancellation, or a medical emergency, to name a few examples—so consider insurance for added protection.

Internet Access   Most large resorts and hotels have Internet access. You can also access the Internet at **Café del Sol,** located on Seven Mile Beach at the Marquee Cinema Shopping Centre on Lawrence Blvd (🕐 **345/946-2233**). See also "Staying Connected," p. 48.

Language   English is the official language of the islands.

Legal Aid   In such a small island country, there are no local resources for legal aid. You must hire a foreign lawyer, and be prepared to post some upfront money.

Lost & Found   Be sure to notify all of your banks and credit card companies immediately upon discovering your wallet has been lost or stolen, and file a report at the nearest police precinct. Your bank, credit card company, or insurer may require a police report number or record of the loss. Most credit card companies have an emergency toll-free number to call if your card is lost or stolen; they may be able to wire you a cash advance immediately or deliver an emergency credit card in a day or two. **Visa**'s emergency number is 📞 **410/581-9994. American Express** cardholders and traveler's-check holders should call 📞 **800/221-7282. MasterCard** holders should call 📞 **800/307-7309** or 636/722-7111. For **other credit cards,** call the toll-free number directory at 📞 **800/555-1212.**

If you need emergency cash over the weekend when all banks are closed, you can have money wired to you via **Western Union** (📞 **800/325-6000;** www.westernunion.com).

Mail   Most airmail between the Cayman Islands and the U.S. mainland takes from 2 to 7 days. The Cayman Islands don't use postal or zip codes. The **main post office** in George Town lies at Edward Street and Cardinal Avenue (📞 **345/949-2474**), between the Royal Bank of Canada and the Bank of Nova Scotia. For information on post offices on Cayman Brac and Little Cayman, see p. 162 and p. 179, respectively.

Sending a postcard to the United States costs CI20¢. An airmail letter to the U.S. costs CI75¢ per half-ounce. Rates to Europe are CI80¢ per half-ounce for an airmail letter. Postcards to Canada, the U.K., Australia, and New Zealand range in price from CI20¢ to CI$1; airmail letters range from CI75¢ to CI$1 per ounce. It's recommended that packages be sent by Federal Express or another trackable delivery service.

Newspapers & Magazines   Published daily, the *Caymanian Compass* is the most popular newspaper on Grand Cayman. The Friday edition is especially helpful because it lists current and upcoming events. Rival papers include *New Caymanian,* published every Friday, and *Cayman Net News,* published Tuesday and Thursday. Available at most hotels, *What's Hot* is a free monthly magazine geared toward visitors. Copies of the *Miami Herald* and the *International Herald Tribune* are available at the big resorts and at most major newsstands in George Town.

Passports   See "Entry Requirements," p. 21. See also **www. frommers.com/tips** for information on how to obtain a passport.

Police   Call ✆ **911** for the police.

Smoking   Smoking is not regulated as carefully in the Cayman Islands as it is in most U.S. cities. However, most major hotels set aside some rooms for nonsmokers. Restaurants often lack nonsmoking sections. When being shown to a table, inform the captain or waiter that you'd like a table as far away from the smoke as possible.

Taxes   A government tourist tax of 10% is added to your hotel bill. A departure tax of CI$20 is also collected when you leave the Caymans; this tax is included in your plane fare. There is no tax on goods and services.

Telephones   See "Staying Connected," p. 48. Telephone and fax services are offered by **Cable & Wireless** (✆ **345/949-7800**) at Anderson Square in George Town.

Time   U.S. Eastern Standard Time (EST) is in effect year-round; daylight saving time is not observed. Greenwich Mean Time (GMT) is 5 hours ahead of EST, so when it's noon in the Cayman Islands, it's 5pm in London (GMT) and 2am the next day in Sydney (or 6pm in London and 3am in Sydney during the summer months).

Tipping   Most restaurants add a 10% to 15% charge that is intended to be in lieu of a tip, so check your bill carefully. Hotels also often add a 10% service charge to your bill. Taxi drivers expect a 10% to 15% tip.

Toilets   Public restrooms are found along Seven Mile Beach on Grand Cayman. Public facilities can be found at most beaches, though they are few and far between and often unpleasant. Visitors usually use the facilities of the resorts, although you should technically be a guest or customer (you can always just purchase a soft drink or a bottle of water).

Visas   See "Entry Requirements," p. 21. Consult **www.cayman islands.ky** for additional visa information.

Useful Phone Numbers   U.S. Dept. of State Travel Advisory: ✆ **202/647-5225** (manned 24 hr.); U.S. Passport Agency: ✆ **202/647-0518;** U.S. Centers for Disease Control: ✆ **800/CDC-INFO** (232-4636).

Visitor Information   Before you go, check out the **Cayman Islands Department of Tourism** website (www.caymanislands.ky), an extensive search engine designed to help you find information about accommodations, dining, shopping, watersports, and other travel services. You can also sign up for printed or e-mail brochures and book vacations directly on this site. Alternatively, write to the Cayman Department of Tourism at PO Box 67, George Town, Grand Cayman, B.W.I., or call ✆ **345/949-0623.** It's located in the Pavilion

Building on Cricket Square in George Town. Hours are Monday to Friday from 8:30am to 5pm.

In the **United States,** the Cayman Islands Department of Tourism maintains the following offices: 6100 Blue Lagoon Dr., Ste. 1202, Miami, FL 33126 (📞 **305/266-2300;** fax 305/267-2932); 9525 West Bryn Mawr, Ste. 160, Rosemont, IL 60018 (📞 **847/678-6446;** fax 847/678-6675); Two Memorial City Plaza, 820 Gessner, Ste. 1335, Houston, TX 77024 (📞 **713/461-1317;** fax 713/461-7409); 420 Lexington Ave., Ste. 2733, New York, NY 10118 (📞 **212/889-9009;** fax 212/889-9125).

In **Canada,** contact Travel Marketing Consultants, 234 Eglington Ave. East, Ste. 306, Toronto, ON M4P1 K5 (📞 **416/485-1550** or 800/263-5808; fax 416/972-5071).

In the **United Kingdom,** contact Cayman Islands, 6 Arlington St., London SW1 1RE (📞 **0207/491-7771;** fax 0207/409-7773).

The **Cayman Islands Government** website (www.gov.ky) provides important tourist and travel information, current local news, and a community and sports calendar. **Destination Cayman** (www.destination.ky) is another great information source, including a Cayman business directory, travel news and local forecasts, annual events, photographs, and more.

Since the Cayman Islands are so small, finding very detailed maps is rarely a problem. All you'll need is the *Cayman Islands Travelers' Road & Dive Map,* which is free. This foldout map also includes good maps of Little Cayman and Cayman Brac if you're planning to visit these satellite islands. Car rental firms distribute this map, and it is available at hotels, condo rentals, tourist attractions, restaurants, dive shops, and the Owen Roberts Airport.

Water   The water in the Cayman Islands is, for the most part, safe to drink. Two desalination plants on Grand Cayman supply good-quality purified tap water to the entire West End, including Seven Mile Beach. If you can determine that you're drinking desalinated water, then it's safe to drink. Just ask. Cayman Brac's desalination plant also supplies purified water to residents, but Little Cayman establishments have their own water systems. If your hotel on Little Cayman relies on rainwater collected in cisterns, it's best to drink only bottled water. When checking into hotels, ask about the water source. Never drink from a river, spring, or stream, regardless of how clean the water might appear.

Index

A

AARP, 44
A.A. Transportation, 33
Access-Able Travel Source, 43
Accessible Journeys, 43
Accommodations, 50–57
  best, 8–10
    to get away from it all, 8–9
    for honeymoons and
      weddings, 8
    luxury hotels, 9–10
  Cayman Brac, 163–168
  Grand Cayman, 58–76
    condos, villas and cottages,
      69–76
    family-friendly, 65
    hotels and resorts, 59–69
  landing the best room, 56
  Little Cayman, 180–184
  off-season discounts, 17–18
  online bookings, 56–57
  saving on your hotel room, 53–55
  telephones, 48
Air Ambulance Card, 43
Air Canada, 25
Airfares, tips for getting the best, 25–28
Airport security, 27
AirTicketsDirect, 27
Air travel, 24–28
Al Ebanks Studio (Grand Cayman), 143
Ambassador Divers (Grand
  Cayman), 112
American Airlines, 25
American Airlines Vacations, 47
American Express
  emergency number, 194
  traveler's checks, 38
American Express Travelers Cheque
  Card, 38
American Foundation for the Blind
  (AFB), 43
American Plan (AP), 54
Animal-friendly issues, 45
Annual Batabano Carnival, 20
Antica Gelateria (Grand Cayman),
  99, 159
Apartment rentals (condo rentals)
  Cayman Brac, 166–168
  Grand Cayman, 69–76
Aqua Beach Restaurant & Bar (Grand
  Cayman), 154
Arabus Clothiers (Grand Cayman), 146
Art galleries, Grand Cayman, 142–144
Art@Government House, 18
Artifacts Ltd. (Grand Cayman), 151
Atlantis Adventures, 2
  Grand Cayman, 114–115
ATMs (automated-teller machines), 36
  Cayman Brac, 162

The Attic Billiard Lounge (Grand
  Cayman), 158
Aunt Sha's Kitchen (Cayman Brac), 175
Australia
  customs regulations, 24
  health-related travel advice, 40
  passports, 21
Avis Rent a Car, 31, 43–44

B

Bamboo Lounge (Grand Cayman), 155
B & S Motor Ventures (Cayman Brac),
  161, 162
Banks
  Cayman Brac, 162
  Little Cayman, 179
Bar at Brac Reef Beach Resort
  (Cayman Brac), 175
Bars, Grand Cayman, 155–156
Batabano (Grand Cayman), 138–139
Batabano Carnival, Annual, 20
Bat Cave (Cayman Brac), 174
Bayside Grocery (Cayman Brac), 174
Bayside Watersports (Grand
  Cayman), 116
Beach Boutique (Grand Cayman), 146
Beaches, 13. *See also specific beaches*
  best, 3
  Cayman Brac, 170–171
  Grand Cayman, 105–107
  Little Cayman, 185–186
Beachwear, Grand Cayman, 144
Bernard K. Passman Gallery (Grand
  Cayman), 148
Beyond the Horizon (Grand
  Cayman), 146
Biking, 33–34
  Cayman Brac, 162
  Little Cayman, 179
Bird-watching, 117
  Governor Michael Gore Bird
    Sanctuary (Grand Cayman), 131
  Little Cayman, 189
  Meagre Bay Pond (Grand
    Cayman), 132
  Parrot Reserve (Cayman Brac), 173
  Queen Elizabeth II Botanic Park
    (Grand Cayman), 125–126
"Blackbeard" (Edward Teach), 139
Black Pearl Skate & Surf Park
  (Grand Cayman), 119
Bloody Bay Marine Park (Little
  Cayman), 186
Blossom Village (Little Cayman), 188
Blowholes (Grand Cayman), 133
Blue Tip golf course (Grand
  Cayman), 118
The Bluff (Cayman Brac), 172
Boating (boat rentals), Grand Cayman,
  113–114
Boatswain's Beach/Cayman Turtle Farm
  (Grand Cayman), 122

Boat trips and tours, Grand Cayman, 108–109

Bodden Town (Grand Cayman), 131–132

Boggy Sand Road (Grand Cayman), 136

Booby Pond (Little Cayman), 189

Booby Pond Visitor's Centre (Little Cayman), 189

The Book Nook (Grand Cayman), 144–145

Bookstores, Grand Cayman, 144–145

Boutique Cartier (Grand Cayman), 148

Brac Freeport (Cayman Brac), 175

Brac Reef Beach Resort (Cayman Brac)
beach, 170
Internet access, 163
scuba diving, 172
tennis, 174

Brazilian Point (Grand Cayman), 144

Breakers (Grand Cayman), 132

Britannia Golf Club (Grand Cayman), 116–117

British Airways, 25

Budget, 31

Bugs and bites, 39

Burtons Taxi Service, 33

Bush, Gladwyn (Miss Lassie), 144

Business hours, 192

Bus travel, 33

C

Cable & Wireless (George Town), 49, 195

Cabs, 32–33
Cayman Brac, 162
Owen Roberts International Airport, 28

Café del Sol (Grand Cayman), 193

Café del Sol/Team Café (Grand Cayman), 49

Calendar of events, 18–21

Camana Bay (Grand Cayman), 128

Cameras, Grand Cayman, 145

Canada
air travel from, 25
customs regulations, 23
health-related travel advice, 40
passports, 21
visitor information in, 196

Canada Border Services Agency, 23

Captain Bryan's (Grand Cayman), 112

Captain Crosby's Watersports (Grand Cayman), 112

Captain Keith Tibbetts (wreck), 171–172

Captain Marvin's Watersports (Grand Cayman), 112

Carbon offsetting, 45, 46

Carib Sands Beach Resort (Cayman Brac), 174

Carnival Cruise Lines, 29

Car rentals, 31–32
Cayman Brac, 161
Little Cayman, 178–179

Car travel, 31–32. See also Driving tours

Casa del Habano (Grand Cayman), 145

Cash, 37

Cathy Church's Underwater Photo Centre & Gallery (Grand Cayman), 143

Cayfest (The National Festival of the Arts), 19–20

Cayman Aggressor IV (Grand Cayman), 112

Cayman Airways
Cayman Brac, 161
Grand Cayman, 25
Little Cayman, 178

Cayman Auto Rentals, 31

Cayman Brac, 160–176
accommodations, 163–168
beaches, 170–171
brief description of, 16–17
exploring by car, 172
getting around, 161–162
getting there, 161
nightlife, 175–176
restaurants, 168–170
shopping, 174–175
visitor information, 161

Cayman Brac Clinic, 162

Cayman Brac Museum (Cayman Brac), 171

Cayman Brac parrot, 173

Cayman Brac Post Office, 163

Cayman Brac Tourist Office, 161, 173

Cayman Cab Team (Grand Cayman), 140

Cayman Camera Ltd. (Grand Cayman), 145

Cayman Cycle Rentals, 34

Cayman Drug (George Town), 192

Caymanian Compass, 152, 194

Cayman Islands Department of Tourism, 50, 110, 195

Cayman Islands International Aviation Week, 20

Cayman Islands Jazz Fest, 19

Cayman Islands Million Dollar Run, 20

Cayman Islands National Museum (Grand Cayman), 122, 124

Cayman Islands Orchid Show, 19

Cayman Islands Pirates Week, 20

Cayman Islands Sailing Club (Grand Cayman), 114

Cayman Islands Tennis Club (Grand Cayman), 120

Cayman Islands Travelers' Road & Dive Map, 196

Cayman Kai Beach Resort (Grand Cayman), 107

Cayman National Bank
Cayman Brac, 162
Little Cayman, 179

Cayman parrot, 117

Cayman Sea Salt, 149

Cayman Turtle Farm (Grand Cayman), 78, 122, 137

Cayman Villas, 52

Cayman Weddings, 55

Cayman Windsurfing (Grand Cayman), 116

Celebrations, 55

Celebrity Cruises, 29–30

Cellphones, 48–49

Cemetery Reef (Grand Cayman), 106

Centers for Disease Control and Prevention (United States), 41, 195

Charles Long (Grand Cayman), 143

Cheapflights.com, 26

Chief Secretary's Office, 54

Children, families with, 44

Cigars, Grand Cayman, 145

Climate, 18

Club Jet (Grand Cayman), 153

Cobalt Coast Resort and Suites (Grand Cayman), 109

Coconut Joe's Beach Bar & Grill (Grand Cayman), 154

Colliers (Grand Cayman), 107

Colombian Emeralds International (Grand Cayman), 149

Columbus, Christopher, 12–13

Conch Club Divers (Little Cayman), 186

Condo rentals, 51–52
    Grand Cayman, 69–76

Connection kit, 50

Consolidators, 26

Continental Airlines, 25

Continental Airlines Vacations, 47

Continental Plan (CP), 54

Convert, HMS (wreck site), 108

Coral Isle Club (Cayman Brac), 175

Coral Stone Stables (Grand Cayman), 118

Corner Pocket Pool Hall (Grand Cayman), 158

Costa Cruises, 30

Cottages, 51–52
    Grand Cayman, 69–76

Country code, 48, 192

Credit cards, 37, 38

Crime and safety, 41–42

Cruise Company, 28

Cruise lines and ships, 28–31

Cruise ship terminal, 30–31

Cruises Inc., 28

CruisesOnly, 28

Currency and currency exchange, 34–35

Customs and Border Protection (CBP), 23

Customs regulations, 22–24

D

D&M (Cayman Brac), 162

Delta Airlines, 25

Delta Vacations, 47

Dentists, Cayman Brac, 162

Departure tax, 21

Destination Cayman (website), 196

Digicel, 49

Dining, 16
    best, 9–11
    Cayman Brac, 168–170
    Grand Cayman, 77–103
        by cuisine, 79–81
        traditional menu items, 78–79
    Little Cayman, 184–185
    Taste of Cayman, 19

Directory assistance, 48

Disabilities, travelers with, 43–44

Divers Alert Network, 41

Divers World Ltd. of Cayman (Grand Cayman), 145–146

The Dive Sites of the Cayman Islands, 107

Divetech (Grand Cayman), 109–110

Diving, 1–2
    best sites, 3, 6–7
    Cayman Brac, 171–172
    Grand Cayman, 107–112
        gear, 145–146
    International Scuba Diving Hall of Fame, 20
    Little Cayman, 186–187
    safety and security for divers, 41

Dolphin Discovery Grand Cayman, 124

Don Foster's Dive (Grand Cayman), 111

Drinking laws, 192

Driving tours, Grand Cayman
    George Town to Rum Point, 128–134
    George Town to West Bay, 134–139

Drugstores, 192
    Cayman Brac, 163
    Little Cayman, 179

E

Earthfoot's Ecotours, 45–46

Easter Regatta, 19

Ebanks, Burton, 91

Eco-tours, 45–46

Eden Rock Diving Center (Grand Cayman), 110

Electricity, 192

Elite Transportation, 33

Elmslie Memorial Church (George Town), 125

Elo's Taxi (Cayman Brac), 162

Emergencies, 192
    Little Cayman, 179

Emerging Horizons, 44

Entry requirements, 21–24

Escorted general interest tours, 48

Etiquette and customs, 192–193

European Plan (EP), 54

Expedia, 26

F

Faith Hospital (Cayman Brac), 162, 179
Families with children, 44
Family Travel Forum, 44
Family Travel Network, 44
Fashion, Grand Cayman, 146
Festivals and special events, 18–21
Fidel Murphy's (Grand Cayman), 156
First Luggage, 26
Fishing, 2
    Cayman Brac, 172
    Grand Cayman, 116
    Little Cayman, 187–188
Fitness Connection (Grand Cayman), 120
Flights.com, 27
Flights International, 26
FlyerTalk, 28
Flying Wheels Travel, 43
Flying with Disability, 43
Fort George (George Town), 125
Foster's Food Fair (Grand Cayman), 146
Foster's Food Fair Pharmacy (Grand Cayman), 192
Four D's Car Rental (Cayman Brac), 161
Frank Sound (Grand Cayman), 133
Frequent-flier clubs, 27
"Frequent-stay" programs, 55

G

Galleria Plaza (Grand Cayman), 150
Gasoline, 193
Gays and lesbians, 42
GayTraveler, 43
George Town, driving tours from, 128–139
George Town (Grand Cayman), historic sites, 125
George Town Hospital (Grand Cayman), 193
Getting Married in the Cayman Islands, 54
Gifts and souvenirs, Grand Cayman, 146–147
Global ATM Alliance, 37
Golf, Grand Cayman, 116–118
Government Information Services, 54
Governor Michael Gore Bird Sanctuary (Grand Cayman), 131
Grand Cayman
    accommodations, 58–76
        condos, villas and cottages, 69–76
        family-friendly, 65
        hotels and resorts, 59–69
    average temperature and rainfall, 18
    beaches, 105–107
    brief description of, 16
    indoor activities, 120
    land-based outdoor pursuits, 116–120
    nightlife, 152–159

    restaurants, 77–103
        by cuisine, 79–81
        traditional menu items, 78–79
    shopping, 141–151
    sights and attractions, 121–140
        driving tours, 128–139
        organized tours, 139–140
        top attractions, 122–126
    watersports, 107–116
        kayaking, 119
        scuba diving and snorkeling, 107–112
Great Cave (Cayman Brac), 174
Guy Harvey's Gallery & Shoppe (Grand Cayman), 147–148
Gyms and fitness facilities, Grand Cayman, 120

H

Handicrafts, Grand Cayman, 147–148
Harbour Place (Grand Cayman), 150
Hard Rock Cafe (George Town), 50
Harley-Davidson of Grand Cayman, 147
The Harquail Theatre (Grand Cayman), 159
Hartford Holidays Travel, 28
Health concerns, 38–41
Health insurance, 40–41
Hell (Grand Cayman), 126, 137
Helmet diving, Grand Cayman, 114
Hertz, 31
Hideaways Aficionado, 53
High season, 17
Hiking and walking
    Cayman Brac, 173
    Grand Cayman, 126–128
Hobbies and Books (Grand Cayman), 151
Holidays, 193
Holiday Taxi (Grand Cayman), 140
Holland America Line, 30
Honeymoon accommodations, best, 8
Honey Suckle Trail Rides (Grand Cayman), 118
Horse Back in Paradise with Nicki (Grand Cayman), 118
Horseback riding, Grand Cayman, 118
Hospitals and clinics, 193
    Cayman Brac, 162
    Little Cayman, 179
HotelChatter, 56
Hotels and resorts, 50–57
    best, 8–10
        to get away from it all, 8–9
        for honeymoons and weddings, 8
        luxury hotels, 9–10
    Cayman Brac, 163–168
    Grand Cayman, 58–76
        condos, villas and cottages, 69–76
        family-friendly, 65
        hotels and resorts, 59–69

landing the best room, 56
Little Cayman, 180–184
off-season discounts, 17–18
online bookings, 56–57
saving on your hotel room, 53–55
telephones, 48
House rentals, 52
Hurricanes, 19
Hutland (Grand Cayman), 134

I

IAMAT (International Association for Medical Assistance to Travellers), 41
Iguanas, rock, 178
Independence from Britain, 13
Indepth Watersports (Cayman Brac), 172
Information sources, 195–196
Cayman Brac, 161
Little Cayman, 178
Inside Flyer, 28
Insurance, 193
International Association for Medical Assistance to Travellers (IAMAT), 41
International Aviation Week, Cayman Islands, 20
International Gay and Lesbian Travel Association (IGLTA), 42
International Scuba Diving Hall of Fame (Grand Cayman), 20, 159
International Society of Travel Medicine, 41
Internet access, 49–50, 193
Cayman Brac, 163
InTouch USA, 49
Ireland, passports, 21

J

Jazz Fest, Cayman Islands, 19
Jewelry, Grand Cayman, 148–149
Jose's Service Center, 32

K

Kaibo Beach Bar & Grill (Grand Cayman), 154–155
Kayak.com, 26
Kayaking
Grand Cayman, 119
Little Cayman, 186, 188
Kelly Cruises, 28
Kennedy Gallery (Grand Cayman), 143–144
Kirk Freeport (Cayman Brac), 175
Kirk Freeport Plaza (Grand Cayman), 150
Kittiwake, USS (wreck site), 109

L

La Casa del Habano (Grand Cayman), 145
La Esperanza (Cayman Brac), 176

Language, 194
La Perfumerie I and II (Grand Cayman), 149–150
Latitude 19 (Grand Cayman), 144
LCB Tours (Little Cayman), 188, 190
Leeward incident, 42
Legal aid, 194
LGBT travelers, 42
The Lighthouse Restaurant at Breakers (Grand Cayman), 88–89
Lighthouse Trail (Cayman Brac), 173
Lime, 49
Limo buses, 33
Lingerie, Grand Cayman, 149
Little Cayman, 3, 177–191
accommodations, 180–184
beaches and outdoor activities, 185–188
brief description of, 17
emergencies, 179
exploring, 188–190
getting around, 178–179
getting there, 178
hospitals and clinics, 179
nightlife, 190–191
restaurants, 184–185
shopping, 190
visitor information, 178
Little Cayman Beach Resort, 188, 190
Little Cayman Beach Resort (Little Cayman), 186
Little Cayman Clinic, 179
Little Cayman Mardi Gras Festival, 19
Little Cayman Museum, 189–190
Little Cayman Post Office, 179
Lodging, 50–57
best, 8–10
to get away from it all, 8–9
for honeymoons and weddings, 8
luxury hotels, 9–10
Cayman Brac, 163–168
Grand Cayman, 58–76
condos, villas and cottages, 69–76
family-friendly, 65
hotels and resorts, 59–69
landing the best room, 56
Little Cayman, 180–184
off-season discounts, 17–18
online bookings, 56–57
saving on your hotel room, 53–55
telephones, 48
Lone Star Bar & Grill (Grand Cayman), 157
Lost and found, 194

M

McCurley's Tours, 33
McLaughlin Enterprises (Little Cayman), 178–179
Mail, 194
Mann Travel and Cruises, 29

Mardi Gras Festival, Little Cayman, 19
Marriages, 54–55
MasterCard
    emergency number, 194
    traveler's checks, 38
Mastic Trail (Grand Cayman), 2, 126–128, 133
Meagre Bay Pond (Grand Cayman), 132
Meal plans, 54
Medical insurance, 40–41
Medical requirements for entry, 24
MedjetAssist, 40
Million Dollar Run, Cayman Islands, 20
Miss Lassie, 144
Mitzi's Fine Jewelry (Grand Cayman), 149
Mobility-Advisor.com, 44
Modified American Plan (MAP), 54
Money and costs, 34–38
Morgan's Harbour Marina (Grand Cayman), 155
MossRehab, 43
My Bar (Grand Cayman), 156

N

National Festival of the Arts, The (Cayfest), 19–20
National Gallery of the Cayman Islands (Grand Cayman), 128
National Trust, 128
Nature Cayman, 50
Nature Spa Health & Beauty (Little Cayman), 190
Nautilus (Grand Cayman), 115
Newspapers and magazines, 194
New Zealand
    customs regulations, 24
    passports, 22
Nightlife, 16
    Cayman Brac, 175–176
    Grand Cayman, 152–159
    Little Cayman, 190–191
North Sound Club (Grand Cayman), 117–118
Now, Voyager, 43

O

O Bar (Grand Cayman), 153
Ocean Frontiers Reef Resort (Grand Cayman), 110
Off season, 17–18
Off the Wall Divers (Grand Cayman), 111
Oh Boy Charters (Grand Cayman), 110–111
Old Courts Building (George Town), 125
Olivia Cruises & Resorts, 43
Opodo, 26
Orbitz, 26
Orchids, 127
Orchid Show, Cayman Islands, 19
Owen Island (Little Cayman), 3, 186

Owen Roberts International Airport, 24
    getting into town from, 28
    Wi-Fi access, 50

P

Package deals, 46–48
Pampered Ponies (Grand Cayman), 118
Panton Square (George Town), 125
Paradise Divers (Little Cayman), 187
Parrot Reserve (Cayman Brac), 173
Passions Boutique (Grand Cayman), 149
Passports, 21–22
Pedro St. James National Historic Site (Grand Cayman), 124–125, 131, 140
Perfumes, Grand Cayman, 149–150
Peter's Cave (Cayman Brac), 174
Petrol, 193
Pharmacies
    Cayman Brac, 163
    Little Cayman, 179
Photographic equipment, Grand Cayman, 145
Pirates, 139
Pirate's Grotto (Grand Cayman), 148
Pirates Point Resort (Little Cayman), 190
Pirates Week, Cayman Islands, 20
Planning your trip, 12–57
    accommodations, 50–57
    calendar of events, 18–21
    crime and safety, 41–42
    entry requirements, 21–24
    getting around, 31–34
    getting there, 24–31
    health concerns, 38–41
    the islands in brief, 12–17
    money and costs, 34–38
    package deals, 46–48
    responsible tourism, 44–46
    specialized travel resources, 42–44
    staying connected, 48–50
    weddings, 54–55
    when to go, 17–18
Point of Sand (Little Cayman), 185–186
Police, 195
Pool hall bars, 158
Population, 13
Post office, 194
    Cayman Brac, 163
    Little Cayman, 179
Prescription medications, 39
Priceline.com, 26
Prospect (Grand Cayman), 130
Pubs, Grand Cayman, 156–158
Pure Art (Grand Cayman), 147

Q

Queen Anne's Revenge, 139
Queen Elizabeth II Botanic Park (Grand Cayman), 125–126, 133–134

Queen's Birthday, 20
Queen's Court Shopping Centre (Grand Cayman), 150

R

Rackham's Waterfront (Grand Cayman), 157
Rainfall, average, 18
Rainy season, 18
Rebecca's Cave (Cayman Brac), 174
Red Sail Sports (Grand Cayman), 107–108, 113
Reef Divers
    Cayman Brac, 172
    Little Cayman, 187
Reef Photo & Video Centre (Little Cayman), 190
Regatta, Easter, 19
Remembrance Day, 20–21
Resorts and hotels, 50–57
    best, 8–10
        to get away from it all, 8–9
        for honeymoons and weddings, 8
        luxury hotels, 9–10
    Cayman Brac, 163–168
    Grand Cayman, 58–76
        condos, villas and cottages, 69–76
        family-friendly, 65
        hotels and resorts, 59–69
    landing the best room, 56
    Little Cayman, 180–184
    off-season discounts, 17–18
    online bookings, 56–57
    saving on your hotel room, 53–55
    telephones, 48
Responsible tourism, 44–46
Restaurants, 16
    best, 10–11
    Cayman Brac, 168–170
    Grand Cayman, 77–103
        by cuisine, 79–81
        traditional menu items, 78–79
    Little Cayman, 184–185
    Taste of Cayman, 19
Ritz-Carlton (Grand Cayman), golf course at, 118
Roadpost, 49
Rock iguanas, 178
Royal Palms Beach Club (Grand Cayman), 153–154
Rum and liqueurs, 96
    Grand Cayman, 150
Rum Point (Grand Cayman), 106, 134

S

Safe Trip Abroad, A (pamphlet), 42
SATH (Society for Accessible Travel & Hospitality), 43
Savannah (Grand Cayman), 131

Savannah Texaco, 32
Scooter rentals, 34
Scooters, Cayman Brac, 162
Scuba diving, 1–2
    best sites, 3, 6–7
    Cayman Brac, 171–172
    Grand Cayman, 107–112
        gear, 145–146
    International Scuba Diving Hall of Fame, 20
    Little Cayman, 186–187
    safety and security for divers, 41
Seamen's Memorial (George Town), 125
Sea Salt, Cayman, 149
Seasons, 17–18
Sea Trek (Grand Cayman), 114
Sea turtles, Grand Cayman, 122
Seaworld Explorer (semisubmarine), 115
Self-catering villas and apartments, Cayman Brac, 166–168
Senior travel, 44
Seven Mile Beach (West Bay Beach; Grand Cayman), 2, 104–106, 136
Seven Mile Watersports (Grand Cayman), 111
Sharon's Hair Clinic (Cayman Brac), 175
Shellections (Grand Cayman), 147
Shipping your luggage, 26
Shopping
    Cayman Brac, 174–175
    Grand Cayman, 141–151
    Little Cayman, 190
Shopping malls, Grand Cayman, 150
Sibley, Joanne, 142–143
Sights and attractions, Grand Cayman, 121–140
    driving tours, 128–139
    organized tours, 139–140
    top attractions, 122–126
Silver Thatch Excursions (Grand Cayman), 140
Silver thatch palm, 127
Skating, Grand Cayman, 119
Skype, 49
SmarterTravel.com, 26
Smith Cove (Grand Cayman), 130
Smith Cove Public Beach (Grand Cayman), 106
Smoking, 195
Snorkeling, 2
    best sites, 7–8
    Grand Cayman, 107–112
        gear, 145–146
    Little Cayman, 186–187
Society for Accessible Travel & Hospitality (SATH), 43
Southern Cross Club (Little Cayman), 187, 188, 191
Special events and festivals, 18–21
Spelunking, Cayman Brac, 173–174
Sports Express, 26
Spotts (Grand Cayman), 130–131
Stamps, Grand Cayman, 150–151

STA Travel, 26–27
Stevenson, Robert Louis, 139
Stingray City (Grand Cayman), 113
Stingrays, 1, 113
Submarine, 2
Submarine rides, Grand Cayman, 114–115
Sun exposure, 39
Surf bikes, Little Cayman, 189
Surfing, Grand Cayman, 119
Surfside Aquasports (Grand Cayman), 119
Sustainable tourism, 44–46

T

Taste of Cayman, 19
Taxes, 195
    departure tax, 21
Taxis, 32–33
    Cayman Brac, 162
    Owen Roberts International Airport, 28
Teach, Edward "Blackbeard," 139
Telephones, 48, 195
Temperature, average, 18
Tennis
    Cayman Brac, 174
    Grand Cayman, 120
    Little Cayman, 188
Texas 7-Mile Beach Star Mart, 32
Thirsty Surfer, 49–50
Thrifty, 31
Time zone, 195
Tipping, 195
Toilets, 195
Tortuga Divers (Grand Cayman), 111–112
The Tortuga Rum Cake Factory (Grand Cayman), 137
Tortuga Rum Company (Grand Cayman), 150
Tourism For All, 44
Tourist information, 195–196
    Cayman Brac, 161
    Little Cayman, 178
TourScan Inc., 47–48
Toys, Grand Cayman, 151
Traveler's checks, 37–38
Travel Health Online, 41
Travelocity, 26
Travel Sentry-certified locks, 27
Travelsupermarket, 26
TravelWithYourKids.com, 44
Treasure Chest (Cayman Brac), 174
Treasure Island (Stevenson), 139
Tropicana Tours (Grand Cayman), 140

U

United Kingdom
    air travel from, 25
    customs regulations, 23–24
    health-related travel advice, 40

    passports, 21, 22
    visitor information in, 196
United States
    air travel from, 25
    customs regulations, 23
    health-related travel advice, 40
    passports, 21, 22
    visitor information in, 196
US Airways, 25
U.S. Customs and Border Protection (CBP), 23

V

Village of Breakers (Grand Cayman), 132
Village of Prospect (Grand Cayman), 130
Village of Savannah (Grand Cayman), 131
Village of Spotts (Grand Cayman), 130–131
Village Square (Little Cayman), 190
Villa rentals, 51–52
    Cayman Brac, 166–168
    Grand Cayman, 69–76
Villas of Distinction, 52
Villas Pappagallo (Grand Cayman), 137–138
Visa
    emergency number, 194
    traveler's checks, 38
Visas, 22
Visitor information, 195–196
    Cayman Brac, 161
    Little Cayman, 178
Volunteer programs, 45
Vonage, 49

W

War Memorial (George Town), 125
Water, drinking, 196
    Little Cayman, 180
Weather, 18
Websites
    online traveler's toolbox, 50
    visitor information, 195–196
Wedding accommodations, best, 8
Weddings, 54–55
West End Point Overlook (Cayman Brac), 173
Westerly Ponds (Cayman Brac), 173
Western Union, 194
West Shore Shopping Centre (Grand Cayman), 150
Windsurfing, Grand Cayman, 116
World Gym (Grand Cayman), 120
Wreck Bar & Grill (Grand Cayman), 106, 157–158
Wreck of the Ten Sails (Grand Cayman), 103, 132